American Drama to 1900

AMERICAN LITERATURE, ENGLISH LITERATURE, AND WORLD LITERATURES IN ENGLISH: AN INFORMATION GUIDE SERIES

Series Editor: Theodore Grieder, Curator, Division of Special Collections, Fales Library, New York University

Associate Editor: Duane DeVries, Associate Professor, Polytechnic Institute of New York, Brooklyn

Other books on American literature in this series:

AMERICAN DRAMA, 1900-1950—Edited by Paul Hurley*

CONTEMPORARY DRAMA IN AMERICA AND ENGLAND, 1950-1970—Edited by Richard H. Harris*

AMERICAN FICTION TO 1900—Edited by David K. Kirby

AMERICAN FICTION, 1900-1950—Edited by James Woodress

CONTEMPORARY FICTION IN AMERICA AND ENGLAND, 1950-1970—Edited by Alfred F. Rosa and Paul A. Echholz

AMERICAN POETRY TO 1900—Edited by Donald Yannella*

AMERICAN POETRY, 1900-1950—Edited by William White*

CONTEMPORARY POETRY IN AMERICA AND ENGLAND, 1950-1970—Edited by Martin E. Gingerich*

AMERICAN PROSE TO 1820—Edited by Donald Yannella and John Roch

AMERICAN PROSE AND CRITICISM, 1820-1900—Edited by Elinore H. Partridge*

AMERICAN PROSE AND CRITICISM, 1900-1950—Edited by Peter A. Brier and Anthony Arthur*

LITERARY JOURNAL IN AMERICA TO 1900—Edited by Edward E. Chielens

LITERARY JOURNAL IN AMERICA, 1900-1950—Edited by Edward E. Chielens

LITTLE MAGAZINES IN AMERICA, 1950-1975—Edited by Robert Bertholf*

AFRO-AMERICAN FICTION, 1853-1976—Edited by Edward Margolies and David Bakish

AFRO-AMERICAN POETRY AND DRAMA, 1760-1975—Edited by William P. French, Michel J. Fabre, Amritjit Singh, and Genevieve Fabre

AUTHOR NEWSLETTERS AND JOURNALS—Edited by Margaret C. Patterson

*in preparation

The above series is part of the
GALE INFORMATION GUIDE LIBRARY

The Library consists of a number of separate series of guides covering major areas in the social sciences, humanities, and current affairs.

General Editor: Paul Wasserman, Professor and former Dean, School of Library and Information Services, University of Maryland

Managing Editor: Denise Allard Adzigian, Gale Research Company

American Drama to 1900

A GUIDE TO INFORMATION SOURCES

Volume 28 in the American Literature, English Literature, and World Literatures in English Information Guide Series

Walter J. Meserve

*Professor, Department of Theatre and Drama
Indiana University
Bloomington*

Gale Research Company
Book Tower, Detroit, Michigan 48226

Library of Congress Cataloging in Publication Data

Meserve, Walter J
    American drama to 1900.

    (American literature, English literature, and
world literatures in English information guide
series ; v. 28) (Gale information guide library)
    Includes index.
    1. American drama—19th century—Bibliography.
2. American drama—Bibliography. I. Title.
Z1231.D7M45   [PS345]   016.812   79-27056
ISBN 0-8103-1365-0

Copyright © 1980 by
Walter J. Meserve

No part of this book may be reproduced in any form without permission in writing from the publisher, except by a reviewer who wishes to quote brief passages or entries in connection with a review written for inclusion in a magazine or newspaper. Manufactured in the United States of America.

Dedicated
to
Those Many Students Who
Through the Years
Have Studied Drama with Me

VITA

Walter J. Meserve is presently a professor of theatre and drama at Indiana University, Bloomington. He received his A.B. from Bates College, Lewiston, Maine; his M.A. from Boston University; and his Ph.D. from the University of Washington. He has been on the editorial board of MODERN DRAMA since 1960.

Meserve is the author of AN OUTLINE HISTORY OF AMERICAN DRAMA; ROBERT E. SHERWOOD: RELUCTANT MORALIST; AN EMERGING ENTERTAINMENT: THE DRAMA OF THE AMERICAN PEOPLE TO 1828; and has edited and compiled numerous books on American drama. He has written articles and reviews for several journals. Meserve is a member of the American Society for Theatre Research, American Theatre Association, and Author's Guild.

CONTENTS

Acknowledgments ix
Introduction xi
    Historical Survey   xii
    Methodology   xiv
Abbreviations of Serial Titles xvii

I. Critical, Historical, and Reference Resources.............. 1
   A. Bibliographies and Checklists 1
   B. Indexes 9
   C. Library and Microreproduced Collections 11
   D. Anthologies and Collected Plays 15
   E. Histories 22
   F. History and Criticism 31
      1. Drama of the Colonies and the Period of the
          Revolution, Beginnings to 1783 31
      2. Drama of a Developing Nation, 1784-1860 36
        a. Surveys and Studies of Individual Authors and
           Plays 36
        b. Critics and Criticism, Dramatic Theory, and
           Nationalism 49
        c. Yankee Drama--Emphasis on Plays Rather Than
           Acting 52
        d. UNCLE TOM'S CABIN as Drama 53
      3. Drama During the Rise of Realism, 1861-1900 55
        a. Surveys and Studies of Individual Authors and
           Plays 55
        b. Critics and Criticism 63

II. Individual Dramatists 67
   James Nelson Barker (1784-1858) 69
   David Belasco (1859-1931) 73
   Robert Montgomery Bird (1806-54) 79
   George Henry Boker (1823-90) 84
   Dion Boucicault (1820-90) 90
   John Brougham (1810-80) 98
   John Daly Burk (1776?-1808) 102
   Bartley Campbell (1843-88) 104

Contents

Samuel Clemens (1835-1910) 106
Augustin Daly (1838-99) 108
William Dunlap (1766-1839) 113
Clyde Fitch (1865-1909) 120
William Gillette (1855-1937) 125
Thomas Godfrey (1736-63) 130
Edward Harrigan (1844-1911) 133
James A. Herne (1839-1901) 137
Bronson Howard (1842-1908) 145
William Dean Howells (1837-1920) 151
Charles H. Hoyt (1859-1900) 158
Henry James (1843-1916) 161
James Morrison Steele MacKaye (1842-94) 166
Robert Munford (ca. 1737-83) 170
Mordecai M. Noah (1785-1851) 172
John Howard Payne (1791-1852) 175
Anna Cora Mowatt Ritchie (1819-70) 182
Richard Penn Smith (1799-1854) 186
John Augustus Stone (1800-1834) 188
Augustus Thomas (1857-1934) 191
Denman Thompson (1833-1910) 196
Royall Tyler (1757-1826) 200
Mercy Otis Warren (1728-1814) 205
John Blake White (1781-1859) 208
Nathaniel Parker Willis (1806-67) 210
Samuel Woodworth (1785-1842) 213

Author Index 217
Title Index 227
Subject Index 241

ACKNOWLEDGMENTS

I am most grateful to those numerous students at the University of Kansas and Indiana University whose term papers, theses, and dissertations turned up bibliographical items that stimulated my own research. For help with the entries on John Brougham and Edward Harrigan I wish to thank Dr. David Hawes and Dr. Richard Moody, respectively, both of Indiana University. Dr. Anthony Shipps, Librarian for English, Indiana University Library, has been exceedingly generous with his time and research skills. Dr. Theodore Grieder not only provided wise and effective solutions to my bibliographical problems but showed considerable patience in the process. Finally, my deep appreciation goes to my wife, Ruth, whose hours of library research toward the completion of this bibliography deserve far more than a brief mention at the end of "acknowledgments."

INTRODUCTION

Writing in the EDINBURGH REVIEW for January 1820, an English critic and wit by the name of Sydney Smith posed some interesting questions: "In the four quarters of the globe," he asked, "who reads an American book? or goes to an American play? or looks at an American picture or statue?" Obviously suggesting a haughty disdain for the artistic and literary achievements of the neighbors across the Atlantic, Smith's words evoked some expected and, perhaps for the modern reader, some unexpected results. There were at this early time, for example, an abundance of Anglophile critics and a substantial part of the cultured citizenry who wholeheartedly agreed with Smith's condemnation of American literature and art. Other people, from both political and cultural points of view, protested vociferously, but the prejudices persisted--even after Ralph Waldo Emerson's eloquent plea in "The American Scholar" (1837). For several decades American literature was considered by many critics simply a minor aspect of English literature.

Smith's reference to dramatic literature in America created little controversy. As most modern critics observe, American drama progressed only slowly toward excellence. In fact, just a hundred and one years after Smith's barbed comment appeared in print, another English critic, William Archer, claimed to find the beginnings of American drama among the sand dunes of Cape Cod with the work of Eugene O'Neill and the productions of the Provincetown Players. By this time, however, there was more of a basis for an argument that an established drama already existed. John Corbin, an American critic, had already observed "The Dawn of American Drama" in 1907, and discussions of its existence, nationality, and quality had been appearing in newspapers and periodicals for many years.

Whatever these comments suggest, either to the beginning student or the teacher whose interests cover American drama in general, they probably do not prepare him for a book-length bibliography of American drama before 1900. Compared to American fiction and poetry, American drama prior to the plays of Eugene O'Neill has seduced the thoughts and energies of few scholars. Indeed, if one became interested in the activities taking place in American theatre during the eighteenth and nineteenth centuries, he was far more likely to be concerned with the art and lives of the performers and managers than with the plays they

Introduction

produced on stage. That is the difference, however, between drama and theatre--between a study of the playwright and his art, and a study of all the skills and crafts necessary to create his vision before an audience. This guide is a bibliography of American drama.

HISTORICAL SURVEY

Idealistically, any bibliography should serve as both a resource to research in an area and a stimulus to further scholarship. The drama of America awaits the scholarly attention that will more accurately place it in that body of literature clearly identified as American by the last part of the nineteenth century. Its beginnings, however, were slight and unabashedly chaotic. The frequently preached view of the theocratic authorities in New England against "Dancing, Stage-playes, and all other Provocations to Uncleanness in our selves or others," as Cotton Mather explained in A CLOUD OF WITNESSES, encouraged neither playwrights nor theatre audiences. Other city fathers from the colonies passed laws forbidding plays and haphazardly prosecuted would-be Thespians until well after the Revolution. But American plays appeared--among the restless joy seekers, in political circles, and as extracurricular activity in colleges. Not until 1767, however, was an American play performed by professional actors--Thomas Godfrey's THE PRINCE OF PARTHIA.

During the years of the Revolution, drama and theatre began to establish a basis in the political arena that would continue in support of nationalism until the issues of the Civil War scattered those forces. The partisan plays of such patriots as Mercy Otis Warren, Hugh Henry Brackenridge, and Robert Munford were opposed by Tory efforts like the anonymous BATTLE OF BROOKLYN (1776). Thereafter, every significant event found its way onto the stage: the war with the Barbary Coast pirates, Jefferson's Embargo Act, the War of 1812, Andrew Jackson's election, border disputes, the war with Mexico, and so on. Nationalism was clearly a major stimulus for the dramatist. Frequently, he created plays around Native American character types; an incredible number of plays were written about the Yankee, the Negro, the Indian, and Mose the Fire B'hoy. Plays about American immigrants featured the Irishman and the German. Nationalism also appeared in those plays that commented on American society. Royall Tyler wrote THE CONTRAST in 1787, a fine comedy with attitudes that future dramatists--James Nelson Barker, Samuel Woodworth, Anna C.M. Ritchie, G.P. Wilkins--emphasized with equal enthusiasm.

Most of the plays that freely exhibited the patriotic and nationalistic fervor of the new and developing nation were unexceptional as drama. Too frequently the comparative few that warrant close study are forgotten. But it must be remembered that there were no professional playwrights during these years. No one could make a living writing plays in America. Some of the cultured few with literary pretensions wrote closet dramas that they tried to foist upon audiences as stage plays, and several successful literary people tried unsuccessfully to write for the stage. Of these latter, only Washington Irving found success, and this in conjunction with John Howard Payne. Generally, plays

Introduction

were written by people with theatre connections--William Dunlap, John Augustus Stone, Anna C.M. Ritchie, John Brougham, and a host of lesser figures. They were actors or theatre managers who needed a play for a particular event or as a personal vehicle, and either wrote it themselves or paid a theatre hack to turn out an evening's entertainment that would soon be lost in history. In 1828 Edwin Forrest started the custom of playwriting contests when he required a vehicle for his particular talents, and other actors followed his lead. Although the idea stimulated some playwriting, it did little for the status of the would-be playwright who found his efforts very poorly rewarded, either with money or with recognition. Throughout the first half of the nineteenth century, however, there was a surprising number of men and women who tried to write for a theatre controlled by actors and managers. Some showed talent, and a number had success with a play or two; but most stopped writing plays early in their careers because there was no economic future in such work. Robert Montgomery Bird is the classic example, but there were others. Not until the last part of the century did playwriting become a recognized profession.

Taking his cue from the best English dramatists of the past, the American dramatist of the early nineteenth century who took his task seriously tried to write poetic drama. Thomas Godfrey accepted the fashion. William Dunlap and John Daly Burk continued it. For many critics the best American drama of, roughly, the second quarter of the nineteenth century was written in poetry--plays by John Howard Payne, James Nelson Barker, Robert Montgomery Bird, John Augustus Stone, Nathaniel Parker Willis, and Epes Sargent, among others. This movement culminated in George Henry Boker's FRANCESCA DA RIMINI (1855), which ironically, was not successful on stage until after 1882, when it was revived by Lawrence Barrett during a period when the requirements of the rise of realism in literature discouraged dramatists from writing poetic dramas, and few, indeed, appeared.

The diverse forces--the discoveries of Sir Charles Lyell; the writings of Marx, Darwin, Comte, and Spenser; the chaos of civil war, expansion to the West, and industrial advance--that directed life and literature in America during the last part of the nineteenth century clearly affected the dramatist; but his position was not sufficiently stable to allow him an authoritative voice in the development of American letters. It was a period of transition in the drama, not particularly helped by the fact that the major writers of the period--Henry James, Samuel Clemens, W.D. Howells--could not write successful plays for the contemporary theatre. And yet this failure was not completely their fault, because the demands of theatre managers made good drama impossible. For example, the most successful theatre manager of the period, Augustin Daly, refused to produce the plays of George Bernard Shaw or Henrik Ibsen.

It was a period of exciting and sensational theatre, however, and the most successful plays exuded theatricality--the melodramas of Boucicault, Daly, Belasco, Bartley Campbell, Steele MacKaye, and William Gillette, or the farces of Edward Harrigan, Denman Thompson, and Charles H. Hoyt. There were also some attempts to look at the developing society, particularly the life of the businessman who was making the new America possible. Bronson Howard dramatized him in several plays. William Dean Howells tried to dramatize

Introduction

the society that he portrayed with such insight and charm in his novels, but whereas the plays retain the charm, they lack the boldness and strength of observation that distinguish his other works. Like other literary people he attempted to adhere to the demands of a theatre that limited the progress of dramatic literature.

By the end of the nineteenth century the American dramatist was beginning to achieve some independence of thought and action. Bronson Howard had shown that one could be a playwright by profession, and Clyde Fitch was about to demonstrate that one could make considerable money writing plays--although both had the help of the Theatrical Syndicate, a commercially cooperative attempt by six major theatre agents to control theatre production in America. The substance of American plays was about to change, a fact dramatized in MARGARET FLEMING (1890) by James A. Herne, who also learned that America was not yet ready for such a play. An admirer of Ibsen, Herne had not accepted the negative message that critics and audiences had accorded GHOSTS during its American production. Nonetheless, changes were being made in the kinds of plays created in America, plays by Fitch, Herne, and Augustus Thomas. Although Eugene O'Neill found little in American drama to stimulate him, preparation for his advent was being made before the turn of the century.

METHODOLOGY

The listing of entries in this bibliography is straightforward and the arrangement, it is hoped, is clear from the table of contents. The emphasis upon collections (I.C) reproduced by microfilm, microprint, and microfiche is basic to any probing research in American drama. The section on History and Criticism (I.F) provides a chronological approach designed to cover all research in American drama that is not specifically related to the individual dramatists considered in Section II. Inclusive dates for subdivisions (II.F.1.2.3) combine historical and recognized literary periods with convenience. One major decision involved which dramatists to place in Section I.F and which to place in Section II. The division finally established is based solely upon the amount of scholarship available on these dramatists. Therefore, regardless of their contemporary reputations in the theatre, dramatists who have attracted substantial comment are listed among the individual dramatists in Section II; otherwise, all dramatists are grouped in Section I.F. Neither Stephen Crane (I.F) nor Samuel Clemens (II), for example, was a successful dramatist, but more has been written about Clemens. Generally, of course, the most important dramatists are listed in Section II. A great many minor playwrights, however, have written a large number of plays but have been forgotten, and the occasional article or book reference to their work appears in the chronological Section I.F.

The reader must always bear in mind that this is a bibliography of American drama, not American theatre. In most circumstances the distinction is clear. There are no entries here concerned specifically with theatre history, theatre architecture and design, actors and actresses, or theatre management. Rather, the entries deal with dramatists and their plays plus discussions of dramatic

Introduction

theory, dramatic criticism, and the critics themselves. In some instances, however, it has been difficult to determine the emphasis of books and essays. For example, a substantial number of the dramatists included were also actors or theatre managers, and writers discussing their activities did not always have the distinction in mind that delimits this bibliography. This problem becomes obvious in the sections on Yankee drama and UNCLE TOM'S CABIN. The Yankee plays were mainly vehicles for actors; UNCLE TOM'S CABIN is the world's greatest stage success; yet both subjects need to be covered in this volume. Although as nearly as possible the entries are concerned only with American drama, some items cover both drama and theatre. Essays on John Brougham's acting or Belasco's management, for example, have been omitted, but some books and essays listed will give information about the acting and the management as well as the dramatic works. For information on the American theatre during this period, readers should refer to THE AMERICAN STAGE TO WORLD WAR I in the Gale Information Guide Series.

To enhance the value of this bibliography, there are frequent cross-references, particularly between Section I.F. and Section II. For books or essays dealing with a period or particular aspect of American drama, page references have been given when the reference or cross-reference is to a substantial discussion; less substantial or minor references in a work are simply listed according to the dramatist whose name may be checked in the Author Index.

Although a list of abbreviations for periodicals and series titles is included, it is not at all indicative of the full range of works listed in the bibliography because most entries carry full titles. It should be noted, too, that when magazine is part of the title of a periodical, such as MUNSEY'S MAGAZINE, it has been omitted.

No bibliography can be complete, alas! Some items have been purposely omitted as they are more pertinent to American theatre than American drama. For other omissions there are only the explanations of human fallibility.

ABBREVIATIONS OF SERIAL TITLES

AL	AMERICAN LITERATURE
ALSA	AMERICAN LITERARY SCHOLARSHIP ANNUAL
AmN&Q	AMERICAN NOTES & QUERIES
APS	AMERICAN PERIODICAL SERIES
AQ	AMERICAN QUARTERLY
BNYPL	BULLETIN OF THE NEW YORK PUBLIC LIBRARY
CLAJ	COLLEGE LANGUAGE ASSOCIATION JOURNAL
CSSJ	CENTRAL STATES SPEECH JOURNAL
DAB	DICTIONARY OF AMERICAN BIOGRAPHY
DAI	DISSERTATION ABSTRACTS INTERNATIONAL
EAL	EARLY AMERICAN LITERATURE
ELLS	ENGLISH LANGUAGE AND LITERATURE STUDIES (TOKYO)
ETJ	EDUCATIONAL THEATRE JOURNAL
MASJ	MID-CONTINENT AMERICAN STUDIES JOURNAL
MD	MODERN DRAMA
MLN	MODERN LANGUAGE NOTES
N&Q	NOTES AND QUERIES
NAR	NORTH AMERICAN REVIEW
NEQ	NEW ENGLAND QUARTERLY
OSUTCB	OHIO STATE UNIVERSITY THEATRE COLLECTION BULLETIN
PMLA	PUBLICATIONS OF THE MODERN LANGUAGE ASSOCIATION
QJS	QUARTERLY JOURNAL OF SPEECH
SM	SPEECH MONOGRAPHS
SSComJ	SOUTHERN SPEECH COMMUNICATIONS JOURNAL

Abbreviations of Serial Titles

SSJ	SOUTHERN SPEECH JOURNAL
TA	THEATRE ARTS
TD	THEATRE DOCUMENTATION
TDR	THE DRAMA REVIEW
TS	THEATRE SURVEY

I. CRITICAL, HISTORICAL, AND REFERENCE RESOURCES

A. BIBLIOGRAPHIES AND CHECKLISTS

1   Adams, William D. A DICTIONARY OF THE DRAMA. A GUIDE TO THE PLAYS, PLAYWRIGHTS, PLAYERS, AND PLAYHOUSES OF THE UNITED KINGDOM AND AMERICA FROM THE EARLIEST TIMES TO THE PRESENT. Philadelphia: Lippincott, 1904.

> Only Volume I, A-G, is published and has limited value.

2   AMERICAN LITERARY REALISM. Arlington: University of Texas at Arlington, Department of English, 1967-- . Quarterly.

> Includes bibliographical studies of American realists.

3   AMERICAN LITERARY SCHOLARSHIP: AN ANNUAL. Durham, N.C.: Duke University Press, 1963-- .

> Section 16 in each volume provides selective evaluation of the year's scholarship--essays and books--in American drama. Essays 1963-65 by Malcolm Goldstein; 1966-73 by Walter J. Meserve; 1974--by Jordan Y. Miller.

4   AMERICAN LITERATURE. Durham, N.C.: Duke University Press, 1929-- . Quarterly.

> Each issue includes a listing of "Articles on American Literature Appearing in Current Periodicals."

5   AMERICAN LITERATURE ABSTRACTS. San Jose, Calif.: San Jose State College, Department of English, 1967-- . Semiannual.

> Each issue contains brief summaries of essays on American literature appearing in scholarly journals.

Critical, Historical, Reference Resources

6   Angotti, Vincent L. AN ANNOTATED BIBLIOGRAPHY AND SUBJECT INDEX TO THE MICROFILM COLLECTION: SOURCE MATERIALS IN THE FIELD OF THEATRE. Ann Arbor, Mich.: University Microfilms Library Service, 1967.

   Providing major references to theatre, both English and American, this bibliography includes such items as Lawrence Hutton's MANUSCRIPT DRAMA DIARY (6 vols., 1870-85).

7   Arata, Esther S., and Nicholas J. Rotoli. BLACK AMERICAN PLAYWRIGHTS, 1800 TO THE PRESENT: A BIBLIOGRAPHY. Metuchen, N.J.: Scarecrow Press, 1976.

   This volume provides an alphabetical listing of playwrights and their plays, plus a general bibliography.

8   ARTICLES IN AMERICAN STUDIES, 1954-1968: A CUMULATION OF THE ANNUAL BIBLIOGRAPHIES FROM AMERICAN QUARTERLY. 2 vols. Ed. Hennig Cohen. Ann Arbor, Mich.: Pierian Press, 1972.

   Basically a reprinting in two volumes of the annual, annotated bibliographies in AQ, the volume includes very few items under "Literature and Drama" or "Literature." Additionally, it is cumbersome to use.

9   Baker, Blanche M. DRAMATIC BIBLIOGRAPHY: AN ANNOTATED LIST OF BOOKS ON THE HISTORY AND CRITICISM OF THE DRAMA AND STAGE AND ON THE ALLIED ARTS OF THE THEATRE. New York: Wilson, 1933.

   This is a basic work, subsequently revised as entry no. 10.

10 _____. THE THEATRE AND ALLIED ARTS: A GUIDE TO BOOKS DEALING WITH THE HISTORY, CRITICISM, AND TECHNIC OF THE DRAMA, AND THEATRE AND RELATED ARTS AND CRAFTS. 1952; rpt. New York: Bloom, 1967.

11 Bergquist, William G. ed. THREE CENTURIES OF ENGLISH AND AMERICAN PLAYS. New York: Hafner, 1963.

   This is an extremely useful checklist of the microcard collection edited by Henry W. Wells, THREE CENTURIES OF DRAMA: AMERICAN (1714-1830) (see entry no. 94).

12 Blanck, Jacob, comp. BIBLIOGRAPHY OF AMERICAN LITERATURE. New Haven, Conn.: Yale University Press, 1955-- .

   A detailed and authoritative bibliography of American literature and its creators, this multivolume project, alphabetically structured, is still in progress. For the some three hundred authors included--from those of the Federal period up to twentieth-

Critical, Historical, Reference Resources

century authors who died before 1930--this is an important, basic bibliographical resource.

13   Brockett, Oscar G., Samuel L. Becker, and Donald C. Bryant. A BIBLIOGRAPHICAL GUIDE TO RESEARCH IN SPEECH AND DRAMATIC ART. Glenview, Ill.: Scott, Foresman, 1963.

    Although the work includes items on American theatre and drama on pages 76-77, the references are few and selective.

14   Busacca, Basil. "Checklist of Black Playwrights: 1823-1970." BLACK SCHOLAR, 5 (1973), 48-54.

15   CATALOGUE OF ADDITIONS TO THE MANUSCRIPTS IN THE BRITISH MUSEUM: PLAYS SUBMITTED TO THE LORD CHAMBERLAIN 1824-1851. London: Published by the Trustees of the British Museum, 1964.

    This is a good source for locating American playscripts.

16   Crick, B.R., and Mirian Alman. A GUIDE TO MANUSCRIPTS RELATING TO AMERICA IN GREAT BRITAIN AND IRELAND. London: Oxford University Press, 1961.

    An Addenda to the GUIDE was published in the BULLETIN of the British Association for American Studies by B.R. Crick, new series, numbers 5, 7, 12. Mainly the items refer to subjects, and the work is of slight value to drama researchers.

17   DRAMATIC COMPOSITIONS COPYRIGHTED IN THE UNITED STATES, 1870-1916. 2 vols. Washington: Copyright Office, Library of Congress, 1918.

    A listing of about sixty-six thousand plays registered for copyright.

18   Eddleman, Floyd E., ed. AMERICAN DRAMA CRITICISM. SUPPLEMENT II. Hamden, Conn.: Shoe String Press, 1976; AMERICAN DRAMA CRITICISM: INTERPRETATIONS, 1890-1977. 2nd ed. Hamden, Conn.: Shoe String Press, 1977.

    SUPPLEMENT II updates Palmer and Dyson (entries nos. 42-43, below) to January 1975. The second edition adds books, articles, and interpretive studies to 1977, but includes few items before 1900.

19   EDUCATIONAL THEATRE JOURNAL. Washington, D.C.: American Theatre Association, 1949-78. Quarterly. Retitled THEATRE JOURNAL with 1979 issue, vol. 31.

    Bibliography and book reviews appear in each issue.

Critical, Historical, Reference Resources

20   Fabre, Geneviève, comp. "Afro-American Drama, 1850-1975." In AFRO-AMERICAN POETRY AND DRAMA. Detroit: Gale Research Co., 1979.

>Fabre's work forms the second part of this guide and includes an introduction to the subject and a treatment and checklist of the Afro-American drama, 1850-1975.

21   Finley, Katherine P., and Paul T. Nolan. "Mississippi Dramas between Wars, 1870-1916: A Checklist and an Argument." JOURNAL OF MISSISSIPPI HISTORY, 26 (1964), 219-28, 299-306.

22   Gohdes, Clarence. BIBLIOGRAPHICAL GUIDE TO THE STUDY OF THE LITERATURE OF THE U.S.A. 2nd ed. Durham, N.C.: Duke University Press, 1963.

>Section 23 on "Drama and Theatre" provides a general but useful annotated bibliography for beginning students.

23   _____. LITERATURE AND THEATRE OF THE STATES AND REGIONS OF THE U.S.A. AN HISTORICAL BIBLIOGRAPHY. Durham, N.C.: Duke University Press, 1967.

>Organized by states and regions, the work is mainly concerned with theatre and its history according to region and community. There are some items on the drama.

24   Hatch, James V., comp. BLACK IMAGES AND THE AMERICAN STAGE, A BIBLIOGRAPHY OF PLAYS AND MUSICALS, 1770-1970. New York: Drama Book Specialists, 1970.

>This volume lists black characters in plays, black playwrights and their plays, plays on black themes. It is, however, difficult to use and of doubtful value.

25   _____. "A Guide to 200 Years of Drama." TDR, 16 (1972), 5-24.

>Concerned with black drama, this listing is divided into two sections: "The Great White Way," plays generally about blacks; and "The Great Black Way," plays by dramatists who demand a theatre only for black people.

26   Hill, Frank Pierce, comp. AMERICAN PLAYS PRINTED, 1714-1830: A BIBLIOGRAPHICAL RECORD. 1934; rpt. New York: Bloom, 1968.

>This early bibliographical listing of 335 play titles and dramatic pieces has been revised but requires further scholarly attention. See entries nos. 50 and 54.

Critical, Historical, Reference Resources

27 Hixon, Don L., and Don A. Hennessee, comps. NINETEENTH-CENTURY AMERICAN DRAMA: A FINDING GUIDE. Metuchen, N.J.: Scarecrow Press, 1977.

> This is a carefully prepared checklist of the approximately 4,000 works by American authors in the Readex Microprint collection of ENGLISH AND AMERICAN DRAMA OF THE NINETEENTH CENTURY (entry no. 84). Appendixes list acting editions of plays, plays with racial and national characters, and plays categorized according to subject and form.

28 Johnson, Albert E., and W.H. Crain, Jr., comps. "A Dictionary of American Dramatic Critics, 1850-1910." TA, 13 (1955), 65-89.

> A valuable identification of critics and their pseudonyms, listed alphabetically with dates, newspaper affiliation, editorships, works.

29 Jones, Joseph, et al., comps. AMERICAN LITERARY MANUSCRIPTS: A CHECKLIST OF HOLDINGS IN ACADEMIC, HISTORICAL, AND PUBLIC LIBRARIES IN THE UNITED STATES. Austin: University of Texas Press, 1960; 2nd ed. comp. J. Albert Robbins et al. Athens: University of Georgia Press, 1977.

> This is a valuable reference text for determining locations of letters, manuscripts, journals, and so forth. Items, however, are not described but are listed only in number. Organized alphabetically by author.

30 Leary, Lewis G., comp. ARTICLES ON AMERICAN LITERATURE APPEARING IN CURRENT PERIODICALS, 1920-1945. Durham, N.C.: Duke University Press, 1947.

> Geared to literature, this volume does not index many drama-theatre journals. Organized according to historical periods with attention to individual authors, it includes a section on "Theatre" with items on theatre and drama.

31 _____. ARTICLES ON AMERICAN LITERATURE, 1900-1950. Durham, N.C.: Duke University Press, 1954.

> An expansion of entry no. 30.

32 Leary, Lewis G., Carolyn Bartholet, and Catharine Roth, comps. ARTICLES ON AMERICAN LITERATURE, 1950-1967. Durham, N.C.: Duke University Press, 1970.

> Further expansion of entries nos. 30 and 31.

Critical, Historical, Reference Resources

33 Litto, Frederic M., comp. AMERICAN DISSERTATIONS ON THE DRAMA AND THE THEATRE, A BIBLIOGRAPHY. Kent, Ohio: Kent State University Press, 1969.

> This computerized bibliography is indexed by author, subject, and key-word-in-context. Essentially, it ends with 1966; it is not complete. For subsequent references see DAI or ALSA.

34 Long, E. Hudson. AMERICAN DRAMA FROM ITS BEGINNINGS TO THE PRESENT. New York: Appleton-Century-Crofts, 1970.

> This brief (78 p.), annotated work is geared to the demands of a survey class in American drama. After basic references, the bibliography lists items by period, region, genre, theme, and subject.

35 McCoskey, John C., comp. "American Satires, 1637-1957: A Selective Checklist. Part I: Drama." SATIRE NEWSLETTER, 2 (1965), 101-09.

> Selected plays listed according to author without commentary.

36 McDowell, John H., and Charles J. McGaw, comps. "A Bibliography on Theatre and Drama in American Colleges and Universities 1937-1947." SM, 16 (1949), 1-124.

> A listing of books, articles, theses, and dissertations published in the United States.

37 Mates, Julian. "The Dramatic Anchor: Research Opportunities in the American Drama before 1800." EAL, 5 (1970-71), 76-79.

> A general bibliographical essay with little specific information.

38 Meserve, Walter J. "The American Periodical Series: Source Material for Theatre and Drama Research." ETJ, 20 (1968), 443-48.

> This essay suggests the scope and quality of resource material available in APS (see entries nos. 59-61).

39 MLA INTERNATIONAL BIBLIOGRAPHY OF BOOKS AND ARTICLES ON THE MODERN LANGUAGES AND LITERATURES. New York: Modern Language Association of America, 1921-- . Annual.

> Bibliography includes items on American literature and drama.

40 MODERN DRAMA. Lawrence, Kans.: A.C. Edwards, 1958-72; Toronto: University of Toronto, Graduate Centre for Study of Drama, Massey College, 1972-- .

Critical, Historical, Reference Resources

Generally, each September issue contains the annual bibliography; occasionally, the bibliography has been omitted.

41 Nolan, Paul T., comp. "Alabama Drama, 1870-1916: A Check List." ALABAMA REVIEW, 18 (1965), 65-72.

42 Palmer, Helen H., and Jane Dyson, comps. AMERICAN DRAMA CRITICISM. INTERPRETATIONS, 1890-1965 INCLUSIVE OF AMERICAN DRAMA SINCE THE FIRST PLAY PRODUCED IN AMERICA. Hamden, Conn.: Shoe String Press, 1967.

> This checklist consists mainly of reviews of plays and articles from commercial magazines, rather than scholarly journals, for a highly selected list of dramatists. Slight value.

43 _____. AMERICAN DRAMA CRITICISM. SUPPLEMENT I. Hamden, Conn.: Shoe String Press, 1970.

> Updated to January 1969. Little value; for example, there are only single entries for Boucicault, Godfrey, Paulding, and Tyler. See also entry no. 18.

44 Roden, Robert F., comp. LATER AMERICAN PLAYS, 1831-1900: BEING A COMPILATION OF THE TITLES OF PLAYS BY AMERICAN AUTHORS PUBLISHED AND PERFORMED IN AMERICA SINCE 1831. 1900; rpt. New York: Burt Franklin, 1969.

> A valuable listing but incomplete.

45 Ryan, Pat M., comp. AMERICAN DRAMA BIBLIOGRAPHY, A CHECKLIST OF PUBLICATIONS IN ENGLISH. Fort Wayne, Ind.: Fort Wayne Public Library, 1969.

> Divided into three sections--"Historical and Reference," "General Background," "Individual Authors"--this checklist includes general criticism and biographical material on significant American playwrights and their plays.

46 Sabin, Joseph, comp. BIBLIOTHECA AMERICANA. A DICTIONARY OF BOOKS RELATING TO AMERICA, FROM ITS DISCOVERY TO THE PRESENT TIME. Begun by Joseph Sabin and continued by Wilberforce Eames for the Bibliographical Society of America. New York: 1868-1936.

> Published under various imprints. Volumes 1-20 by Sabin-Eames; Volumes 21-29 completed by R.W.G. Vail. A basic text for bibliography of selected American authors. See also entries nos. 70 and 75.

Critical, Historical, Reference Resources

47 Salem, James M. A GUIDE TO CRITICAL REVIEWS: PART I: AMERICAN DRAMA, 1909-1969. 2nd ed. Metuchen, N.J.: Scarecrow Press, 1973.

   Reviews of American plays on New York stage. The volume contains a few entries for eighteenth- and nineteenth-century dramatists, but is marred by a misleading table of contents.

48 Spiller, Robert E., et al., eds. LITERARY HISTORY OF THE UNITED STATES. 4th ed. 2 vols. New York: Macmillan, 1974.

   This is a major source for general information on American dramatists. Volume 2 is a bibliography.

49 Stoddard, Roger E., comp. "A Catalogue of the Dramatic Imprints of David and Thomas Longworth, 1802-1821." PAPERS OF THE AMERICAN ANTIQUARIAN SOCIETY, 84 (1975), 317-406.

   Stoddard locates, collates, and describes all dramatic imprints of this very active publisher; he lists 429 editions of 374 plays.

50 _____. "Some Corrigenda and Addenda to Hill's AMERICAN PLAYS PRINTED IN 1714-1839." PUBLICATIONS OF THE BIBLIOGRAPHICAL SOCIETY OF AMERICA, 65 (1971), 278-95.

   Stoddard provides a serious and scholarly criticism of Hill's work (see entry no. 26) and offers corrections and additions as a first step toward a necessary revision.

51 Stratman, Carl J. AMERICAN THEATRICAL PERIODICALS, 1798-1967. Durham, N.C.: Duke University Press, 1970.

   This book lists name, place, dates, editors, changes in name of periodicals which treat theatre. Although incomplete, it is still a valuable source book.

52 _____, comp. BIBLIOGRAPHY OF THE AMERICAN THEATRE, EXCLUDING NEW YORK CITY. Chicago: Loyola University Press, 1965.

   Mainly concerned with historical theatre research, listed by states, this work pays some attention to dramatic criticism.

53 Watson, Charles S. "Eighteenth and Nineteenth Century Drama." In A BIBLIOGRAPHICAL GUIDE TO THE STUDY OF SOUTHERN LITERATURE. Ed. Louis D. Rubin, Jr. Baton Rouge: Louisiana State University Press, 1969, pp. 92-99.

54 Wegelin, Oscar, comp. EARLY AMERICAN PLAYS, 1714-1830. New York: Dunlap Society, 1900.

Critical, Historical, Reference Resources

This early basic text, improved by Hill (entry no. 26) is a compilation of titles of plays and dramatic poems written by people born or residing in North America.

55 Woodress, James, comp. DISSERTATIONS IN AMERICAN LITERATURE, 1891-1966. Durham, N.C.: Duke University Press, 1968.

Revised and enlarged from 1957 issue, this includes nearly forty-seven hundred entries listed alphabetically by American authors or genre; "Drama" entries, 2926-3281.

B. INDEXES

57 Adkins, Nelson F., comp. EARLY AMERICAN PERIODICALS INDEX TO 1850. New York: Readex Microprint, 1964.

Consisting of approximately 650,000 cards based upon a close analysis of about 340 American magazines published from about 1730 to 1860, this project was originally conceived and sponsored by the English Department of New York University, the New York City Board of Education, and the New York University libraries. Staff was provided by the Works Progress Administration which reproduced a part of the work, undated. Turned over to the New York University library in 1939, the index was continued and published: INDEX TO EARLY AMERICAN PERIODICAL LITERATURE, 1728-1870. New York: Pamphlet Distributing Co., 1941-42. It now consists of eight boxes of cards arranged under six catagories; the material relevant to this bibliography are A. General Prose, authors and anonymous titles (1 box) and F. Subjects (2 boxes).

58 _____. INDEX OF EARLY AMERICAN PERIODICALS. New York: Readex Microprint Corp., 1968.

A continuation of entry no. 57.

59 AMERICAN PERIODICAL SERIES, 19TH CENTURY--1800-1850. A CONSOLIDATED INDEX TO THE MICROFILM SERIES OF 18TH CENTURY PERIODICALS AND TO THE FIRST 10 YEARS OF THE 1800-1850 SERIES. Ann Arbor, Mich.: University Microfilms, 1956.

60 AMERICAN PERIODICAL SERIES, 1800-1850. A GUIDE TO YEARS 21-31 OF THE MICROFILM COLLECTION, REELS 817-1151 WITH TITLE INDEX TO YEARS 1-31. Ann Arbor, Mich.: University Microfilms, 1972.

Critical, Historical, Reference Resources

61   AMERICAN PERIODICAL SERIES, 1800-1850. A GUIDE TO THE MICROFILM COLLECTION, REELS 1152-1408 WITH TITLE INDEX TO YEARS 1-37. Ann Arbor, Mich.: University Microfilms, 1974.

62   Blitgen, Sister Carol, comp. "An Index to: A RECORD OF THE BOSTON STAGE by William W. Clapp, Jr." TD, 1 (1968), 35-68.

       See also Clapp's RECORD OF THE BOSTON STAGE, entry no. 123.

63   Chicorel, Marietta, ed. CHICOREL THEATER INDEX TO PLAYS IN ANTHOLOGIES, PERIODICALS, DISCS AND TAPES. New York: Chicorel Library Publishing Co., 1970-- .

       A multivolume indexing relative to drama and theatre. A continuing project.

64   Clough, Peter H., comp. "A Subject Index to: DRAMA SURVEY, 1961-1968." TD, 3 (1970), 81-100.

65   Cornyn, Stan, comp. A SELECTIVE INDEX TO THEATRE MAGAZINE. Metuchen, N.J.: Scarecrow Press, 1964.

       Index covers years 1900-30.

66   DRAMATIC INDEX FOR 1909-49; COVERING ARTICLES AND ILLUSTRATIONS CONCERNING THE STAGE AND ITS PLAYERS IN THE PERIODICALS OF AMERICA AND ENGLAND AND INCLUDING THE DRAMATIC BOOKS OF THE YEAR. 41 vols. Boston: Boston Book Co., 1910-18; Boston: F.W. Faxon Co., 1919-52.

       This index is continued in BULLETIN OF BIBLIOGRAPHY through August 1953; later as BULLETIN OF BIBLIOGRAPHY AND MAGAZINE NOTES.

67   Firkins, Ina Ten Eyck, comp. INDEX TO PLAYS 1800-1926. New York: H.W. Wilson, 1927.

68   Hamar, Clifford E., comp. "American Theatre History, A Geographical Index." ETJ, 1 (1949), 164-94.

       Inaccurate list of doubtful significance.

69   Keller, Dean H., comp. INDEX TO PLAYS IN PERIODICALS. Metuchen, N.J.: Scarecrow Press, 1971.

       This work indexes 103 magazines through 1969 providing both author and title indexes. A few entries refer to pre-1900 plays.

Critical, Historical, Reference Resources

70 Marder, Carl J. III, comp. "An Index to: PERSONAL RECOLLECTIONS OF THE DRAMA by Henry Dickinson Stone." TD, 3 (1970), 65-80.

71 Molnar, John Edgar, comp. AUTHOR-TITLE INDEX TO SABIN'S BIBLIOTHECA AMERICANA. 3 vols. Metuchen, N.J.: Scarecrow Press, 1974.

> See also Sabin's BIBLIOTHECA AMERICANA, entry no. 46.

72 Ottemiller, John H., comp. INDEX TO PLAYS IN COLLECTIONS. AN AUTHOR AND TITLE INDEX TO PLAYS APPEARING IN COLLECTIONS PUBLISHED BETWEEN 1900 AND 1956. 4th ed., rev. and enl. New York: Scarecrow Press, 1964.

> The 6th edition, revised and enlarged, covers 1900 to early 1975, compiled by John M. Connor and Billie M. Connor (Metuchen, N.J.: Scarecrow Press, 1976).

73 Pence, James H., comp. THE MAGAZINE AND THE DRAMA. AN INDEX. New York: Dunlap Society, 1896.

> A list of articles on the drama published in nineteenth-century periodicals.

74 Srnka, Alfred H., comp. "An Index to: PERSONAL RECOLLECTIONS OF THE STAGE by William Burke Wood." TD, 2 (1969), 51-73.

75 Thompson, Lawrence S., comp. THE NEW SABIN. BOOKS DESCRIBED BY JOSEPH SABIN AND HIS SUCCESSORS, NOW DESCRIBED AGAIN ON THE BASIS OF EXAMINATION OF ORIGINALS, AND FULLY INDEXED BY TITLE, SUBJECT, JOINT AUTHORS, AND INSTITUTIONS AND AGENCIES. 4 vols. Troy, N.Y.: Whitston Publishing Co., 1974-- .

> Volume 1, entries 1-2484, plus index, 1974; volume 2, entries 2485-5802, plus index, 1975; volume 3, entries 5803-8443, plus index, 1976; volume 4, entries 8444-11225, plus index, 1977. See also Sabin's BIBLIOTHECA AMERICANA, entry no. 46.

C. LIBRARY AND MICROREPRODUCED COLLECTIONS

76 Ash, Lee, with assistance of William Miller and Alfred Waltermire, Jr., comps. SUBJECT COLLECTIONS: A GUIDE TO SPECIAL BOOK COLLECTIONS AND SUBJECT EMPHASES AS REPORTED BY UNIVERSITY, COLLEGE, PUBLIC AND SPECIAL LIBRARIES IN THE UNITED STATES, THE TERRITORIES, AND CANADA. 4th ed., rev. and enl. New York: R.R. Bowker, 1974.

Critical, Historical, Reference Resources

77 BIBLIOGRAPHIC GUIDE TO THEATRE ARTS: 1975, 1976, 1977. Boston: G.K. Hall,

   These annually published bibliographies list in a computer-produced format all materials cataloged during any given year by the New York Public Library Theatre and Drama Collections, with additional entries from the Library of Congress. They serve as an annual supplement to the CATALOG OF THE THEATRE AND DRAMA COLLECTIONS. See entries nos. 88 and 89.

78 DICTIONARY CATALOGUE OF THE HARRIS COLLECTION OF AMERICAN POETRY AND PLAYS. 13 vols. (Providence, R.I.: Brown University Library); Boston: G.K. Hall, 1972.

   Two hundred years of American plays, 1765-1964; this catalog was established to celebrate the bicentennial of the first printing of THE PRINCE OF PARTHIA.

79 Downs, Robert Bingham. AMERICAN LIBRARY RESOURCES: A BIBLIOGRAPHICAL GUIDE. Chicago: American Library Association, 1951. SUPPLEMENT, 1950-1961, 1962. SUPPLEMENT, 1961-1970, 1972.

80 Engle, Gary. "The Atkinson Collection of Ethiopian Dramas at the University of Chicago." RESOURCES FOR AMERICAN LITERARY STUDY, 1 (1971), 181-91.

   A description of the Atkinson Collection; this collection and the Morton Collection at the University of Chicago Library contain some sixteen hundred plays, 1850-1910.

81 Evans, Charles, comp. AMERICAN BIBLIOGRAPHY: A CHRONOLOGICAL DICTIONARY OF ALL BOOKS, PAMPHLETS AND PERIODICAL PUBLICATIONS PRINTED IN THE UNITED STATES OF AMERICA, FROM THE GENESIS OF PRINTING IN 1639 DOWN TO AND INCLUDING THE YEAR 1820; WITH BIBLIOGRAPHICAL AND BIOGRAPHICAL NOTES. 12 vols. Chicago: Blakely Press, 1903-34.

   Evans completed his ambitious task only through 1799; Shipton and Bristol have completed the work through 1820, while others (Shaw, Shoemaker, etc.) are endeavoring to extend the bibliography beyond that date:

   a. Shipton, Clifford K., comp. THE AMERICAN BIBLIOGRAPHY OF CHARLES EVANS. Vol. 13. Worcester, Mass.: American Antiquarian Society, 1955.

   b. Bristol, Roger Pattrell, comp. THE AMERICAN BIBLIOGRAPHY OF CHARLES EVANS. Vol. 14. Worcester, Mass.: American Antiquarian Society, 1959.

c. _____. SUPPLEMENT TO CHARLES EVANS' AMERICAN BIBLIOGRAPHY. Charlottesville: University Press of Virginia, 1962, 1970.

> This bibliography adds 11,200 items which escaped Evans and Shipton.

d. Shaw, Ralph R., and Richard H. Shoemaker, comps. AMERICAN BIBLIOGRAPHY: A PRELIMINARY CHECKLIST FOR 1801-1819. 22 vols. New York: Scarecrow Press, 1958-66.

> This project is being continued by Scarecrow Press under the title A CHECKLIST OF AMERICAN IMPRINTS as follows:
>
> Shoemaker, 1820-1825. 1964-69.
>
> Shoemaker, assisted by Gayle Cooper. 1828-1829. 1970-71. M. Frances Cooper has prepared a TITLE INDEX, 1972, and an AUTHOR INDEX (with corrections and sources), 1973, to the CHECKLIST OF AMERICAN IMPRINTS FOR 1820-1829.
>
> Cooper, Gayle. 1830. 1972.
>
> Bruntjen, Scott and Carol. 1831. 1975.
>
> Bruntjen, Scott and Carol. 1932. 1977.

e. Readex Microprint undertook to reproduce the items in the Evans's AMERICAN BIBLIOGRAPHY and its continuation by other scholars:

> Shipton, Clifford K., ed. EARLY AMERICAN IMPRINTS (FIRST SERIES, EVANS) 1639-1800. Worcester, Mass.: American Antiquarian Society, 1955-57. (26 boxes)
>
> Shipton, Clifford K., James E. Mooney, and John B. Hench, eds. EARLY AMERICAN IMPRINTS (SECOND SERIES, SHAW-SHOEMAKER) 1801-1819. Worcester, Mass.: American Antiquarian Society, 1964.
>
> Shipton, Clifford K., and James E. Mooney, comps. NATIONAL INDEX OF AMERICAN IMPRINTS THROUGH 1800. 2 vols. Worcester, Mass.: American Antiquarian Society, 1969.

82 Fracchia, Charles Anthony, ed. GLEESON LIBRARY ASSOCIATES, UNIVERSITY OF SAN FRANCISCO, no. 5 (February 1965).

> An unnumbered eight-page supplement to this newsletter contains a checklist of the George W. Poultney Collection of Theatre Manuscripts which include mainly late nineteenth-century and early twentieth-century American plays.

Critical, Historical, Reference Resources

83   Freedley, George. "The New York Public Library's Theatre Collection." WILSON LIBRARY BULLETIN, 38 (1964), 636-39.

> A brief history and description of the theatre collection and its major additions from 1895 to the present.

84   Freedley, George, and Allardyce Nicoll, eds. ENGLISH AND AMERICAN PLAYS OF THE 19TH CENTURY. AMERICAN PLAYS 1831-1900. New York: Readex Microprint Corp., 1964-- .

> An extremely valuable collection; a continuing project. Microprint reproductions of the items listed in the bibliography of Arthur Hobson Quinn's A HISTORY OF THE AMERICAN DRAMA (see entries nos. 163 and 164). See also entry no. 94.

85   Gilder, Rosamond, and George Freedley, comps. THEATRE COLLECTIONS IN LIBRARIES AND MUSEUMS. New York: Theatre Arts, 1936.

> A standard early work now out of date.

86   Haskell, David C., comp. "List of American Dramas in the New York Public Library." BNYPL, 19 (1915), 739-86.

> A list of approximately twelve hundred plays; useful but badly out of date.

87   Hunter, Frederick J., comp. A GUIDE TO THE THEATRE AND DRAMA COLLECTION AT THE UNIVERSITY OF TEXAS. Austin: University of Texas, 1967.

> Most relevant to American drama is the small G.C. Howard Collection of nineteenth-century plays.

88   New York Public Library. CATALOG OF THE THEATRE AND DRAMA COLLECTIONS. PART 1, DRAMA COLLECTION: AUTHOR LISTING. 6 vols. Boston: G.K. Hall, 1967.

89   _____. CATALOG OF THE THEATRE AND DRAMA COLLECTIONS. PART 1, DRAMA COLLECTION: FIRST SUPPLEMENT, LISTING OF CULTURAL ORIGINS. Boston: G.K. Hall, 1973.

90   Sarlos, Robert K. "The Facilities in Support of Dramatic Art at the University of California, Davis." TD, 4 (1971-72), 37-40.

91   _____. "The Theatrical Collection at Davis." AMERICAN SOCIETY FOR THEATRE RESEARCH NEWSLETTER, n.s. 3 (Fall 1974), 1-2, 9, 10.

Critical, Historical, Reference Resources

92 Sperber, Ann. "Lincoln Center's Library and Museum for Performing Arts." LIBRARY JOURNAL, 15 April 1972, pp. 1493-99.

> A general essay for the interested, beginning student.

93 Von Chorba, Albert, Jr., comp. "Checklist of American Drama Published in the English Colonies of North America and the United States through 1865 in the Possession of The Library, University of Pennsylvania." Philadelphia: University of Pennsylvania Library, 1951. Mimeo.

> A listing of 592 items, some of which are different editions of the same play.

94 Wells, Henry W., ed. THREE CENTURIES OF ENGLISH AND AMERICAN PLAYS, 1500-1830. New York: Readex Microprint Corp., 1953.

> Includes American plays, 1714-1830. With the Freedley-Nicoll collection (entry no. 84) these microprints are the most readily available source of American plays--beginnings to 1900. See also Bergquist, entry no. 11.

95 Young, William C., comp. AMERICAN THEATRICAL ARTS: A GUIDE TO MANUSCRIPTS AND SPECIAL COLLECTIONS IN THE UNITED STATES AND CANADA. Chicago: American Library Association, 1971.

> Describes collections in 138 U.S. and Canadian libraries. Lists all types of theatre and gives information on actors, directors, playwrights, and so forth.

D. ANTHOLOGIES AND COLLECTED PLAYS

96 Bates, Alfred, ed. THE DRAMA. 22 vols. New York: Smart and Stanley, 1903.

> Volume 19, AMERICAN DRAMA, contains a synopsis and quotations from A CURE FOR THE SPLEEN, attributed to Jonathan Sewall, a scene from THE FATHER OF AN ONLY CHILD by William Dunlap, THE SPANISH STUDENT by H.W. Longfellow, THÉRÈSE, THE ORPHAN OF GENEVA by John Howard Payne, a dramatization of J.F. Cooper's THE WEPT OF WISH-TON-WISH, and RIP VAN WINKLE by Charles Burke.

> Volume 20, AMERICAN DRAMA, contains SOLON SHINGLE by J.S. Jones, PO-CA-HON-TAS by John Brougham, and THE 'FORTY-NINERS by T.W. Hanshew.

97 Booth, Michael, ed. HISS THE VILLAIN. New York: Blom, 1964.

> Includes UNDER THE GASLIGHT by Augustin Daly and TEN NIGHTS IN A BAR-ROOM by William W. Pratt.

Critical, Historical, Reference Resources

98   Cerf, Bennett, and Van H. Cartmell, comps. S.R.O. THE MOST SUCCESSFUL PLAYS OF THE AMERICAN STAGE. New York: Doubleday, 1944.

>   Includes UNCLE TOM'S CABIN by A.E. Thomas, EAST LYNNE by Mrs. Henry Wood, THE OLD HOMESTEAD by Denman Thompson, and RIP VAN WINKLE as played by Joseph Jefferson.

99   Chapman, John, and Garrison P. Sherwood, eds. THE BEST PLAYS OF 1894-99. New York: Dodd, Mead, 1955.

>   Includes commentary and abbreviated versions of THE HEART OF MARYLAND by David Belasco and SECRET SERVICE by William Gillette.

100   Clark, Barrett H., general ed. AMERICA'S LOST PLAYS. 20 vols. Princeton, N.J.: Princeton University Press, 1940-41; reissued in 10 vols. plus an additional (21st) vol., Bloomington: Indiana University Press, 1963-65, 1969.

>   The twenty-one volumes are listed below with their editors and pertinent plays noted. Each volume contains an introductory essay and notes.
>
>   I. Allardyce Nicoll and F. Theodore Cloak, eds. Dion Boucicault's FORBIDDEN FRUIT, LOUIS XI, DOT, FLYING SCUD, MERCY DODD, and ROBERT EMMET.
>
>   II. Oral Sumner Coad, ed. William Dunlap's FALSE SHAME and THIRTY YEARS.
>
>   III. Sculley Bradley, ed. George H. Boker's THE WORLD A MASK, THE BANKRUPT, and GLAUCUS
>
>   IV. Isaac Goldberg and Hubert Heffner, eds. ROSEDALE by Lester Wallack, ACROSS THE CONTINENT by James McCloskey, DAVY CROCKETT by Frank Murdoch, SAM'L OF POSEN by George H. Jessop, and OUR BOARDING HOUSE by Leonard Grover.
>
>   V. Codman Hislop and W.R. Richardson, eds. John H. Payne's TRIAL WITHOUT JURY, MOUNT SAVAGE, THE BOARDING SCHOOLS, THE TWO SONS-IN-LAW, MAZEPPA, and THE SPANISH HUSBAND.
>
>   VI. Codman Hislop and W.R. Richardson, eds. John H. Payne's THE LAST DUEL IN SPAIN, WOMAN'S REVENGE, THE ITALIAN BRIDE, ROMULUS THE SHEPHERD KING, and THE BLACK MAN.
>
>   VII. Arthur Hobson Quinn, ed. James A. Herne's WITHIN AN INCH OF HIS LIFE, "THE MINUTE MEN" OF 1774-1775, DRIFTING APART, and THE REVEREND GRIFFITH DAVENPORT (Act IV).

Critical, Historical, Reference Resources

VIII. Garrett H. Leverton, ed. A ROYAL SLAVE by Clarence Bennett, THE GREAT DIAMOND ROBBERY by Edward M. Alfriend and A.C. Wheeler, FROM RAGS TO RICHES by Charles A. Taylor, NO MOTHER TO GUIDE HER by Lillian Mortimer, and BILLY THE KID by Walter Woods.

IX. Douglas L. Hunt, ed. Charles Hoyt's A BUNCH OF KEYS, A MIDNIGHT BELL, A TRIP TO CHINATOWN, A TEMPERANCE TOWN, and A MILK WHITE FLAG.

X. Allan G[ates] Halline, ed. Bronson Howard's HURRICANE, OLD LOVE LETTERS, THE BANKER'S DAUGHTER, BARON RUDOLPH, KNAVE AND QUEEN, and ONE OF OUR GIRLS.

XI. Percy MacKaye, ed. Steele MacKaye's ROSE MICHEL, WON AT LAST, IN SPITE OF ALL, and AN ARRANT KNAVE.

XII. Edward H. O'Neill, ed. R.M. Bird's THE COWLED LOVER, CARIDORF, NEWS OF THE NIGHT, and 'TWAS ALL FOR THE BEST.

XIII. Ralph H. Ware and H.W. Schoenberger, eds. R.P. Smith's THE SENTINELS, THE BOMBARDMENT OF ALGIERS, WILLIAM PENN, SHAKESPEARE IN LOVE, A WIFE AT A VENTURE, and THE LAST MAN.

XIV. Eugene R. Page, ed. METAMORA (with the fourth act supplied in the I.U. Press issue), TANCRED, KING OF SICILY, by J.A. Stone, THE SPY by Charles P. Clinch, THE BATTLE OF STILLWATER by H.J. Conway, THE USURPER by J.S. Jones, THE CROCK OF GOLD by S.S. Steele, JOB AND HIS CHILDREN by J.M. Field, SIGNOR MARC by J.H. Wilkins, and THE DUKE'S MOTTO by John Brougham.

XV. Arthur Wallace Peach and George Floyd Newbrough, eds. Royall Tyler's THE ISLAND OF BARRATARIA, THE ORIGIN OF THE FEAST OF PURIM, JOSEPH AND HIS BRETHREN, and THE JUDGEMENT OF SOLOMON.

XVI. J.B. Russak, ed. MONTE CRISTO as played by James O'Neill, HIPPOLYTUS by Julia Ward Howe, MISTRESS NELL by George C. Hazelton, BECKY SHARP by Langdon Mitchell, and THE WARRENS OF VIRGINIA by William C. DeMille.

XVII. Robert Hamilton Ball, ed. THE MAIN LINE by Henry C. DeMille and Charles Barnard and THE WIFE, LORD CHUMLEY, THE CHARITY BALL, and MEN AND WOMEN by DeMille and David Belasco.

Critical, Historical, Reference Resources

        XVIII. Glenn Hughes and George Savage, eds. THE GIRL I LEFT BEHIND ME by David Belasco and Franklin Fyles and LA BELLE RUSE, THE STRANGLERS OF PARIS, THE HEART OF MARYLAND, and NAUGHTY ANTHONY by David Belasco.

        XIX. Napier Wilt, ed. Bartley Campbell's THE VIRGINIAN, MY PARTNER, THE GALLEY SLAVE, FAIRFAX, and THE WHITE SLAVE.

        XX. Catherine Sturtevant, ed. Augustin Daly's MAN AND WIFE, DIVORCE, THE BIG BONANZA, PIQUE, and NEEDLES AND PINS.

        XXI. Walter J. Meserve and William R. Reardon, eds. ANDROBOROS by Robert Hunter, the anonymous THE TRIAL OF ATTICUS BEFORE JUSTICE BEAU FOR A RAPE, the anonymous THE BATTLE OF BROOKLYN, DARBY'S RETURN by William Dunlap, and PO-CA-HON-TAS by John Brougham.

101   _____, ed. FAVORITE AMERICAN PLAYS OF THE NINETEENTH CENTURY. Princeton, N.J.: Princeton University Press, 1943.

        METAMORA by John A. Stone, DAVY CROCKETT by Frank Murdock, MONTE CRISTO by Charles Fechter, FLYING SCUD by Dion Boucicault, THE BANKER'S DAUGHTER by Bronson Howard, MY PARTNER by Bartley Campbell, A TRIP TO CHINATOWN by Charles H. Hoyt, THE GREAT DIAMOND ROBBERY by Edward Alfriend and A.C. Wheeler, THE HEART OF MARYLAND by David Belasco, and THE MIGHTY DOLLAR by Benjamin E. Woolf.

102   Coyle, William, and Harry G. Damaser, eds. SIX EARLY AMERICAN PLAYS, 1798-1900. Columbus, Ohio: Charles E. Merrill, 1968.

        Weak and confused introduction. Includes ANDRÉ by William Dunlap, METAMORA by John A. Stone, FASHION by Anna Cora Mowatt, THE OCTOROON by Dion Boucicault, SHENANDOAH by Bronson Howard, and MARGARET FLEMING by James A. Herne.

103   Downer, Alan S. AMERICAN DRAMA. New York: Thomas Y. Crowell, 1960.

        Includes THE CONTRAST by Royall Tyler and SHORE ACRES by James A. Herne.

104   Gassner, John, and Mollie Gassner, eds. BEST PLAYS OF THE EARLY AMERICAN THEATRE. New York: Crown, 1967.

Critical, Historical, Reference Resources

Includes THE CONTRAST by Royall Tyler, SUPERSTITION by James N. Barker, CHARLES II by Payne-Irving, UNCLE TOM'S CABIN by George L. Aiken, THE OCTOROON by Dion Boucicault, COUNT OF MONTE CRISTO by Charles Fechter, THE MOUSE TRAP by W.D. Howells, and SECRET SERVICE by William Gillette.

105   Halline, Allan G[ates], ed. AMERICAN PLAYS. New York: American Book Co., 1935.

Includes THE BUCKTAILS by James K. Paulding, THE GLADIATOR by Robert M. Bird, BIANCA VISCONTI by Nathaniel P. Willis, HORIZON by Augustin Daly, THE DANITES IN THE SIERRAS by J. Miller, THE HENRIETTA by Bronson Howard, THE CONTRAST by Royall Tyler, ANDRÉ by William Dunlap, SUPERSTITION by James N. Barker, FASHION by Anna C.M. Ritchie, and FRANCESCA DA RIMINI by George H. Boker.

106   Lovell, John, Jr., comp. DIGESTS OF GREAT AMERICAN PLAYS. New York: Thomas Y. Crowell, 1961.

A useful reference work; complete, act-by-act summaries of 34 plays through 1900; 102 plays summarized in book.

107   Matlaw, Myron, ed. THE BLACK CROOK AND OTHER NINETEENTH-CENTURY AMERICAN PLAYS. New York: Dutton, 1967.

Includes FASHION by Anna C.M. Ritchie, FRANCESCA DA RIMINI by George H. Boker, THE OCTOROON by Dion Boucicault, Jefferson's version of RIP VAN WINKLE, THE BLACK CROOK by Charles Barras, SHENANDOAH by Bronson Howard, and MARGARET FLEMING by James A. Herne.

Very selective bibliography.

108   Moody, Richard, ed. DRAMAS FROM THE AMERICAN THEATRE, 1762-1909. New York: World, 1966.

Excellent bibliography and introductory essays to plays; includes twenty-four plays prior to 1900: A DIALOGUE AND ODE by Francis Hopkinson, A DIALOGUE BETWEEN AN ENGLISHMAN AND AN INDIAN by John Smith, A LITTLE TEATABLE CHITCHAT by John Smith, THE CANDIDATES by Robert Munford, THE CONTRAST by Tyler, BUNKER-HILL by John Daly Burk, THE GLORY OF COLUMBIA: HER YEOMANRY! by William Dunlap, SHE WOULD BE A SOLDIER by M.M. Noah, THE FOREST ROSE by Samuel Woodworth, A TRIP TO NIAGARA by William Dunlap, THE GLADIATOR by Robert M. Bird, THE DRUNKARD by William Smith, FASHION

Critical, Historical, Reference Resources

by Anna C.M. Ritchie, UNCLE TOM'S CABIN by George L. Aiken, METAMORA by Stone, PO-CA-HON-TAS by John Brougham, FRANCESCA DA RIMINI by George H. Boker, ACROSS THE CONTINENT by James J. McCloskey, THE MULLIGAN GUARD BALL by Edward Harrigan, SHENANDOAH by Bronson Howard, A LETTER OF INTRODUCTION by W.D. Howells, A TEMPERANCE TOWN by Charles H. Hoyt, and SHORE ACRES by James A. Herne.

109 Moses, Montrose J., ed. REPRESENTATIVE AMERICAN DRAMAS, NATIONAL AND LOCAL. Boston: Little, Brown, 1925.

Plays from 1894-1924 period including A TEXAS STEER by Charles Hoyt.

110 _____. REPRESENTATIVE AMERICAN DRAMAS, NATIONAL AND LOCAL. Rev. Joseph Wood Krutch. Boston: Little, Brown, 1941.

111 _____. REPRESENTATIVE PLAYS BY AMERICAN DRAMATISTS. 3 vols. 1918-25; rpt. New York: Blom, 1964.

Good introduction to each volume. Includes a number of nineteenth-century plays, as noted below.

Volume I: THE PRINCE OF PARTHIA by Thomas Godfrey, PONTEACH by Robert Rogers, THE GROUP by Mercy Warren, THE BATTLE OF BUNKER'S HILL by H.H. Brackenridge, THE FALL OF BRITISH TYRANNY by John Leacock, THE POLITICIAN OUTWITTED by Samuel Low, THE CONTRAST by Royall Tyler, ANDRÉ by William Dunlap, THE INDIAN PRINCESS by James N. Barker, and SHE WOULD BE A SOLDIER by M.M. Noah.

Volume II: FASHIONABLE FOLLIES by Joseph Hutton, BRUTUS by John H. Payne, SERTORIUS by D.P. Brown, TORTESA THE USURER by N.P. Willis, THE PEOPLE'S LAWYER by J.S. Jones, JACK CADE by R.T. Conrad, FASHION by A.C.M. Ritchie, UNCLE TOM'S CABIN by G.L. Aiken, SELF by Mrs. Sidney Bateman, and HORSESHOE ROBINSON by C.W. Tayleure.

Volume III: RIP VAN WINKLE by Charles Burke, FRANCESCA DA RIMINI by George H. Boker, LOVE IN '76 by O.B. Bunce, PAUL KAUVAR by Steele MacKaye, SHENANDOAH by Bronson Howard, IN MISSOURA by Augustus Thomas, THE MOTH AND THE FLAME by Clyde Fitch, and THE RETURN OF PETER GRIMM by David Belasco.

Critical, Historical, Reference Resources

112   NEW YORK DRAMA, A CHOICE COLLECTION OF TRAGEDIES, COMEDIES, FARCES, COMEDIETTAS, ETC. 5 vols. New York: Wheat and Cornett, 1876-78.

   An interesting assortment of plays produced in New York, ranging from Shakespeare through the present day. Includes a few American plays: Volume 1, BRUTUS by John H. Payne and THE PERSECUTED DUTCHMAN by S. Barry; Volume 2, CHARLES THE SECOND by Payne-Irving, RIP VAN WINKLE by Charles Burke, and THE YANKEE PEDDLER by Morris Barnett; Volume 4, THE STAGE-STRUCK YANKEE by O.E. Durivage; and Volume 5, HANDY ANDY by W.R. Floyd.

113   Philbrick, Norman, ed. TRUMPETS SOUNDING: PROPAGANDA PLAYS OF THE AMERICAN REVOLUTION. New York: Blom, 1972.

   Seven plays with full introductions setting them in the period: anonymous, A DIALOGUE BETWEEN A SOUTHERN DELEGATE, AND HIS SPOUSE, ON HIS RETURN FROM THE GRAND CONTINENTAL CONGRESS; THE FALL OF BRITISH TYRANNY by John Leacock; THE BLOCKHEADS, attributed to Mercy Warren; anonymous, THE BATTLE OF BROOKLYN; THE DEATH OF GENERAL MONTGOMERY by H.H. Brackenridge; THE PATRIOTS by Robert Munford; and THE MOTLEY ASSEMBLY, attributed to Mercy Warren.

114   Quinn, Arthur Hobson, ed. REPRESENTATIVE AMERICAN PLAYS. 7th ed. New York: Appleton-Century-Crofts, 1953.

   Excellent introductions, notes, and texts of plays "from 1767 to the Present Day." Includes seventeen plays through 1900: THE PRINCE OF PARTHIA by Thomas Godfrey, THE CONTRAST by Royall Tyler, ANDRÉ by William Dunlap, SUPERSTITION by James N. Barker, CHARLES THE SECOND by Payne and Irving, POCAHONTAS by G.W.P. Custis, THE BROKER OF BOGOTA by Robert M. Bird, TORTESA THE USURER by N.P. Willis, FASHION by Anna C.M. Ritchie, FRANCESCA DA RIMINI by George H. Boker, THE OCTOROON by Dion Boucicault, RIP VAN WINKLE as played by Jefferson, HAZEL KIRK by Steele MacKaye, SHENANDOAH by Bronson Howard, MARGARET FLEMING by James A. Herne, SECRET SERVICE by William Gillette, and MADAME BUTTERFLY by David Belasco and Luther Long.

115   THEATRICAL COMICALITIES, WHIMSICALITIES, ODDITIES AND DROLLERIES. N.p., 1828.

   An interesting and typical early nineteenth-century collection of skits, sketches, and amateur acts.

Critical, Historical, Reference Resources

E. HISTORIES

116   THE AMERICAN THEATRE: A SUM OF ITS PARTS. New York: Samuel French, 1971.

>A collection of papers delivered at the first American College Theatre Festival, Washington, D.C. (1969). Although mainly on theatre, a few papers consider the drama. Ralph G. Allen's "Our Native Theatre: Honky-Tonk, Minstrel Shows, Burlesque" (pp. 273-316) is chiefly concerned with burlesque and includes scripts of "Four Burlesque Bits." Elliot Norton's "Puffers, Pundits and Other Play Reviewers: A Short History of American Dramatic Criticism" (pp. 317-38) is sketchy, mainly personal, and falls far short of its suggested objective. Randolph Edmonds' "Black Drama in the American Theatre: 1700-1970" (pp. 379-428) focuses chiefly on modern plays about Negroes.

117   Anderson, John. THE AMERICAN THEATRE. New York: Dial Press, 1938.

>See chapter II, "The Apprentice" (pp. 31-56), an interesting but slight commentary on nineteenth-century American drama.

118   Atkinson, Brooks. BROADWAY. New York: Macmillan, 1970.

>Reminiscences of a major drama and theatre critic with references to and brief discussions of the work of turn-of-the-century dramatists.

119   Bates, Alfred, ed. THE DRAMA. 22 vols. New York: Smart and Stanley, 1903.

>Volume 19, AMERICAN DRAMA is a general history of the drama and the theatre from colonial times through the opening of the nineteenth century. Largely dated in its comments but valuable for the analysis of particular plays, and the reprinting of dialogue, scenes, and complete plays. See entry no. 96 for a list of the plays included.
>
>Volume 20, AMERICAN DRAMA is concerned with drama and theatre from 1830 through the end of the century. Details of acting and management plus considerable information on playwrights. See entry no. 96 for a list of the plays included.

120   Bradley, [Edward] Sculley. "The Emergence of the Modern Drama." In LITERARY HISTORY OF THE UNITED STATES. Ed. Robert E. Spiller et al., II. pp. 1000-1015. See entry no. 48.

>A brief survey of nineteenth-century American drama.

Critical, Historical, Reference Resources

121 Brockett, Oscar G., and Robert R. Findlay. CENTURY OF INNOVATION; A HISTORY OF EUROPEAN AND AMERICAN THEATRE AND DRAMA SINCE 1870. Englewood Cliffs, N.J.: Prentice-Hall, 1973.

   Little evaluation of American drama prior to 1915; see pages 179-84.

122 Burton, Richard. THE NEW AMERICAN DRAMA. New York: Thomas Y. Crowell, 1913.

   Most emphasis on drama since 1870. Burton notes three stages in the drama: neglect, imitation of foreign models, and independence. Largely outdated by more recent studies.

123 Clapp, William W., Jr. A RECORD OF THE BOSTON STAGE. Boston: James Munroe, 1853.

   A chronological record of Boston theatre but also valuable for comments on American plays and playwrights as well as quoted letters and reviews. See also entry no. 62, an index to this work.

124 Clark, Barrett H. THE BRITISH AND AMERICAN DRAMA OF TO-DAY. Cincinnati: Stewart and Kidd, 1912.

   Includes biography, bibliography, and general study of important plays and playwrights.

125 _____. A STUDY OF THE MODERN DRAMA. New York: D. Appleton, 1928.

   Brief discussions of several turn-of-the-century American dramatists.

126 Clark, Barrett H., and George Freedley, eds. A HISTORY OF MODERN DRAMA. New York: D. Appleton-Century, 1947.

   Barrett Clark's essay in chapter XIII, "The United States" (pp. 639-54), comments intelligently on late nineteenth-century American dramatists and attempts to place them in the world perspective.

127 Coad, Oral Sumner, and Edwin Minns, Jr. THE AMERICAN STAGE. The Pageant of America series, vol. 14. New Haven, Conn.: Yale University Press, 1929.

   The authors provide a history of the theatre with peripheral commentary on plays and playwrights.

Critical, Historical, Reference Resources

128 Cowie, Alexander. "The Beginnings of Fiction and Drama." In LITERARY HISTORY OF THE UNITED STATES. Ed. Robert E. Spiller et al., I. pp. 171-91. See entry no. 48.

    Brief and slight reference to early American drama.

129 Crawford, Mary Caroline. THE ROMANCE OF THE AMERICAN THEATRE. Boston: Little, Brown, 1913.

    A popularly written approach to theatre and drama trends during the nineteenth century; of little lasting value.

130 Drama League of America. BRIEF SURVEY COURSE ON AMERICAN DRAMA. Comp. Mrs. A. Starr Best. Study Course, No. 30. Drama League of America, 1926.

    Nine lessons, of which two refer to the nineteenth century.

131 Dunlap, William. HISTORY OF THE AMERICAN THEATRE. 1832; rpt. New York: Burt Franklin, 1963.

    A basic text for the study of early American drama by America's first major playwright. Important not for the facts, which are sometimes in error, but for the atmosphere the author reveals, his anecdotes, and his commentary, which must also be recognized as biased.

132 Duyckinck, Evert A., and George L. Duyckinck. CYCLOPAEDIA OF AMERICAN LITERATURE. 2 vols. 1875; rpt. Detroit: Gale Research, 1965.

    This text, of historical interest only, does not recognize American drama as separate from English drama.

133 Gallagher, Kent G. THE FOREIGNER IN EARLY AMERICAN DRAMA: A STUDY IN ATTITUDES. The Hague: Mouton, 1966.

    Contains comments on a variety of plays under such headings as "Anti-Foreign Sentiments," "The Sympathetic Foreigner," and "Cosmic Foreigners."

134 Geisinger, Marion. PLAYS, PLAYERS AND PLAYWRIGHTS, AN ILLUSTRATED HISTORY OF THE THEATRE. New York: Hart, 1971.

    With less than half of the volume on American theatre and drama and a few comments on eighteenth- and nineteenth-century drama, this work reveals little knowledge of American drama. It is written for a popular audience.

Critical, Historical, Reference Resources

135 Grimsted, David. MELODRAMA UNVEILED: AMERICAN THEATRE AND CULTURE, 1800-1850. Chicago: University of Chicago Press, 1968.

Emphasis is on the cultural background and dramatic structure of melodrama as illustrated by major writers. Chapter 7, "American Playwrights: In Search of a National Drama," provides a sound discussion of problems and intentions. Chapter 1, "The Corruption of An Enlightened Age," considers the work of William Dunlap.

136 Hapgood, Norman. THE STAGE IN AMERICA (1897-1900). New York: Macmillan, 1901.

Scattered comments on turn-of-the-century playwrights.

137 Hartman, John Geoffrey. THE DEVELOPMENT OF AMERICAN SOCIAL COMEDY, 1787-1936. 1939; rpt. New York: Octagon Books, 1971.

This very useful and broad historical survey of social comedy in America discusses a large number of comedies under such headings as the "Period of Caricature" and "Transition Period." The latter includes the work of Clyde Fitch who, according to Hartman, established social comedy in America.

138 Hartnoll, Phyllis, ed. THE OXFORD COMPANION TO THE THEATRE. 3rd ed. London: Oxford University Press, 1967.

Brief biographies of many American dramatists, with some reference to the American drama.

139 Havens, Daniel F. THE COLUMBIAN MUSE OF COMEDY: THE DEVELOPMENT OF A NATIVE TRADITION IN EARLY AMERICAN SOCIAL COMEDY, 1787-1845. Carbondale: Southern Illinois University Press, 1973.

The subtitle is misleading in that the emphasis is not on development but on certain aspects of social comedy: the Jonathan character, three selected plays (THE FATHER, TEARS AND SMILES, and CITY LOOKING GLASS), and FASHION. The author offers no concluding assessment of the period.

140 Herron, Ima Honaker. THE SMALL TOWN IN AMERICAN DRAMA. Dallas: Southern Methodist University Press, 1969.

Through selected topics the author shows how American playwrights reflect social and historical movements in their work. Laced with peripheral observations of uneven insight, the book's major value is the commentary on little-known American plays.

Critical, Historical, Reference Resources

141   Hewitt, Barnard. THEATRE U.S.A. 1668-1957. New York: McGraw-Hill, 1959.

> A summary view with the emphasis on theatre rather than dramatists. A major value of the book lies in the inclusion of numerous and long contemporary reviews and commentary.

142   Hodge, Francis. YANKEE THEATRE: THE IMAGE OF AMERICA ON THE STAGE, 1825-1850. Austin: University of Texas Press, 1964.

> The most thorough treatment of the subject to date, this work is limited by the years treated and the author's point of view, which is primarily that of acting. Excellent list of plays.

143   Hornblow, Arthur. A HISTORY OF THE THEATRE IN AMERICA FROM ITS BEGINNINGS TO THE PRESENT TIME. 2 vols. 1919; rpt. New York: Blom, 1965.

> Many passing comments on plays and playwrights by a man who edited the THEATRE MAGAZINE for nineteen years.

144   Hoyt, Harlowe R. TOWN HALL TONIGHT. Englewood Cliffs, N.J.: Prentice-Hall, 1955.

> A book of reminiscences and excerpts from American melodramas and entertainments as they were presented in Beaver Dam, Wisconsin, during the last two decades of the nineteenth century.

145   Hughes, Glenn. A HISTORY OF THE AMERICAN THEATRE, 1700-1950. New York: Samuel French, 1951.

> Organized under innumerable subheadings in chapters covering ten to twenty-five years, this work concentrates on actors and theatre activities but includes sections on playwrights (e.g., pp. 282-99). Text marred by inaccuracies.

146   Hutton, Laurence. CURIOSITIES OF THE AMERICAN STAGE. New York: Harper and Brothers, 1891.

> An invaluable study of nineteenth-century drama from several points of view: Indian, frontier, Negro, and other native character types. Also material on American burlesque and actors.

147   _____. PLAYS AND PLAYERS. New York: Hurd and Houghton, 1875.

> Mainly on theatres and actors but includes material on drama. Good section on the plays of John Brougham.

Critical, Historical, Reference Resources

148   Isaacs, Edith J.R. THE NEGRO IN THE AMERICAN THEATRE. New York: Theatre Arts, 1947.

         Parts reprinted from THEATRE ARTS magazine. First two chapters comment on Negro theatre and plays with Negro characters appearing prior to 1917.

149   Lewis, Philip C. TROUPING: HOW THE SHOW CAME TO TOWN. New York: Harper and Row, 1973.

         Popularly styled sketch of American drama with references to actors and popular plays and playwrights. Not of scholarly value.

150   Mayorga, Margaret G. A SHORT HISTORY OF THE AMERICAN DRAMA. New York: Dodd, Mead, 1932.

         This brief study of American plays, eclectically organized according to influences (foreign, actor, etc.), content (domestic plays), form (minstrelsy), and history (period of expansion), is the weakest of existing full-length studies.

151   Meserve, Walter J. "The Dramatists and Their Plays." In AMERICAN DRAMA. Vol. 8 of THE REVELS HISTORY OF DRAMA IN ENGLISH. Ed. T.W. Craik. London: Methuen, 1977, pp. 147-296.

         A survey of the major dramatists and the development of American drama, beginnings to present. Valuable chronological table and bibliography.

152   _____. AN EMERGING ENTERTAINMENT: THE DRAMA OF THE AMERICAN PEOPLE TO 1828. Bloomington: Indiana University Press, 1977.

         This chronological study and critical evaluation of American plays, relates the drama to the cultural and historical progress of the country and analyzes the drama as a literary genre contributing to the American theatre. It treats colonial attitudes and experiments with the drama, drama and the "War of the Belles Lettres," early plays as dramatists met the demands of a growing theatre, variety of creativity among dramatists, and the prejudices encountered prior to Edwin Forrest's play contests. A basic text which includes a discussion of dramatic criticism in America. Notes and bibliography.

153   _____. AN OUTLINE HISTORY OF AMERICAN DRAMA. Totowa, N.J.: Littlefield, Adams, 1965.

         A brief study of the major trends in American drama, with summarized play plots and slight critical assessment. Of value as a reference work.

Critical, Historical, Reference Resources

154   Miller, Jordan Y. AMERICAN DRAMATIC LITERATURE. New York: McGraw-Hill, 1961.

   Part 1 (pp. 3-73), "The Backgrounds of Modern American Drama," provides a good if brief survey of important developments in American drama.

155   Moody, Richard. AMERICA TAKES THE STAGE: ROMANTICISM IN AMERICAN DRAMA AND THEATRE, 1750-1900. Bloomington: Indiana University Press, 1955.

   A substantial study of native themes (war and the frontier) and characters (Negro, Indian, Yankee) in the drama as a reflection of the romantic spirit. Also treats romanticism in acting and scene design. Notes, bibliography, playlist.

156   Morris, Lloyd. CURTAIN TIME. New York: Random House, 1953.

   An informal "story of the American theatre" from the early nineteenth century with occasional commentary on American plays and playwrights.

157   Moses, Montrose J. THE AMERICAN DRAMATIST. 1911; rev. ed. 1925; rpt. New York: Blom, 1964.

   An early and important history of the drama organized according to native types and major dramatists; best part deals with material after the Civil War. Emphasis on drama reflecting a developing America makes Moses' approach a good companion to Arthur Hobson Quinn's history of the drama (entries no. 163 and 164). The revised edition greatly improves the first.

158   _____. "The Drama, 1860-1918." In THE CAMBRIDGE HISTORY OF AMERICAN LITERATURE. Ed. William P. Trent et al. New York: Macmillan, 1933. III, pp. 266-98.

   Survey of an important period by a major historian.

159   Nannes, Caspar Harold. POLITICS IN THE AMERICAN DRAMA. Washington: Catholic University of America, 1960.

   A popularly written treatment of slight value; the first two chapters comment briefly on the nineteenth century with emphasis on the final decade.

160   Nolan, Paul T. PROVINCIAL DRAMA IN AMERICA, 1870-1916: A CASEBOOK OF PRIMARY MATERIALS. Metuchen, N.J.: Scarecrow Press, 1967.

   With a checklist of southern playwrights, three reprinted

Critical, Historical, Reference Resources

short plays, and essays of slight critical value, this work attempts to interest students in the fifty thousand plays copyrighted during the period considered.

161 Pollock, Thomas Clark. THE PHILADELPHIA THEATRE IN THE EIGHTEENTH CENTURY. Philadelphia: University of Pennsylvania Press, 1933.

Includes comments on plays by Americans.

162 Quinn, Arthur Hobson. "The Early Drama, 1756-1860." In THE CAMBRIDGE HISTORY OF AMERICAN LITERATURE. Ed. William P. Trent et al. New York: Macmillan, 1933. III, pp. 215-32.

A brief survey by a major drama historian.

163 _____. A HISTORY OF THE AMERICAN DRAMA FROM THE BEGINNING TO THE CIVIL WAR. 2nd ed. New York: Appleton-Century-Crofts, 1943.

A basic history of the period, fusing the drama and theatre during the early years. Organization geared to major dramatists with emphasis upon poetic drama--that is, the plays of Dunlap, Barker, Payne, Bird, and Boker. Other chapters deal with drama in the colonies and during the Revolution, early comedy and comedy types, politics and history on the stage, tragedy and melodrama, and the plays of Boucicault. Gives careful attention to production information and analysis of selected plays. Bibliography and list of plays, 1665-1860.

164 _____. A HISTORY OF THE AMERICAN DRAMA FROM THE CIVIL WAR TO THE PRESENT DAY. 2 vols in 1. Rev. ed. New York: Appleton-Century-Crofts, 1936.

The first volume treats the last part of the nineteenth century and emphasizes the contributions of Daly, Howard, Howells, Hoyt, Herne, Belasco, Gillette, Thomas, and Fitch. There are also chapters on frontier drama and romantic drama. A basic text combining drama and theatre history, and concerned with the major contributors to a developing drama.

165 _____, ed. THE LITERATURE OF THE AMERICAN POEPLE. New York: Appleton-Century-Crofts, 1951.

This historical and critical survey is divided into four major parts: Kenneth B. Murdock, in part I, "The Colonial and Revolutionary Period," comments only briefly on the drama (pp. 161-65); Quinn, in part II, "The Establishment of National Literature," includes chapters on "Early Fiction and Drama"

Critical, Historical, Reference Resources

and "Revolt and Celebration in the Drama;" Clarence Gohdes, in part III, "The Later Nineteenth Century," discusses "Amusements on the Stage" (pp. 790-809); Part IV by George F. Whicher considers "The Twentieth Century."

166 Rahill, Frank. THE WORLD OF MELODRAMA. University Park: Pennsylvania State University Press, 1967.

Roughly a third of this book considers American plays. Most perceptive on French and English melodrama, the work emphasizes popular style and interesting information, but lacks critical analysis. Its value is as introduction to the genre of melodrama and the inclusion of innumerable play plots.

167 Reed, Perley I. THE REALISTIC PRESENTATION OF AMERICAN CHARACTERS IN NATIVE AMERICAN PLAYS PRIOR TO 1870. Ohio State University BULLETIN XXII, no. 26. Columbus: Ohio State University, 1918.

An early but still valuable discussion; includes bibliography (pp. 144-68).

168 Rees, James. THE DRAMATIC AUTHORS OF AMERICA. Philadelphia: G.B. Zieber, 1845.

A collection of essays, previously published in the DRAMATIC MIRROR AND LITERARY COMPANION, with a preface sympathetic to the drama and bemoaning the paucity of good dramatists. Basic source for information on early dramatists and their plays.

169 Sievers, W. David. FREUD ON BROADWAY: A HISTORY OF PSYCHOANALYSIS AND THE AMERICAN DRAMA. New York: Hermitage House, 1955.

Some discussion of a number of turn-of-the-century American dramatists.

170 Strang, Lewis C. PLAYERS AND PLAYS OF THE LAST QUARTER CENTURY. 2 vols. Boston: L.C. Page, 1903.

Volume II has a section (IV) on playwriting; and there is further brief discussion of Bronson Howard (Section V) as well as Gillette, Herne, Fitch, and Thomas (Section VI).

171 Taubman, Howard. THE MAKING OF THE AMERICAN THEATRE. New York: Coward, McCann, 1965.

This broad historical commentary includes many references to American playwrights and their plays but lacks footnotes and bibliography.

Critical, Historical, Reference Resources

172 Walbridge, Earle F. "Drames à Clef: A List of Plays with Characters Based on Real People. Part II: American Drama." BNYPL, 60 (1956), 159 ff, 235-47.

>An introduction followed by a list of plays with commentary quoted from histories. Relevant periods are Revolutionary, post-Revolutionary, and nineteenth century.

173 Wilson, Garff B. THREE HUNDRED YEARS OF AMERICAN DRAMA AND THEATRE. Englewood Cliffs, N.J.: Prentice-Hall, 1973.

>This ambitious attempt to discuss in "fictional form" the drama, all aspects of theatre, dramatic criticism, and radio and television in America is perceptive and easily read, but weak in documentation. Pertinent chapters treat early American playwriting, playwriting 1800-50, playwriting 1850-1900, and playwriting at the turn of the nineteenth century.

174 Wright, Richardson. REVELS IN JAMAICA, 1682-1838. New York: Dodd, Mead, 1937.

>Some references to plays written by actors whose careers matured in America.

F. HISTORY AND CRITICISM

1. Drama of the Colonies and the Period of the Revolution, Beginnings to 1783

175 [Aston, Anthony]. THE FOOL'S OPERA; OR, THE TASTE OF THE AGE. WRITTEN BY MAT MEDLEY. AND PERFORMED BY HIS COMPANY IN OXFORD, TO WHICH IS PREFIX'D A SKETCH OF THE AUTHOR'S LIFE. WRITTEN BY HIMSELF. London: N.p., 1731.

>Brief but unique information on the man who may have written the first play in English in America.

176 Austin, Mary. "Spanish Drama in Colonial America." TA, 19 (1935), 705.

>One-page excerpt from "Folk Plays of the Southwest" by Austin, TA, 17 (1933), 599-610. The essay refers to a play by Farfán and to THE MOORS AND THE CHRISTIANS, a traditional Catholic play, which was performed on 10 July 1598 at San Juan Pueblo in what is now New Mexico.

177 Avery, Laurence G. "A Proposal Concerning the Study of Early American Drama." ETJ, 29 (1977), 243-50.

Critical, Historical, Reference Resources

> Using two opposing views of drama--the Calvinist and the sentimental--Avery concludes that a common purpose of drama is to produce an emotional effect in the audience.

178 Bridenbaugh, Carl, and Jessica Bridenbaugh. REBELS AND GENTLE-MEN, PHILADELPHIA IN THE AGE OF FRANKLIN. New York: Reynal and Hitchcock, 1942.

> Pages 137-46 have commentary on early American plays produced in Philadelphia.

179 Brown, Herbert. "Sensibility in Eighteenth-Century American Drama." AL, 4 (1932), 49-60.

> Mainly a recognition of, with little comment on, the many plays written and produced in America at this time.

180 Bruce, Philip A. "An Early Virginia Play." NATION, 11 February 1909, p. 136.

> Bruce refers to a letter that describes part of the judge's action with reference to YE BEARE AND YE CUB.

181 Cairns, W.B. "American Drama of the 18th Century." DIAL, 15 July 1915, pp. 60-62.

> Reaction to Nevins' introduction to Robert Rogers' PONTEACH, mainly supporting his conclusions regarding the poetry and English reception of play; see entry no. 206.

182 Colby, Elbridge. "Early American Comedy." BNYPL, 23 (1919), 427-35; rpt. August 1919 by the New York Public Library.

> Brief comments on dramatists of the Revolution and afterwards, with list of plays.

183 Culp, Ralph Borden. "Drama and Theatre as a Source of Colonial American Attitudes toward Independence, 1758-1776." Ph.D. dissertation, Cornell University, 1951.

184 _____. "Drama and Theatre in the American Revolution." SM, 32 (1965), 79-86.

> Through a discussion of the rhetoric, persuasive techniques, and dramatic situations devised by Whig and Tory playwrights, Culp concludes that Whig playwrights were more skillful than their Tory competitors.

Critical, Historical, Reference Resources

185   Curvin, Jonathan. "Realism in Early American Art and Theatre." QJS, 30 (1944), 450-55.

      Refers to PONTEACH and THE CONTRAST in comparing theatre realism with portraiture of the period.

186   Dallett, Frances J. "John Leacock and THE FALL OF BRITISH TYRANNY." PENNSYLVANIA MAGAZINE OF HISTORY AND BIOGRAPHY, 78 (1954), 456-75.

      A well-documented identification of Leacock and an excellent discussion of his play.

187   Dolmetsch, Carl R. "William Byrd II: Comic Dramatist?" EAL, 6 (1971), 18-30.

      The author concludes that "Byrd could have had something to do with the composition of THE CARELESS HUSBAND," thus replacing Hunter as first American dramatist.

188   Drummond, A.M., and Richard Moody. "Indian Treaties." QJS, 39 (1953), 15-22.

      Authors contend that Indian treaties provide first evidence of theatrical and dramatic activity in America and, as recorded, constitute the first American drama.

189   Ford, Paul Leicester. "The Beginnings of American Dramatic Literature." NEW ENGLAND MAGAZINE, n.s. 9 (1894), 673-87.

      Essay provides information and background for the 1606-1789 period.

190   Gay, F.L. "The First American Play." NATION, 11 February 1909, p. 136.

      Responding to a previous note on early American drama by W.J. Neidig (see entry no. 203), Gay refers to THEATRE OF NEPTUNE and corrects the date of presentation.

191   Henderson, Archibald. "Early Drama and Amateur Entertainment in North Carolina, Part 1." REVIEWER, 5 (October 1925), 68-77.

      Author describes the activity of Thomas Godfrey in Wilmington and the amateurs of the Thalian Association; notes that THE PRINCE OF PARTHIA may have been produced there on 11 June 1847.

192   _____. "Early Drama and Professional Entertainment in North Carolina." REVIEWER, 5 (July 1925), 47-57.

Critical, Historical, Reference Resources

        Author comments on Tony Aston, the activities of the American Company in North Carolina in 1787, theatre advertising, and wax works entertainment.

193   Hubbell, Jay B. "The Smith-Pocahontas Story in Literature." VIRGINIA MAGAZINE OF HISTORY AND BIOGRAPHY, 65 (1957), 275-300.

        This essay includes a discussion of the story in dramatic form.

194   Hurley, Doran. "Our First Dramatist." AMERICA, 29 November 1941, pp. 213-14.

        A brief comment on the playwriting career of George Henry Miles from a Catholic point of view.

195   Johnston, W. "Entertainments of the Spanish Explorers." CHRONICLES OF OKLAHOMA, 8 (March 1930), 89-93.

        Johnston refers to Farfán's work and concludes that the Southwest owes a long tradition of entertainment to the Spanish.

196   Kussrow, Van Carl, Jr. "On with the Show: A Study of Public Arguments in Favor of Theatre in America during the Eighteenth Century." Ph.D. dissertation, Indiana University, 1959.

197   Law, Robert A. "Notes on Some Early American Dramas." UNIVERSITY OF TEXAS STUDIES IN ENGLISH, 5 (1925), 96-100.

        Adds to plays listed in Quinn's history (see entries nos. 163 and 164); corrects some errors.

198   Leder, Lawrence H. "Robert Hunter's ANDROBOROS." BNYPL, 60 (1964), 153-60.

        This scholarly essay provides a background for the play and an identification of the characters; the text of play is reproduced.

199   Lescarbot, Marc. THE THEATRE OF NEPTUNE IN NEW FRANCE. Trans. and introd. Harriette Taber Richardson. Boston: Houghton Mifflin, 1927.

        First English translation of Lescarbot's seventeenth-century play, with good commentary on the author and picture of the site.

200   McNicall, Robert E. "The Caloosa Village TEQUESTA: A Miami of Sixteenth Century." TEQUESTA, 1 (March 1941), 11-20.

        Most extensive reference to Brother Villareal's comment on plays produced at the Spanish Mission in Florida.

Critical, Historical, Reference Resources

201 Mayorga, Margaret M. "The First Theatre Performance in North America." AmN&Q, 2 (Summer 1942), 84.

   Author contends that Brother Villareal's performance at the Spanish Mission, Tequesta, Florida, are the first plays in America.

202 Menelly, John Henry. "A Study of American Drama Prior to 1801." Ph.D. dissertation, New York University, 1911.

203 Neidig, William J. "The First Play in America." NATION, 28 January 1909, pp. 86-88.

   Neidig comments on playhouses in New York, 1733; Charleston, 1738; Quebec, 1640; and on Villeneuve's POUCHA-HOUMMA, 1752-58. See entry no. 190.

204 Quinn, Arthur Hobson. "The Authorship of the First American College Masque." GENERAL MAGAZINE AND HISTORICAL CHRONICLE, 28 (1926), 313-16.

   Concerned with the authorship of THE MASQUE OF ALFRED, which Quinn once attributed to Francis Hopkinson and now, after further study of available manuscripts, correctly identifies as the work of William Smith.

205 Robinson, Alice Jean McDonnell. "The Developing Ideas of Individual Freedom and National Unity as Reflected in American Plays and Theatre, 1722-1819." Ph.D. dissertation, Stanford University, 1965.

206 Rogers, Robert. PONTEACH; OR, THE SAVAGES OF AMERICA; A TRAGEDY. Ed. and introd. Allen Nevins. 1914; rpt. New York: Burt Franklin, 1971.

   Biographical and critical commentary; suggests questionable authorship. See entry no. 181.

207 Rugg, Harold G. "The Dartmouth Plays, 1779-1782." THEATRE ANNUAL, 1 (1942), 55-57.

   A brief discussion of John Smith (1752-1809) and his two dialogues: DIALOGUE BETWEEN AN ENGLISHMAN AND AN INDIAN and A LITTLE TEA TABLE CHITCHAT.

208 Teunissen, John J. "Blockheadism and the Propaganda Plays of the American Revolution." EAL, 7 (1972), 148-62.

   A discussion of Whig and Tory plays by Jonathan Sewall, Mercy Warren, and others during blockade of Boston.

Critical, Historical, Reference Resources

209   Ticki, Cecelia. "Thespis and the 'Carnall Hipocrite': A Puritan Motive for Aversion to Drama." EAL, 4 (1969), 86-103.

>   Ticki argues that the Puritan attitude toward imagination not only discouraged playwrights but elicited public condemnation of actors.

210   Wise, Jennings C. YE KINGDOME OF ACCAWMACKE ON THE EASTERN SHORE OF VIRGINIA IN THE SEVENTEENTH CENTURY. Baltimore: Regional Publishing Co., 1967.

>   Volume provides interesting details on production of YE BARE AND YE CUBB.

211   Wroth, Laurence C. "The Indian Treaty as Literature." YALE REVIEW, 17 (1928), 748-66.

>   A discussion of Indian treaties as dramatic literature.

2. Drama of a Developing Nation, 1784-1860

a. SURVEYS AND STUDIES OF INDIVIDUAL AUTHORS AND PLAYS

212   Abrahamson, Doris M. "William Wells Brown: America's First Negro Playwright." ETJ, 20 (1968), 370-75.

>   An analysis of Brown's antislavery play, THE ESCAPE; OR, A LEAP FOR FREEDOM.

213   Adkins, Nelson F. "James K. Paulding's LION OF THE WEST." AL, 3 (1931), 249-58.

>   Written before the text of the play was discovered and based on a two-page outline (which is included), this basic essay also gives production information.

214   Amacher, Richard E. "Behind the Curtain with the Noble Savage: Stage Movement of Indian Plays, 1825-1860." TS, 7 (1966), 101-14.

>   Sketchy comments on production of popular Indian plays by Custis, Stone, Dunlap, Brougham, and Hatton.

215   Angotti, Vincent L. "American Dramatic Criticism, 1800-1820." Ph.D. dissertation, University of Kansas, 1967.

216   Arndt, K.J. "Poe's 'Politian' and Goethe's 'Mignon.'" MLN, 49 (1934), 101-04.

>   Author compares the fourth scene of POLITIAN to MIGNON and argues that their closeness shows plagiarism.

Critical, Historical, Reference Resources

217 Blanc, Robert E. "James McHenry (1785-1845), Playwright and Novelist." Ph.D. dissertation, University of Pennsylvania, 1939.

218 Booth, Michael R. "The Drunkard's Progress: Nineteenth-Century Temperance Drama." DALHOUSIE REVIEW, 44 (1964), 205-12.

   Essay summarizes the essence of the temperance play (American and British) from 1830 on: drunkard as criminal, the pledge scene, and the recovery.

219 Briggs, H.E., and E.B. Briggs. "The Early Theatre on the Upper Mississippi." MID-AMERICA, 31 (1948), 131-62.

   A review of theatre activity with comments on many American plays.

220 Chaplin, Leila Bowie. "Life and Works of Nathaniel Deering." University of Maine Studies, No. 32. MAINE BULLETIN, 37 (1934), 145-52, 226-33.

   Includes texts of Deering's plays CARABASSET and THE CLAIRVOYANTS.

221 Clifford, James L. "Robert Merry--A Pre-Byronic Hero." BULLETIN OF THE JOHN RYLANDS LIBRARY, 27 (1942), 74-96.

   A good basic essay on a writer who may be considered to have contributed to early American drama.

222 Coad, Oral Sumner. "An Old American College Play." MLN, 37 (1922), 157-63.

   Author argues that THE MERCENARY MATCH by Barnabas Bidwell is a unique and rare composition among early American plays.

223 Comstock, Sarah. "Early American Drama." NAR, 225 (1928), 469-75.

   A popularly written comment on amateur productions of plays by Payne, Dunlap, Tyler, and Barker.

224 Davis, Blanche E. "The Hero in American Drama, 1787-1900." Ph.D. dissertation, Columbia University, 1951.

225 "Death of Edward G.P. Wilkins." SPIRIT OF THE TIMES, 11 May 1861, p. 224.

   Obituary comments on author (1829-61) of YOUNG NEW YORK.

Critical, Historical, Reference Resources

226 Dewsnap, James W. "William Gilmore Simms as Playwright." Ph.D. dissertation, University of Georgia, 1971.

227 Doddridge, Joseph. NOTES ON THE SETTLEMENT AND INDIAN WARS, OF THE WESTERN PARTS OF VIRGINIA AND PENNSYLVANIA FROM THE YEAR 1763 UNTIL THE YEAR 1783 INCLUSIVE. Ed. Alfred Williams. With a memoir of the author by his daughter. 1824; rpt. New York: Burt Franklin, 1973.

    Valuable for comments on the author of LOGAN.

228 Dorson, Richard M. "Mose the Far-famed and World-renowned." AL, 15 (1943), 288-300.

    General historical and descriptive essay of popular character in mid-nineteenth-century American drama.

229 "The Drama." UNITED STATES DEMOCRATIC REVIEW, 42 (July 1858), 16-39.

    A general review of American stage and plays which condemns "prostitution of the stage."

230 "Dramatic Reminiscences." NEW ENGLAND MAGAZINE, 2 (1832), 369-73, 483-90; (1832), 33-40, 507-10.

    Scattered memories of plays and actors in Boston theatres; includes some prologues and addresses.

231 Eaton, Walter Pritchard. "Our Humble Dramatic Origins." LITERARY DIGEST, 11 March 1916, pp. 641-42.

    A brief comment on early drama.

232 Elfenbein, Josef Aaron. "American Drama, 1782-1812, As an Index to Social Thought." Ph.D. dissertation, New York University, 1951.

233 Ellis, Milton. "Puritans and the Drama." AmN&Q, 2 (July 1942), 64.

    A single-paragraph reference to prologues and epilogues written by Judith Sargent Murray and first printed in MASSACHUSETTS MAGAZINE of March, April, and June 1790, and March and April 1791.

234 Enkvist, Nils Erik. CARICATURES OF AMERICANS ON THE ENGLISH STAGE PRIOR TO 1870. Commentationes Humanarum Litterarum, XVIII, 1. Helsingfors: Centraltryckeri Och Bokbinderi ab, 1951.

    A detailed commentary on the transference of American plays and American characters to the English stage. Emphasis on frontiersman, Yankee, Negro minstrel, Rip Van Winkle, and FASHION.

Critical, Historical, Reference Resources

235   Ewing, Robert. THE THEATRICAL CONTRIBUTIONS OF "JACQUES" TO THE UNITED STATES GAZETTE. Philadelphia: N.p., 1826.

   Criticisms of performances at New Theatre in Philadelphia, 1825-26 season, including American plays CHARLES II, TEARS AND SMILES, MARMION, BRUTUS, and THE MAID AND THE MAGPIE.

236   Fagin, N. Bryllion. "Isaac Harby and the Early American Theatre." AMERICAN JEWISH ARCHIVES, 8 (1956), 3-13.

   A discussion of Harby's two major plays, his contribution to American dramatic criticism, and his difficulties in the theatre.

237   Falk, Armand E. "Theatrical Criticism in the New York Evening Post, 1807-1830." Ph.D. dissertation, Michigan State University, 1969.

238   Farrison, W.E. "Brown's First Drama." CLAJ, 2 (1958), 104-10.

   A carefully written essay on EXPERIENCE; OR, HOW TO GIVE A NORTHERN MAN A BACKBONE by William W. Brown, who read his play throughout New England from April 1856 to the summer of 1857.

239   _____. WILLIAM WELLS BROWN: AUTHOR AND REFORMER. Chicago: University of Chicago Press, 1969.

   An important critical biography of the first American black dramatist.

240   Fox, D.R. "The Development of the American Theater." NEW YORK HISTORY, 17 (1936), 22-41.

   Survey of drama and theatre from beginnings to mid-nineteenth century.

241   Gafford, Lucile. "The Boston Stage and the War of 1812." NEQ, 7 (1934), 327-35.

   A brief discussion, almost a listing, of numerous war plays that came to Boston; some quotations from programs are included.

242   _____. "Transcendentalist Attitudes toward Drama and Theatre." NEQ, 13 (1940), 442-66.

   Gafford reveals that the group at Brook Farm read plays, that transcendentalist journals reviewed drama, and such transcendentalists as Very, Judd, Emerson, and Fuller commented on the drama.

Critical, Historical, Reference Resources

243   Glenn, Stanley. "The Development of the Negro Character in American Comedy before the Civil War." SSJ, 26 (1960), 133-48.

> A summary of Negro character with attitudes he portrayed discussed under various headings: vulgar clown, faithful servant, and so forth.

244   _____. "Ludicrous Characterization in American Comedy from the Beginning until the Civil War." Ph.D. dissertation, Stanford University, 1955.

245   Hazelrigg, Charles Tabb. AMERICAN LITERARY PIONEER: A BIOGRAPHICAL STUDY OF JAMES A. HILLHOUSE. New York: Bookman Associates, 1953.

> A discussion of Hillhouse's ambitions as a playwright and an analysis of his several plays; it is the most thorough study available.

246   Herold, Amos L. JAMES KIRK PAULDING: VERSATILE AMERICAN. New York: Columbia University Press, 1926.

> The only modern biography of Paulding, this work includes bibliography of works.

247   Hill, George H. SCENES FROM THE LIFE OF AN ACTOR. 1853; rpt. New York: Blom, 1969.

> An autobiography that includes a scene from THE GREEN MOUNTAIN BOY.

248   Hodge, Francis. "Biography of a Lost play: LION OF THE WEST." THEATRE ANNUAL, 12 (1954), 48-61.

> The author traces the creation of this play through the work of Hackett, Paulding, Stone, W.B. Bernard, Prosper Wetmore, and George Morris. He compares the play with Hackett's THE KENTUCKIAN.

249   Holman, C.H. "Simms and the British Dramatists." PMLA, 65 (1950), 346-59.

> Mainly on work of British dramatists as sources for Simms's novels, this essay also mentions Simms's work as a dramatist.

250   Hoole, William Stanley. THE ANTI-BELLUM CHARLESTON THEATRE. University: University of Alabama Press, 1946.

> Includes comments on plays.

Critical, Historical, Reference Resources

251 _____. "Simms's MICHAEL BONHAM, A 'Forgotten Drama' of the Texas Revolution." SOUTHWEST HISTORICAL QUARTERLY, 46 (1942), 255-61.

    The essay provides background of the play plus details of production and reception.

252 "The Irish Drama." SPIRIT OF THE TIMES, 14 January 1854, p. 472.

    Beginning with Tyrone Power, the essayist refers to many actors and Irish-character plays on the American stage.

253 Jorgenson, C.E. "Gleanings from Judith Sargent Murray." AL, 12 (1940), 73-78.

    With slight reference to her plays, the author discusses the ideas Murray expressed in her essays and the kind of mind she possessed.

254 "Julian." NORTH AMERICAN MAGAZINE, 1 (December 1832), 24-27.

    A review of the play by Charles Jared Ingersoll. Much plot, little criticism.

255 Kibles, James E., Jr. PSEUDONYMOUS PUBLICATIONS OF WILLIAM GILMORE SIMMS. Athens: University of Georgia Press, 1976.

    This work includes scattered references to Simms's comments on the drama.

256 Lancaster, A.E. "Historical American Plays." CHAUTAUQUAN, 31 (1900), 359-64.

    Author questions why there were so few historical plays as of 1900, then surveys treatment of history in drama from mid-eighteenth century onward.

257 Leary, Lewis. "John Blair Linn." WILLIAM AND MARY QUARTERLY, 3 (1947), 148-76.

    Good background on life and works, mainly poetry and essays. Brief reference to his play.

258 Linn, John Blair. VALERIAN, A NARRATIVE POEM INTENDED, IN PART, TO DESCRIBE THE EARLY PERSECUTION OF CHRISTIANS AND TO ILLUSTRATE THE INFLUENCE OF CHRISTIANITY ON THE MANNERS OF NATIONS. With a Sketch of the Life and Character of the Author by Charles Brockden Brown. Philadelphia: Printed by Thomas and George Palmers, 1805.

    Valuable for the sketch by Brown.

Critical, Historical, Reference Resources

259   Lown, Charles R., Jr. "Business and the Businessman in American Drama Prior to the Civil War." Ph.D. dissertation, Stanford University, 1957.

260   _____. "The Businessman in Early American Drama." ETJ, 15 (1963), 47-54.

   Typical characteristics of businessmen displayed in American drama before 1810.

261   Mabbett, T.O. "The Text of Poe's Play 'Politian.'" N&Q, 189 (July 1945), 20.

   A brief correction to the 1923 edition of the play after seeing newly discovered manuscript pages.

262   Marchiafava, Bruce T. "The Influence of Patriotism in the American Drama and Theatre, 1773-1830." Ph.D. dissertation, Northwestern University, 1970.

263   Marder, Daniel. HUGH HENRY BRACKENRIDGE. New York: Twayne Publishers, 1967.

   Slight discussion of his plays (pp. 68-73).

264   Mates, Julian. THE AMERICAN MUSICAL STAGE BEFORE 1800. New Brunswick, N.J.: Rutgers University Press, 1962.

   Mainly on production aspects of musicals but includes comments on the plays.

265   Maxwell, William Bulloch. THE MYSTERIOUS FATHER. Ed. and introd. Gerald Kahan. Athens: University of Georgia Press, 1965.

   An Italianate melodrama in style, compared to Dunlap's RIBBEMONT by editor.

266   Meserve, Walter J. "'An Earnest Purpose': American Drama at Mid-19th Century." PLAYERS, 48 (1973), 60-64.

   An analysis of FASHION, UNCLE TOM'S CABIN, FRANCESCA DA RIMINI, and THE OCTOROON pointing toward the historical significance of these dramas.

267   Moise, Abraham. "A Memorie of His Life." In A SELECTION FROM THE MISCELLANEOUS HISTORY OF THE LATE ISAAC HARBY, ESQ. Charleston, N.C.: Printed by J.S. Burges, 1829.

   Personal observations with a brief but clear commentary on Harby's plays. Includes essay "Defense of the Drama" (pp. 248-61).

Critical, Historical, Reference Resources

268   Moise, Lusius Clifton. BIOGRAPHY OF ISAAC HARBY. Columbia: University of South Carolina Press, 1931.

        A sympathetic portrayal of early South Carolina dramatist and critic: "With an Account of the Reformed Society of Israelites of Charleston, South Carolina, 1824-1833."

269   Montgomery, Evelyn. "Proverbial Materials in THE POLITICIAN OUTWITTED and Other Comedies of Early American Drama, 1789-1829." MIDWEST FOLKLORE, 11 (1961-62), 215-24.

        Lists forty-eight proverbs and proverbial expressions in the play, mainly delivered by Humphrey Cubb. Also provides lists for A COUNTRY CLOWN and HOW TO TRY A LOVER.

270   Moses, Montrose J. "American Plays of Our Forefathers." NAR, 215 (1922), 790-804.

        Moses finds little value in plays written prior to 1870 as he stresses the self-expression of nationalistic-minded dramatists.

271   "Mrs. H.L. Bateman." NEW YORK CLIPPER, 22 January 1881, p. 9.

        Obituary of the author of SELF.

272   Nelligan, Murray H. "American Nationalism on Stage: The Plays of George Washington Parke Custis (1781-1857)." VIRGINIA MAGAZINE OF HISTORY AND BIOGRAPHY, 58 (1950), 299-323.

        An extensive commentary on Custis' dramatic works plus historical background.

273   "The New England Tragedies." NEW ENGLANDER, 28 (1869), 201-04.

        Detailed commentary on plays by H.W. Longfellow.

274   Nichols, Harold, J. "The Prejudice against Native American Drama from 1778-1830." QJS, 60 (1975), 279-88.

        Nichols emphasizes the distinct prejudices, the patriotism during the War of 1812, and the changing atmosphere brought by Forrest's Prize Play Contests. Sensible essay.

275   Ota, Thomas. "Student Dramatic Activities at Yale College during the Eighteenth Century." THEATRE ANNUAL, 3 (1944), 47-59.

        On dialogues and plays, some written by Yale students and produced by Linonia Society and Brothers of Unity.

Critical, Historical, Reference Resources

276 Page, E.R. "Rediscovering the American Drama." AMERICAN SCHOLAR, 8 (1939), 250-52.

> A preview of the then forthcoming twenty-volume edition of AMERICA'S LOST PLAYS (entry no. 97) by one of its editors.

277 Pagel, Carol Ann Ryan. "A History and Analysis of Representative American Dramatizations from American Novels, 1800-1860." Ph.D. dissertation, University of Denver, 1970.

278 Parks, Edd Winfield. WILLIAM GILMORE SIMMS AS LITERARY CRITIC. Athens: University of Georgia Press, 1961.

> Chapter IV, "On Dramas and Dramatists" (pp. 68-88), treats Simms's criticism of the drama and makes only brief comment on his plays.

279 Paulding, James K. THE LION OF THE WEST. Ed. and introd. James Tidwell. Stanford, Calif.: Stanford University Press, 1954.

> A good background for this play, written in 1830, revised in 1831 and 1833, and now published from manuscripts in British Museum entitled THE KENTUCKIAN; OR, A TRIP TO NEW YORK, a farce in two acts, revised by J.A. Stone and William Bayle Bernard.

280 Paulding, James K., and William Irving Paulding. AMERICAN COMEDIES. Philadelphia: Carey and Hart, 1847.

> Includes THE BUCKTAILS, THE NOBLE EXILE, MADMEN ALL, and ANTIPATHIES.

281 Paulding, William I. LITERARY LIFE OF JAMES KIRK PAULDING. New York: Charles Scribner, 1867.

> Discussion of THE LION OF THE WEST (pp. 218-20).

282 Peavy, C.D. "The American Indian in the Drama of the United States." MCNEESE REVIEW, 10 (1958), 68-86.

> A general introduction to nineteenth-century plays dealing with Indians; most valuable for list of forty-seven plays (1821-58).

283 Perkins, Alice J. FRANCES WRIGHT, FREE ENQUIRER. Philadelphia: Porcupine Press, 1972.

> Slight work on Frances Wright's liberal tendencies.

Critical, Historical, Reference Resources

284 Pray, Isaac C., Jr. "The First Scene of an unpublished tragedy entitled THE NOBLE ROMANS." NEW YORK MIRROR, 12 March 1837, p. 310.

> An example of the way contemporary newspapers help the drama historian.

285 Rappolo, Joseph. "American Themes, Heroes and History on the New Orleans Stage, 1806-1865." TULANE STUDIES IN ENGLISH, 5 (1955), 151-81.

> This essay emphasizes local interest, for example, the War of 1812 with Jackson in New Orleans, but reflects national popular appeal.

286 _____. "Local and Topical Plays in New Orleans, 1806-1865." TULANE STUDIES IN ENGLISH, 4 (1954), 91-124.

> Author refers to over seven hundred plays in New Orleans, all but four lost, and provides commentary on major plays and production data.

287 Reardon, William R. "Banned in Boston. A Study of Theatrical Censorship in Boston from 1630 to 1950." Ph.D. dissertation, Stanford University, 1953.

288 [Rees, James]. "Dramatic Authors of America." DRAMATIC MIRROR AND LITERARY COMPANION, 1 (August 1841), 18.

> Concerned with the life and career of N.H. Bannister.

289 "Review of James A. Hillhouse's Dramas, Discourses, and Other Pieces." NEW ENGLANDER, 16 (1858), 705-41.

> An extensive contemporary analysis; Hillhouse's collected work was published in 1839.

290 Rossman, K.R. "The Irish in American Drama in Mid-19th Century." NEW YORK HISTORICAL SOCIETY NOTES, 21 (January 1940), 39-53.

> Author emphasizes Boucicault, Brougham, Barney Williams, and Irish actors more than plays.

291 Sargent, M.E. "Susanna Rowson." MEDFORD HISTORICAL REGISTER, 7 (April 1904), 25-40.

> Some biographical information. The article mentions plays but emphasizes Rowson's nondramatic writings and her school in Medford.

Critical, Historical, Reference Resources

292   Sawyer, Lemuel. THE AUTOBIOGRAPHY OF LEMUEL SAWYER. New York: Privately printed, 1844.

      Basic information presented with a certain straight forward naivete of style.

293   _____. BLACKBEARD. Facsimile ed. Introd. Richard Walser. Raleigh, N.C.: State Department of Archives and History, 1952.

      Historical background provided.

294   Scherting, John A. "Partisan Drama and the American Stage, 1783-1807." Ph.D. dissertation, Washington State University, 1970.

295   Schoenberger, Harold William. "American Adaptations of French Plays on the New York and Philadelphia Stages from 1790 to 1833." Ph.D. dissertation, University of Pennsylvania, 1924.

296   Shillingsburg, Miriam J. "The West Point Treason in American Drama, 1791-1891." ETJ, 30 (1978), 73-89.

      A discussion of the plays treating Major André as a spy. Emphasis upon William Dunlap's ANDRÉ.

297   Shockley, Martin S. "American Plays in the Richmond Theatre, 1819-1838." STUDIES IN PHILOLOGY, 37 (1940), 100-19.

      Author mentions forty plays, mainly by Dunlap, Payne, Noah, Stone, and Barker but also several local playwrights; some seventeen American dramatists listed.

298   Simms, William Gilmore. "Our Early Authors and Artists." XIX CENTURY, 1 (1869), 273-83.

      Biographical information, personal reflections, and commentary on plays of Ioor, Harby, Holland, White.

299   Sitton, Fred. "The Indian Play in America, 1750-1900." Ph.D. dissertation, Northwestern University, 1962.

300   Snowden, Yates. SOUTH CAROLINA PLAYERS AND PLAYWRIGHTS. Columbia, S.C.: n.p., 1936.

301   _____. "South Carolina Plays and Playwrights." CAROLINIAN, November 1909, pp. 1-13.

      Good basic essay on group of dramatists in early nineteenth century. Largely superseded by the book-length study by Charles S. Watson (entry no. 312).

Critical, Historical, Reference Resources

302   Streubel, Ernest J. "The Pocahontas Story in Early American Drama."
      COLONNADE, 10 (September 1915), 68-77.

      Argues that theatre managers tended to determine the nature
      of plays, to legislate music, declamation, and so forth.

303   Stone, Henry Dickinson. PERSONAL RECOLLECTIONS OF THE DRAMA
      OR THEATRICAL REMINISCENCES EMBRACING SKETCHES OF PROMI-
      NENT ACTORS AND ACTRESSES, THEIR CHIEF CHARACTERISTICS,
      ORIGINAL ANECDOTES OF THEM, AND INCIDENTS CONNECTED
      THEREWITH. Albany: Charles Van Benthysen and Sons, 1873.

      See entry no. 70.

304   Thompson, Laurance. "Longfellow Sells THE SPANISH STUDENT." AL,
      6 (1934), 141-50.

      Thompson explains Longfellow's difficulties in publishing his
      play in GRAHAM'S MAGAZINE, his correspondence with
      editor, and his care in launching drama.

305   "A Tragedy." NATIONAL ERA, 28 June, 1855, p. 101.

      Scene from an unpublished play by Louis F. Thomas,
      based on conquest of Mexico by Spaniards.

306   "Uncle Ben Baker." NEW YORK DRAMATIC MIRROR, 13 September
      1890, p. 5.

      A good account of the life, playwriting, and theatre activity
      of the author of the first "Mose" play--Benjamin A. Baker.

307   Vail, R.W.G. SUSANNA HASWELL ROWSON: THE AUTHOR OF
      CHARLOTTE TEMPLE: A BIBLIOGRAPHICAL STUDY. Worcester, Mass.:
      American Antiquarian Society, 1933.

      A basic source for study of Rowson as novelist and dramatist.

308   Van Lennep, William. "John Adams to a Young Playwright: An Un-
      published Letter to Samuel Judah." HARVARD LITERARY BULLETIN, 1
      (1947), 117-18.

      Having read Judah's "horrible" ODOFRIEDE, THE OUTCAST
      and noted that it diminishes "human happiness" as do HAMLET
      and MACBETH, Adams advises Judah to change his habits.

309   "Velasco: A Tragedy, in Five Acts." NEW YORK REVIEW, 4 (1839),
      243.

      A substantial review of the play by Epes Sargent (New York:
      Harper and Brothers, 1838).

Critical, Historical, Reference Resources

310   Walser, Richard. "Negro Dialect in Eighteenth Century American Drama." AMERICAN SPEECH, 30 (1955), 269-76.

    An analysis of ten plays (including THE DISAPPOINTMENT, THE CANDIDATE, TRIAL OF ATTICUS, YORKER'S STRATEGEM, and TRIUMPS OF LOVE) in which the author sees no consistency in dialect except for plays by John Murdock, but finds the beginning of the literature of Negro dialect.

311   Waterman, W.R. FRANCES WRIGHT. Studies in History, Economics, and Public Law, Vol. 115, No. 1. New York: Columbia University Press, 1924.

    A general and slight biography.

312   Watson, Charles S. ANTEBELLUM CHARLESTON DRAMATISTS. University: University of Alabama Press, 1976.

    A history of the drama in one of the major theatre centers of pre-Civil War America. Emphasis on Ioor, White, Harby, and Simms. Invaluable source for drama research.

313   _____. "A Denunciation on the Stage of Spanish Rule: James Workman's LIBERTY IN LOUISIANA (1804)." LOUISIANA HISTORY, 11 (1970), 245, 58.

    A thorough analysis of the play in terms of the author's political objectives and the historical period.

314   _____. "Jeffersonian Republicanism in William Ioor's INDEPENDENCE, the First Play of South Carolina." SOUTH CAROLINA HISTORICAL MAGAZINE, 69 (1968), 194-203.

    Discussing INDEPENDENCE as an early example of agrarianism in American literature, Watson notes changes from source, James Thompson's THE SEASONS.

315   Weggelin, Oscar. "Micah Hawkins and the SAW-MILL." MAGAZINE OF HISTORY WITH NOTES AND QUERIES, 32, iii, Extra No. 127 (1927), 153-210.

    An excellent study of an interesting author and his play.

316   Wright [D'Arusmont], Frances. BIOGRAPHY AND NOTES. Boston: Privately printed, 1848.

    Life, adventures and travels of the free-thinking author of ALTORF; various people quoted.

Critical, Historical, Reference Resources

317   Wood, William Burk. PERSONAL RECOLLECTIONS OF THE STAGE, EMBRACING NOTICES OF ACTORS, AUTHORS, AND AUDITORS, DURING A PERIOD OF FORTY YEARS. Philadelphia: Henry Carey Baird, 1855.

   See entry no. 74.

318   Wyld, Lionel D. "The Miracle Play in America: An Aspect of Folk Theatre." DRAMA CRITIQUE, 1 (November 1958), 13-18.

   Concerned with Indian plays and the relationship of nativity plays to Spanish-Catholic-Christian scenes, the author pulls together contributions of other folk researchers.

b. CRITICS AND CRITICISM, DRAMATIC THEORY, AND NATIONALISM

319   "American Actors and Dramatic Authors." SPIRIT OF THE TIMES, 7 March 1840, p. 12.

   Author bemoans lack of attention to American drama and points out causes for the poor character of dramatic literature. He emphasizes the plays of Dunlap.

320   "The Decline of the Drama." SPIRIT OF THE TIMES, 13 November 1858, p. 473.

   Writer deplores lack of good tragedy, American or European, and good theatre companies. Mainly on Forrest as one who helped American drama.

321   "Decline of the Modern Drama, By the Author of 'Truth, A Gift for Scribblers.'" NEW ENGLAND MAGAZINE, 8 (1835), 105-07.

   After a bitter commentary revealing that talented dramatists must tailor plays for star actors, the author reviews the tastes of audiences and concludes that good plays fail and that past masters of the drama cannot be used as models.

322   "The Drama." NATIONAL REGISTER, 27 July 1816, pp. 339-40.

   An enthusiastic defense of the abused American dramatist whose work is frequently "superior to many of the European dramas" but who is denied reputation and pecuniary advantage. Particular reference to Barker.

323   "The Drama." NATIONAL REGISTER, 10 April 1819, pp. 225-27.

   Concerned with the spread of drama throughout the Union and its tendency to "improve the human character," the author provides a vindication of the drama against prejudice.

Critical, Historical, Reference Resources

324   "Dramatic Copyright." SPIRIT OF THE TIMES, 20 January 1849, p. 576.

> Sympathetic view of the dramatist and the unfair advantage taken of him by both actors and managers.

325   "Dramatic Criticism." SPIRIT OF THE TIMES, 9 December 1837, p. 1

> A credo for SPIRIT OF THE TIMES drama critics or reviewers. Refers to plays, actors, and theatre companies.

326   "Dramatic Literature." AMERICAN QUARTERLY REVIEW, 12 (March 1830), 134.

> Author urges playwrights to create a dramatic structure for a new country but still reserves the right to criticize all literature.

327   "Editor's Cabinet--The American Drama." NATIONAL REGISTER, 12 July 1817, pp. 30-32.

> Author sees improved taste among theatre audiences but warns that nonsense upon the stage will not be countenanced simply because it is written by a native American. Admits that American drama is essentially English but feels that native playwrights, after the period of imitation, will contribute to world drama.

328   Fagin, N. Bryllion. "Poe--Drama Critic." THEATRE ANNUAL, 5 (1946), 23-28.

> Author presents Poe, author of eight reviews, as a severe critic who was sympathetic to American drama. One of the few good essays on nineteenth-century drama criticism.

329   Leggett, William. "The Drama." CRITIC, 22 November 1823, p. 62.

> As part of a review of James Lawson's GIORDANO, this astute editor comments on the value of native American drama and enumerates subjects appropriate to native plays, but insists on good drama not just American drama.

330   Moses, Montrose J., and John Mason Brown, eds. THE AMERICAN THEATRE AS SEEN BY ITS CRITICS, 1752-1934. New York: W.W. Norton, 1934.

> A collection of contemporary reviews by substantial critics, mainly on acting but including many reviews of American plays. Valuable resource.

Critical, Historical, Reference Resources

331 Moss, James E. "Dramatic Criticism in Frontier St. Louis, 1835-1838." MISSOURI HISTORICAL REVIEW, 58 (1964), 191-216.

>A summary of theatre production in St. Louis as reviewed in the COMMERCIAL BULLETIN through editorial comments, which are mainly on manners and morals, and anonymous letters to the newspaper.

332 [Oakes, James]. "Letters from Acorn." SPIRIT OF THE TIMES, 17 March 1855, p. 49.

>This review of Epes Sargent's PRIESTESS becomes a plea for national drama.

333 _____. "Letters from Acorn." SPIRIT OF THE TIMES, 6 September 1856, p. 349.

>A strong comment in support of the Dramatic Author's Copyright Law passed by Congress.

334 "Originality in Dramatic Writing." SPIRIT OF THE TIMES, 7 April 1855, p. 89.

>The author surveys dramatic literature from the Greeks through Shakespeare in order to make a comment on contemporaries.

335 "THE POLITICIANS, a Comedy in Five Acts. By Cornelius Mathews." NEW YORK REVIEW, 7 (1840), 430-39.

>Emphasizing national drama, author refutes Lord Kames's view of comedy in ELEMENTS OF CRITICISM (1762). Quotations from Mathews' play.

336 Reardon, William R. "The American Drama and Theatre in the Nineteenth Century: A Retreat from Meaning." EMERSON SOCIETY QUARTERLY, 20 (1974), 170-86.

>As reasons for weak drama, author suggests lack of talented dramatists, audiences' craving for farce and plays dealing with economic problems, and the growth of the nation.

337 Sederholm, Frederick L. "The Development of Theories of Dramatic Comedy in America through 1830." Ph.D. dissertation, State University of Iowa, 1961.

338 Smeal, J.F.S. "The Idea of Our Early National Drama." NORTH DAKOTA QUARTERLY, 42, i[1974], 5-27.

>A poorly written essay with some good research on the idea that drama went westward with the nation.

Critical, Historical, Reference Resources

339 [Walsh, Robert?]. "American Drama." AMERICAN QUARTERLY REVIEW, 1 (1827), 331-57.

> The single most important contemporary essay on early nineteenth century American drama. Using a review of THE FATHER OF AN ONLY CHILD, MARMION, and SUPERSTITION as a basis, the author writes an intelligent, persuasive, and sensibly sympathetic argument for the support of native American drama. The identity of the writer is uncertain; Walsh owned the magazine.

340 Watson, Charles S. "Stephen Cullen Carpenter, First Drama Critic of the Charleston COURIER." SOUTH CAROLINA HISTORICAL MAGAZINE, 69 (1968), 243-52.

> A short biography of Carpenter with a discussion of his intentions as a critic: to provide informal dramatic criticism, to improve the quality of drama and drama companies, and to increase public support of the theatre. Clearly written and substantial essay.

341 Whitman, Walt. "As a Very Average Proof." BROOKLYN EAGLE, 7 October 1846; rpt. in THE GATHERING OF FORCES. Ed. Cleveland Rogers and John Black. New York: G.C. Putnam's Sons, 1920. II, 341-42.

> Author warns against reviewing plays prior to production.

342 _____. "Miserable State of the Stage. Why Can't We Have Something Worth the Name of American Drama!" BROOKLYN EAGLE, 8 February 1847; rpt. in THE GATHERING OF FORCES. Ed. Cleveland Rogers and John Black. New York: G.C. Putnam's Sons, 1920. II, 310-11. Also rpt. in THE AMERICAN THEATRE AS SEEN BY ITS CRITICS, 1752-1934. Ed. Montrose J. Moses and John Mason Brown, pp. 70-72. See entry no. 330.

> Condemnation of puffs, lack of good theatres (except for occasional plays at the Park), and the star system. Whitman wants to encourage American talent: "give us American plays."

c. YANKEE DRAMA—EMPHASIS ON PLAYS RATHER THAN ACTING

343 Balch, Marston. "Jonathan the First, The Origin of the Stage Yankee." MLN, 46 (1931), 281-88.

> This early essay provides the correct background and stage interest, but arrives at incorrect conclusions.

344 Dorson, Richard M. "The Yankee on the Stage--A Folk Hero of the American Drama." NEQ, 13 (1940), 467-93.

Author describes the Yankee--his character and relation to country scene--from beginnings to present and refers to such plays as THE CONTRAST, THE OLD HOMESTEAD, and JOHNNY JOHNSON while emphasizing American plays of the 1830s, 1840s, and 1850s.

345   Eich, Louis M. "The Stage Yankee." QJS, 27 (1941), 16-25.

Author uses publications of THE OLD HOMESTEAD and SHORE ACRES to dramatize the climax of his survey of the Yankee on stage.

346   Hodge, Francis. YANKEE THEATRE: THE IMAGE OF AMERICA ON THE STAGE, 1825-1850. See entry no. 142.

347   Kernodle, Portia. "The Yankee Types on the London Stage, 1824-1880." SM, 14 (1947), 139-47.

Good, basic essay on English response to early Yankee plays and other American characters, such as Davy Crockett and Colonel Sellers.

348   Killheffer, Marie. "A Comparison of the Dialect of the 'Bigelow Papers' with the Dialect of Four Yankee Plays." AMERICAN SPEECH, 3 (1928), 222-36.

Mainly on dialect and "Bigelow Papers," this essay includes brief references to THE CONTRAST, THE YANKEY IN ENGLAND, THE PEOPLE'S LAWYER, and THE OLD HOMESTEAD.

349   Leggett, William. "The Drama." CRITIC, 27 December 1828, p. 141.

Leggett includes an analysis of the Yankee character in a review of Hackett's Solomon Swap in WHO WANTS A GUINEA?

350   LIFE AND RECOLLECTIONS OF YANKEE HILL: TOGETHER WITH ANECDOTES AND INCIDENTS OF HIS TRAVELS. Ed. W.K. Northall. New York: N.p., 1850.

Largely anecdotal biography but with numerous references to Yankee plays acted by Hill.

d. UNCLE TOM'S CABIN AS DRAMA

351   Birdoff, Harry. THE WORLD'S GREATEST HIT: UNCLE TOM'S CABIN. New York: Vanni, 1947.

This is the most complete study of the dramatization of the novel that Mrs. Stowe declared the world was not ready to accept.

Critical, Historical, Reference Resources

352   Corbett, Elizabeth. "A Footnote to 'The Drama.'" DRAMA, 16 (1926), 285-86.

         A discussion of the traditional and impromptu aspects of the acted play, "our one folk play . . . entitled to its little niche in dramatic history."

353   Drummond, A.M., and Richard Moody. "The Hit of the Century: UNCLE TOM'S CABIN--1852-1952." ETJ, 4 (1952), 315-22.

         A history of the early development of the play and its phenomenal success in the theatre. Good, basic essay.

354   Grimsted, David. "Uncle Tom from Page to Stage: Limitations of Nineteenth Century Drama." QJS, 56 (1970), 235-44.

         Author compares play with novel, comments on Aikens' version and the strange popularity of a serious play treating a controversial issue.

355   Laurie, Joe, Jr. "The Theatre's All-Time Hit." AMERICAN MERCURY, 60 (1945), 469-72.

         The story of UNCLE TOM'S CABIN as dramatized and presented through Tom Shows.

356   Lippman, Monroe. "Uncle Tom and His Poor Relations: American Slavery Plays." SSJ, 28 (1963), 183-97.

         With the background and explanation of success of UNCLE TOM'S CABIN, the author notes French, German, Spanish, Finnish, Italian, and Polish versions along with burlesque and variations on slavery themes.

357   Meserve, Walter J., and Ruth I. Meserve. "Uncle Tom's Cabin and Modern Chinese Drama." MD, 17 (1974), 57-66.

         A discussion of the dramatization of UNCLE TOM'S CABIN by members of the Chinese Spring Willow Society that helped bring Western drama to China in 1907. Re-created version (10 scenes) in 1957 is compared to novel and discussed scene by scene. Brief portions translated.

358   Moody, Richard. "Uncle Tom, The Theatre, and Mrs. Stowe." AMERICAN HERITAGE, 6 (1955), 28-33, 102-03.

         A commentary on the play and players and the continuing popularity of UNCLE TOM plus an interesting glimpse of Mrs. Stowe who saw the play in Boston at the National Theatre in 1854.

Critical, Historical, Reference Resources

359   Roppolo, Joseph P. "Uncle Tom in New Orleans: Three Lost Plays." NEQ, 17 (1954), 213-26.

> An interesting commentary based on contemporary accounts of southern versions of UNCLE TOM'S CABIN.

3. Drama During the Rise of Realism, 1861-1900

a. SURVEYS AND STUDIES OF INDIVIDUAL AUTHORS AND PLAYS

360   [Beaumont Fletcher]. "Bret Harte's 'Sue' on Stage." GODEY'S, 133 (1896), 580-85.

> Author comments on play as badly structured, a mixture of charm and wretchedness; provides plot; and declares that the era of American playwright will surely come.

361   _____. "The Coming Dramatic Season." GODEY'S, 135 (1897), 352-60.

> Author comments on novels adapted to stage and to opera and emphasizes importance of American plays and actors. Particular reference to Gillette's work.

362   Bennison, Martin J., and Barry B. Witham. "Sentimental Love and the Nineteenth-Century American Drama." PLAYERS, 49 (1974), 127-29.

> Authors attempt to show differences within the sentimental tradition in nineteenth-century drama. Particular concern for FRANCESCA DA RIMINI and MARGARET FLEMING.

363   Brockett, O.G., and L. Brockett. "Civil War Theatre: Contemporary Treatments." CIVIL WAR HISTORY, 1 (1955), 229-50.

> An excellent survey of the numerous Civil War plays that appeared in American theatres; discussion of the events that stimulated the dramatists.

364   Clapp, H.A. "Reminiscences of a Dramatic Critic." ATLANTIC MONTHLY, 88 (1901), 155-65; 344-54; 490-501; 622-34.

> Commentary on plays, actors, and theatres, American and English; the first part of reminiscences is most significant for the subject in hand.

365   Coleman, William S.E. "Buffalo Bill on Stage." PLAYERS, 47 (1971), 80-91.

> An excellent article on the various Buffalo Bill plays and the ways in which they were produced.

Critical, Historical, Reference Resources

366   Davis, Owen. MY FIRST FIFTY YEARS IN THE THEATRE: Boston: Walter H. Baker, 1950.

> A playwright-author comments on the major playwrights and their plays when he started writing in 1897.

367   Eaton, Walter Prichard. "'Why Do You Fear Me, Nellie?': The Melodrama of Forty Years Ago." HARPER'S MONTHLY, 183 (1941), 164-70.

> A well-written bit of nostalgia for the melodrama of the past with sarcastic comments for the "scholarly" resurrections in the twenty-volume edition of AMERICA'S LOST PLAYS. Observations on past favorites.

368   Fine, L.H. "THE FIRE-TRIBE AND THE PALE FACE: An Unfinished and Unpublished Play by Stephen Crane." MARKHAM REVIEW, 3 (1972), 37-38.

> A brief analysis of the manuscript and the plot of the play.

369   _____. "Two Unpublished Plays by Stephen Crane." RESOURCES FOR AMERICAN LITERARY STUDY, 1 (1971), 200-216.

> A brief commentary. The plays are THE FIRE TRIBE AND THE PALEFACE, unfinished, and an untitled play.

370   Frohman, Daniel. DANIEL FROHMAN PRESENTS. New York: Lee Furman, 1937.

> The autobiography of a major theatre person whose memories, like those of other such people, invariably shed light on various aspects of American drama. Comments on HAZEL KIRKE, William Gillette, and Bartley Campbell in Chapter 7, on Mark Twain in Chapter 8.

371   _____. "The Tendencies of the American Stage." COSMOPOLITAN, 38 (1904), 15-22.

> Optimistic about present drama, Frohman refers to plays by Howard, Gillette, Thompson, and Boucicault.

372   Gaffney, Fannie H. "Modern Dramatic Realism." ARENA, 29 (1903), 390-96.

> Concerned with realistic characters on stage, the author attacks the motives of playwrights, the permissive and money-minded managers, and the public.

373   Garland, Hamlin. "Under the Wheel." ARENA, 2 (1890), 182-288.

> The text of Garland's major dramatic work.

374 Gordan, John D. "THE GHOST at Brede Place." BNYPL, 56 (1952), 591-96.

> An interesting comment on a lost play entitled THE GHOST, created by Crane and nine others (including Henry James, Joseph Conrad, and H.G. Wells) and presented at Crane's house in England, Brede Place, on 28 December 1899.

375 Hall, Roger A. "THE BROOK: America's Germinal Musical?" ETJ, 27 (1975), 323-29.

> Author argues that this Texas production used the traditional musical comedy form.

376 Haskins, William. "Image-wise, Man, That's the Way it Was!" SHOW, 2 (October 1962), 13-20.

> Author refers to nineteenth-century plays by Joaquin Miller, Bronson Howard, and Augustus Thomas to indicate effect of American drama, "image-wise," on Europe.

377 Hennequin, Alfred. "Characteristics of American Drama." ARENA, 1 (1890), 700-709.

> A long comment on Greek, English, and French drama introduces this essay on social realism in America. Such characteristics as strong melodramatic situations, farcical scenes, horse-play and songs, moral sentiment, and poetic justice are emphasized. A good general essay although it lacks reference to particular plays.

378 Heydrick, Benjamin A. "The American Drama." CHAUTAUQUAN, 65 (1911), 25-48.

> Author surveys the drama since 1870 in terms of plays dealing with society, local color, Americans at work, and national problems.

379 Heywood, Blanche E. "Tally-ho, the Mountain Play." OVERLAND MONTHLY, n.s. 73 (1919), 469-71.

> A brief personal glimpse, with pictures, of Joaquin Miller and his play, TALLY-HO.

380 Holman, C. Hugh. "The Literature of the Old South." In FIFTEEN AMERICAN AUTHORS BEFORE 1900. Ed. Robert A. Rees and Earl N. Harbert. Madison: University of Wisconsin Press, 1971, pp. 387-400.

> A bibliographical essay with a brief section on drama and theatre.

Critical, Historical, Reference Resources

381   Hornblow, Arthur. "The Leading Contemporary Dramatists." NEW YORK DRAMATIC MIRROR, 22 December 1894, p. 3.

   Author points out that although America had had a literature of its own for more than half a century, it was just beginning to have a national drama.

382   _____. "Our American Dramatists." MUNSEY'S 12 (1894), 159.

   A brief comment on successful contemporary playwrights: B. Howard, Edward Kidder, Augustus Thomas, H.G. Carleton, Belasco, Gillette, Hoyt, Harrigan, and Herne. Good illustrations.

383   Howells, W.D. "Drama." ATLANTIC MONTHLY, 35 (1875), 749-50.

   Mainly on Raymond's version of Mark Twain's THE GILDED AGE.

384   _____. "Some New American Plays." HARPER'S WEEKLY, 16 January 1904, pp. 89-90. Rpt. in AMERICAN DRAMA AND IT CRITICS. Ed. Alan S. Downer. Chicago: University of Chicago Press, 1965, pp. 10-17.

   A comment on dramas of the late nineteenth century.

385   Hutton, Laurence. "The American Play." LIPPINCOTT'S, 37 (1886), 289. Rpt. in A LIBRARY OF AMERICAN LITERATURE FROM THE EARLIEST SETTLEMENT TO THE PRESENT TIME. Ed. Edmund Clarence Steadman and Ellen Mackay. New York: Charles L. Webster, 1889. X, 217-18.

   A brief review of eighteenth- and nineteenth-century American drama with the conclusion that the "American play" has yet to be written.

386   Johnson, Albert E. "American Dramatizations of American Literary Materials from 1850 to 1900." Ph.D. dissertation, Cornell University, 1948.

387   Kalb, Deborah S. "The Rise and Fall of the American Woman in American Drama." ETJ, 27 (1975), 149-60.

   Author includes a discussion of women in late nineteenth-century plays; particular reference is made to Herne's MARGARET FLEMING.

388   Koster, Donald Nelson. THE THEME OF DIVORCE IN AMERICAN DRAMA, 1871-1939. Philadelphia: Privately printed, 1942.

   A published dissertation, reasonably well researched, on a theme popular among dramatists.

Critical, Historical, Reference Resources

389   Logan, Olive. "The Ancestry of Brudder Bones." HARPER'S MONTHLY, 58 (1879), 687-98.

        Author suggests a background for American minstrel in French, Greek, and Chinese sources.

390   Mabie, Hamilton W. "American Plays, Old and New." OUTLOOK, 102 (1912), 945-55.

        A commentary on the plays of several late nineteenth century dramatists.

391   Marshall, T.F. "The Birth Date of Nathaniel Harrington Bannister." AL, 8 (1936), 306-07.

        Author takes date from family Bible (1813-47); Harrington married Amelia Stone, widow of J.A. Stone, in 1835.

392   Mathews, F. Annie. "A Plea for the Play-writer." GODEY'S, 127 (1893), 466-68.

        Mathews argues that although the printed play has no copyright protection and therefore few plays exist, a reading audience would help American drama.

393   Meserve, Walter J. "American Drama and the Rise of Realism." JAHRBÜCH FÜR AMERIKASTUDIEN, 9 (1964), 152-59.

        Author studies the parallel development of drama and fiction during the rise of realism, emphasizing local color drama, novels adapted for the stage, and Herne's MARGARET FLEMING.

394   Millard, Bailey. "The Merriwold Dramatists." BOOKMAN, 29 (1909), 627-33.

        Personal observations on the several dramatists who wrote plays at Merriwold--William C. DeMille, Charles Klein, J.I. Clarke, and Martha Morton. Good illustrations.

395   Montgomery, George E. "Bartley Campbell." THEATRE, 14 June 1886, pp. 348-49.

        Campbell is presented as a man of a pathetic life who failed as a manager, wrote many plays, but remains "a mechanic, not a thinker, and his plays . . . will be forgotten."

396   Moses, Montrose J. "Is There an American Drama?" DRAMA LEAGUE MONTHLY, 2 (1917), 505-09.

        Author considers drama since Bronson Howard, emphasizing its rightful place in the study of American literature.

Critical, Historical, Reference Resources

397   Naeseth, Henriette. "Drama in Early Deadwood, 1869-1879." AL, 10 (1938), 289-312.

>   A well-researched essay on theatre and drama in Deadwood, South Dakota. Author notes forty-four American plays and provides plays lists for each summer season.

398   Nardin, James T. "A Study in Popular American Farce, 1865-1914." Ph.D. dissertation, University of Chicago, 1950.

399   Nolan, Paul T. "Bright American Minds, British Brains, and Southern Drama." SSJ, 24 (1959), 129-34.

>   Mainly on Espy Williams as revealed through a letter (1902) by actor-director Clarence Brune.

400   _____. "Drama in the Lower Mississippi States." MISSISSIPPI QUARTERLY, 19 (1965), 20-28.

>   The work of an active researcher. Plays are grouped into four parts: (1) prior to the Civil War (very few plays), (2) to World War I (perhaps 250 plays in Library of Congress), (3) between world wars, and (4) since World War II.

401   _____. "Espy Williams: New Orleans Playwright." BULLETIN OF THE MISSISSIPPI LIBRARY ASSOCIATION, 21 (1959), 133-39.

>   Biographical essay on Williams.

402   _____. "Williams' DANTE: The Death of Nineteenth-Century Heroic Drama." SSJ, 25 (1960), 255-63.

>   A discussion of play by Espy Williams (1852-1908) based on the Dante-Beatrice legend and written in blank verse as commissioned by Lawrence Barrett on whom the article concentrates.

403   _____, ed. LIFE ON THE BORDER: A BORDER DRAMA. Written especially for Buffalo Bill. Cody, Wyo.: Pioneer Drama Service, 1965.

>   One of the old Wild West Shows with Captain Jack Crawford playing Buffalo Bill. Authorship undetermined.

404   "Our Colonial View of the Drama." LITERARY DIGEST, 23 November 1912, pp. 959-60.

>   This essay is not concerned with Colonial drama; author refers to Brander Matthews' objection to Howells' pervasive interest in plays on American subjects.

Critical, Historical, Reference Resources

405 Palmer, A.M. "Why Theatrical Managers Reject Plays." FORUM, 15 (1893), 614-20.

   A comment on American plays by a theatre manager who claimed to receive five hundred manuscripts a year. The essay indicates the power and bias of a theatre manager.

406 Pawley, Thomas D. "The First Black Playwrights." BLACK WRITERS, 21 (1972), 16-24.

   A historical view of early black plays, playwrights, and theatre companies. Carefully researched and written.

407 Potter, Helen. "The Drama of the Twentieth Century." ARENA, 23 (1900), 157-66.

   An idealized view and argument to cure all of the growing pains of nineteenth-century American drama.

408 Rahill, Frank. "Melodrama." THEATRE ARTS, 16 (1932), 285-94.

   Author considers melodrama from its beginnings in France through England to America. Although he concentrates on English drama, he mentions the works of Boucicault and Herne.

409 Reardon, William, and John Foxen. "The Propaganda Play." CIVIL WAR HISTORY, 1 (1955), 281-93.

   A brief comment on UNCLE TOM'S CABIN prior to an emphasis on modern drama.

410 Scanlan, Tom. "The Domestication of Rip Van Winkle: Joe Jefferson's Play as Prologue to Modern American Drama." VIRGINIA QUARTERLY REVIEW, 50 (1974), 51-62.

   Author attempts, unconvincingly, to show that RIP VAN WINKLE foreshadows plays by Eugene O'Neill, Arthur Miller, and Tennessee Williams.

411 Schneider, Robert W. "Stephen Crane and the Drama of Transition." JOURNAL OF CENTRAL MISSISSIPPI VALLEY AMERICAN STUDIES ASSOCIATION, 2 (1961), 1-16.

   This essay does not treat Crane's plays but rather the fin-de-siecle dramatic situation which Crane's writings reflect.

412 Slout, William L. "THE BLACK CROOK: First of the Nudies." PLAYERS, 50 (1975), 16-19.

   A popular account of this 1866 musical success and its contemporary reception.

Critical, Historical, Reference Resources

413   Stallings, Roy. "The Drama in Southern Illinois (1865-1900)." JOURNAL OF THE ILLINOIS STATE HISTORICAL SOCIETY, 33 (1940), 190-202.

         Theatre activity after Civil War in Cairo-Carbondale area; mainly a list of plays and actors with comments on theatre.

414   Stallman, Robert W. "Stephan Crane as Dramatist." BNYPL, 67 (1963), 495-511.

         The text of Crane's DRAMA IN CUBA with brief introduction describing Crane's other efforts in drama and his lack of success.

415   Stallman, Robert W., and E.R. Hagemann, eds. THE WAR DISPATCHES OF STEPHEN CRANE. New York: New York University Press, 1964.

         Includes Crane's play DRAMA IN CUBA (pp. 318-34).

416   Waterman, Arthur F. "Joseph Jefferson as Rip Van Winkle." JOURNAL OF POPULAR CULTURE, 1 (1968), 371-78.

         A discussion of the play and the role as it absorbed Jefferson's life.

417   Watson, Margaret G. SILVER THEATRE, AMUSEMENTS OF THE MINING FRONTIER IN EARLY NEVADA, 1850-1864. Glendale, Calif.: Arthur H. Clark Co., 1964.

         Author mentions plays and playwrights as well as actors, mainly during the 1860-64 period. The emphasis is on Mark Twain.

418   Wegelin, Oscar. "An Early Iowa Playwright." NEW YORK HISTORICAL SOCIETY QUARTERLY BULLETIN, 27 (1944), 42-44.

         A bibliographical list of six plays by Orestes Augustus Brownson: ANNIE, 1869 (probably first original American play printed in Iowa); CAROLINE, 1870; THE TEN SQUAWS, 1870; SIMPSON, 1870; THE FOREIGNERS IN AMERICA, 1870; and CARL EHRLICHKEIT, 1870.

419   Welsh, Willard. "The War in Drama." CIVIL WAR HISTORY, 1 (1955), 251-80.

         Author groups plays according to the issue of war, the contemporary reactions, and the patriotic effusions that appeared during the following twenty years.

420   Whitford, Kathryn. "MILLER OF BOSCOBEL: Hamlin Garland's Labor Play." MASJ, 8 (Fall 1967), 33-42.

         Illustrating a turning point in Garland's career, Whitford de-

Critical, Historical, Reference Resources

scribes the play in terms of plot, productions, and Garland's sympathy for labor.

421 Wills, J. Richard. "Olive Logan vs. the Nude Woman." PLAYERS, 47 (1971), 36-43.

> A well-written essay on an author-playwright-lecturer-actress who campaigned against nudity.

b. CRITICS AND CRITICISM

422 "American Playwrights on the American Drama." HARPER'S WEEKLY, 2 February 1889, pp. 97-99.

> One of the most significant contemporary essays on American drama. It gives the views of Augustin Daly, Edward Harrigan, Bronson Howard, William Gillette, John Grosvenor Wilson, and Steele MacKaye, with a final comment by William Winter.

423 Archer, William. "American Drama Revisited." INDEPENDENT, 27 June 1907, pp. 1519-25.

> This significant British critic sees birth of American drama in work of Howard, Herne, Thomas, and Fitch. Gives an account of drama, 1900-07.

424 Bender, Jack E. "Brander Matthews: Critic of the Theatre." ETJ, 12 (1960), 169-76.

> An evaluation of Matthews as a critic, his contributions to drama criticism, particularly after 1890, and his view of theatre as a means to an end--that is, as a criticism of life.

425 Garland, Hamlin. CRUMBLING IDOLS: TWELVE ESSAYS ON ART DEALING CHIEFLY WITH LITERATURE, PAINTING, AND THE DRAMA. Ed. Jane Johnson. Cambridge, Mass.: Harvard University Press, 1960.

> Essay no. 7, "The Drift of the Drama," was first published in IDOLS (Boston: Stone and Kimball, 1894, pp. 69-78). Viewing drama in this essay in terms of his theory of veritism and contemporary values, Garland sees great promise in American drama.

> In Essay no. 8, "The Influence of Ibsen" (pp. 81-93), Garland says that Ibsen's work helps in "our war against conventionalism" but must not dominate or be a model for American drama which must be "more human."

426 Mantle, Burns. AMERICAN PLAYWRIGHTS OF TODAY. New York: Dodd, Mead, 1929.

Critical, Historical, Reference Resources

"A Salaam to the Past" includes comments on Augustus Thomas, Charles H. Hoyt, and others.

427 Marsh, John L. "Michael Valentine Ball--Faithful Diarist, Passionate Playgoer." PLAYERS, 50 (1975), 38-43.

> The subject is a play-going doctor from Warren, Pennsylvania, who wrote of plays he saw from 1884 to 1886.

428 Matthews, Brander. "The American on the Stage." SCRIBNER'S 18 (1879), 321-33.

> A survey of the major American character types, emphasizing the Yankee, Davy Crockett, Colonel Sellers, and Judge Slote in Woolf's THE MIGHTY DOLLAR.

429 _____. "The Dramatic Outlook in America." HARPER'S MONTHLY, 78 (1889), 430.

> General observation that the season's plays indicate a beginning for dramatic literature in America.

430 _____. "The Literary Merit of Our Latter-Day Drama." SCRIBNER'S, 34 (1903), 607-12.

> A continuation of Matthews' usual optimistic view of contemporary plays in terms of literature.

431 _____. "The Relation of Drama to Literature." FORUM, 24 (1898), 630-40.

> Matthews emphasizes the distinction between the written and spoken word, shows his sympathy for dramatists, and opens a mild attack on contemporary critics.

432 Miller, Tice L. "John Ranken Towse: The Last of the Victorian Critics." ETJ, 22 (1970), 161-78.

> Mainly on Towse's treatment of actors and post-1900 theatre but also concerned with his activities, critical standards, and reaction to such individual playwrights as Herne.

433 _____. "Towse on Reform in the American Theatre." CSSJ, 23 (1972), 254-60

> Towse believed in the repertory stock system, one change of bill, and performances of popular as well as classical drama.

434 Rothman, John. THE ORIGIN AND DEVELOPMENT OF DRAMATIC CRITICISM IN THE "NEW YORK TIMES," 1851-1880. 1953; rpt. New York: Arno Press, 1970.

Critical, Historical, Reference Resources

Biographies of men who wrote reviews; analyses of sample reviews; and an attempt to identify the reviewers.

435 Schwab, Arnold T. JAMES GIBBONS HUNEKER, CRITIC OF THE SEVEN ARTS. Stanford, Calif.: Stanford University Press, 1963.

Biography of a major American critic, whose opinions on American drama are referred to on page 75.

436 Scott, Clement. "The Advance of American Dramatic Art." MUNSEY'S, 20 (1899), 556-60.

Mainly on actors--Booth, Bateman, Jefferson, Broughman, Raymond, and Godwin--whom he considers the "success of American art." This English critic thinks American actors and plays must now be recognized in England.

437 Syle, L. Dupont. ESSAYS IN DRAMATIC CRITICISM WITH IMPRESSIONS OF SOME MODERN PLAYS. New York: William R. Jenkins, 1898.

This view of theatre and drama as seen in San Francisco in 1898 is pretentiously prepared for future historians. Part II, "Impressions," is of some interest, offering observations on a musical version of RIP VAN WINKLE, Herne's SHORE ACRES, and a play by Belasco and Henry Guy Carleton. A mixed moral and academic approach.

438 Towse, John Ranken. SIXTY YEARS OF THE THEATRE. New York: Funk and Wagnalls, 1916.

A few scattered comments on American plays.

439 Trent, W.P. "Brander Matthews as a Dramatic Critic." INTERNATIONAL, 4 (1901), 289-93.

440 Winter, William. "American Playwrights on the American Drama."

See entry no. 422. Winter provides a brief view of American playwriting from THE PRINCE OF PARTHIA to the work of Howells.

441 _____. OTHER DAYS: BEING CHRONICLES AND MEMORIES OF THE STAGE. New York: Moffat, Yaud, 1908.

As a prominent critic of the late nineteenth-century theatre and drama, Winter's views are a source of information for the student of drama.

Critical, Historical, Reference Resources

442 _____. SHADOWS OF THE STAGE. New York: Macmillan, 1892.

> Reprinted theatre reviews including numerous comments on American plays and playwrights.

443 Wright, Thomas K. "Nym Crinkle: Gadfly Critic and Male Chauvinist." ETJ, 24 (1972), 370-82.

> Quotations from and comments on reviews by Nym Crinkle (Andrew Carpenter Wheeler, 1832-1903), presented as a serious critic who espoused views contrary to Towse and Winter and, seemingly, had little influence on theatre.

II. INDIVIDUAL DRAMATISTS

Essentially, all American dramatists who have been subjected to scholarly attention are included in this bibliography, but only those who have attracted substantial work are listed among the thirty-four individual dramatists in Section II. For playwrights whose names do not appear in this section, the researcher should consult Section I.F, which provides a listing, under three chronologically devised headings, of all works concerned with dramatists and the drama during the eighteenth and nineteenth centuries. There are also entries in this section treating critics and their criticism of American drama, and one should refer always to the basic histories listed in Section I.E.

In Section II the major plays of each dramatist are listed first; dates provided are either the first publication date or the earliest known production date. In some instances this listing comprises the entire output of the dramatist, but in the main only the names of those plays for which the dramatist is best known appear. Likewise, the listing of editions and collections of individually published plays concentrates on those plays that are considered the dramatist's best. Generally, this listing is exhaustive, but for Payne, whose best plays were published several times during the nineteenth century, or for such prolific dramatists as Boucicault or Brougham, who wrote dozens of plays, many of which were published in acting editions, a complete listing would serve no purpose. Except for particular circumstances, such as the absence of other publication of a major play, acting editions are not included in this bibliography.

Plays listed under "Collected Plays" and "Plays in Anthologies" are cross-referenced to Section I.D, where all plays in collections--those of plays by one author or by a number of authors--are listed under "Anthologies and Collected Plays." For students and teachers trying to find a play, the "Plays in Anthologies" may be one of the more frequently used parts of this volume. Certainly, however, microform resources noted particularly in I.C, must not be forgotten as basic materials for the study of the plays of the period.

The listings of plays for each of the dramatists in Section II are followed by "Nondramatic Works" (the dramatist's comments on his plays or his writings about the drama in general); by available bibliographies and checklists; and by

Individual Dramatists

biographical and critical studies (essays and books that treat his life and work). At the beginning of each section on "Biography and Criticism" there is a listing of cross-references. Mainly, these refer the reader to the histories in Section I.E, which include comments on the dramatist. When a history or reference work contains a substantial discussion, that volume is listed separately under "Biography and Criticism," with page references. When necessary, cross-references will be made to any entry in this bibliography, as, for example, when an essay treats two dramatists. In all instances it is hoped that the annotations will help to assess the value of books and essays by describing their contents and the objectives of their authors.

JAMES NELSON BARKER (1784-1858)

MAJOR PLAYS

TEARS AND SMILES, 1807.
THE INDIAN PRINCESS, 1808.
MARMION, 1812.
HOW TO TRY A LOVER, 1817.
SUPERSTITION, 1824.

PUBLISHED PLAYS

A. Individual Titles

444   HOW TO TRY A LOVER. New York: David Longworth, 1817.

445   THE INDIAN PRINCESS. Philadelphia: G.E. Blake; New York: David Longworth, 1808.

446   MARMION; OR, FLODDEN FIELD. New York: Longworths, 1812; New York: D. Longworth, 1816; Philadelphia: A.R. Poole; New York: E.M. Murden, 1826.

447   TEARS AND SMILES. Philadelphia: G.E. Blake; New York: D. Longworth, 1808.

448   THE TRAGEDY OF SUPERSTITION. Philadelphia: A.R. Poole, 1826.

B. Plays in Anthologies

449   THE INDIAN PRINCESS. In REPRESENTATIVE PLAYS BY AMERICAN DRAMATISTS. Ed. Montrose J. Moses. I, pp. 565-628. See entry no. 111.

James Nelson Barker

450 SUPERSTITION. In AMERICAN PLAYS. Ed. Allan Gates Halline, pp. 117-51. See entry no. 105.

451 SUPERSTITION. In REPRESENTATIVE AMERICAN PLAYS. Ed. Arthur Hobson Quinn, pp. 113-40. See entry no. 114.

452 TEARS AND SMILES. In JAMES NELSON BARKER, 1784-1858. By Paul H. Musser, pp. 138-207. See entry no. 466.

NONDRAMATIC WORKS

453 "The Drama." Eleven critical essays published in the DRAMATIC PRESS (Philadelphia), 18 December 1816--19 February 1817.

454 "To William Dunlap, Esq." Letter, 10 June 1832. In HISTORY OF THE AMERICAN THEATRE. By William Dunlap. II, 308-16. See entry no. 131.

    Barker's account of his playwriting.

BIBLIOGRAPHY

455 See entries nos. 4, 12, 29, 30, 31, 32, 33, 34, 45, 48, 466, 467.

BIOGRAPHY AND CRITICISM

456 See entries nos. 133, 135, 142, 155, 157, 165, 168, 223.

457 Crowley, John W. "James Nelson Barker in Perspective." ETJ, 24 (1972), 363-69.

    Author sees Barker as one whose crusade for nationalism never reached his ideal; emphasizes SUPERSTITION as epitome of his work.

458 Earnhart, Phyllis H. "The First American Play in England?" AL, 31 (1959), 326-29.

    Earnhart argues that English production of POCAHONTAS (Drury Lane, 15 December 1820) was not Barker's play.

459 "From the New York Courier--The Critic, No. 1, American Literature." NATIONAL REGISTER, 22 June 1816, pp. 258-59.

    A discussion of Barker's work, particularly MARMION.

James Nelson Barker

460   Havens, Daniel F. THE COLUMBIAN MUSE OF COMEDY. See entry no. 139.

   A discussion of TEARS AND SMILES and MARMION (pp. 62-64).

461   Herron, Ima Honaker. THE SMALL TOWN IN AMERICAN DRAMA. See entry no. 140.

   A commentary on TEARS AND SMILES and SUPERSTITION (pp. 9-12), plus other references.

462   Kuhn, John G. "James Nelson Barker's Play of Ideas in 1812 and 1824; or, How He Got Scott Free." Ph.D. dissertation, University of Pennsylvania, 1969.

   On MARMION and SUPERSTITION.

463   Mayorga, Margaret G. A SHORT HISTORY OF THE AMERICAN DRAMA. See entry no. 150.

   A discussion with quotations from major plays (pp. 76-82); other references.

464   Meserve, Walter J. AN EMERGING ENTERTAINMENT: THE DRAMA OF THE AMERICAN PEOPLE TO 1828. See entry no. 152

   A substantial discussion of contribution to American drama. Particular analysis of early career (pp. 177-84) and later work with SUPERSTITION (pp. 259-63).

465   _____. AN OUTLINE HISTORY OF AMERICAN DRAMA. See entry no. 153.

   A commentary on poetic drama (pp. 64-66); on an Indian play (pp. 76-77); on comedy (pp. 83-84); and other references.

466   Musser, Paul H. JAMES NELSON BARKER, 1784-1858. Philadelphia: University of Pennsylvania, 1929.

   Standard biography, using best sources; good bibliography.

467   Quinn, Arthur Hobson. A HISTORY OF THE AMERICAN DRAMA FROM THE BEGINNING TO THE CIVIL WAR. See entry no. 163.

   A solid survey discussion of Barker's entire work (pp. 136-51).

468   Sata, Mansanori. "SUPERSTITION (1824) to WINTERSET (1935): Romeo-Juliet theme kara no kosatsu." ELLS, 6 (1969), 131-46.

James Nelson Barker

469 Wilson, Garff B. THREE HUNDRED YEARS OF AMERICAN DRAMA AND THEATRE. See entry no. 173.

Mainly concerned with SUPERSTITION (pp. 112-14).

DAVID BELASCO (1859-1931)

MAJOR PLAYS

HEARTS OF OAK (with James A. Herne), 1879.
MAY BLOSSOM, 1882.
LORD CHUMLEY (with H.C. DeMille), 1888.
THE GIRL I LEFT BEHIND ME (with Franklyn Fyles), 1893.
THE HEART OF MARYLAND, 1895.
MADAME BUTTERFLY (with L. Long), 1900.
THE GIRL OF THE GOLDEN WEST, 1905.
THE RETURN OF PETER GRIMM, 1911.

PUBLISHED PLAYS

A. Individual Titles

470 THE GIRL OF THE GOLDEN WEST. New York: Samuel French, 1915, 1933.

471 THE RETURN OF PETER GRIMM. New York: Samuel French, 1915.

472 THE ROSE OF THE RANCHO. New York: Samuel French, 1915.

B. Collected Plays

473 THE HEART OF MARYLAND AND OTHER PLAYS. Eds. Glenn Hughes and George Savage. Vol. 18 of AMERICA'S LOST PLAYS. Ed. Barrett H. Clark. See entry no. 100.

> Contains LA BELLE RUSSE, THE STRANGLERS OF PARIS, THE GIRL I LEFT BEHIND ME, THE HEART OF MARYLAND, NAUGHTY ANTHONY. Brief introduction with notes to each play concerning production.

David Belasco

474   THE PLAYS OF HENRY C. DEMILLE WRITTEN IN COLLABORATION WITH DAVID BELASCO. Ed. Robert Hamilton Ball. Vol. 17 of AMERICA'S LOST PLAYS. Ed. Barrett H. Clark. See entry no. 100.

   Contains THE MAIN LINE, THE WIFE, LORD CHUMLEY, THE CHARITY BALL, MEN AND WOMEN. Introductory essay.

475   SIX PLAYS. Introd. Montrose J. Moses. Boston: Little, Brown, 1929.

   Contains MADAME BUTTERFLY, DUBARRY, THE DARLING OF THE GODS, ADREA, THE GIRL OF THE GOLDEN WEST, THE RETURN OF PETER GRIMM.

C. Plays in Anthologies

476   THE GIRL OF THE GOLDEN WEST. In REPRESENTATIVE AMERICAN DRAMAS, NATIONAL AND LOCAL. Ed. Montrose J. Moses, pp. 47-97. See entry no. 109.

477   THE HEART OF MARYLAND. In THE BEST PLAYS OF 1894-99. Ed. John Chapman and Garrison P. Sherwood, pp. 20-31. See entry no. 99.

478   THE HEART OF MARYLAND. In FAVORITE AMERICAN PLAYS OF THE NINETEENTH CENTURY. Ed. Barrett H. Clark, pp. 405-82. See entry no. 101.

479   MADAME BUTTERFLY. In REPRESENTATIVE AMERICAN PLAYS. Ed. Arthur Hobson Quinn, pp. 621-36. See entry no. 114.

480   THE RETURN OF PETER GRIMM. In THE MASTERPIECES OF MODERN DRAMA. Vol. I, ENGLISH AND AMERICAN. Ed. John H. Pierce. Garden City, N.Y.: Doubleday, 1916, pp. 253-66.

   Abbreviated scenes.

481   THE RETURN OF PETER GRIMM. In MODERN AMERICAN PLAYS. Ed. George P. Baker. New York: Harcourt, Brace & Howe, 1920, pp. 101-213.

482   THE RETURN OF PETER GRIMM. In REPRESENTATIVE PLAYS BY AMERICAN DRAMATISTS. Ed. Montrose J. Moses. II, pp. 815-915. See entry no. 111.

NONDRAMATIC WORKS

483   "Beauty As I See It." ARTS AND DECORATION, 19 (July 1923), 9-10.

   Concerned with realism.

David Belasco

484 "The Great Opportunity of the Woman Dramatist." GOOD HOUSE-KEEPING, 53 (1911), 626-32.

    An optimistic view with evidence.

485 "How I Write a Play." CHICAGO JOURNAL, 19 July 1912, pp. 5-6.

    Belasco asserts his determination to imitate real life and to pay attention to minute details. Essay appeared in several newspapers.

486 "How 'The Girl of the Golden West' Was Written." GREAT BOOKS MONTHLY ALBUM, 5 (1911), 334-38.

487 "The Meaning of the Theatre." MUNSEY'S, 50 (1914), 645.

    Concerned with drama as a means for teaching.

488 "The Playwright and the Box Office." CENTURY, 84 (1912), 883-90.

    How to market a play that can be judged only at the box office.

489 THE THEATRE THROUGH ITS STAGE DOOR. Ed. Louis V. Defoe. New York: Harper, 1919.

    Accounts of Belasco's numerous productions. Certain chapters reprinted from various periodicals.

BIBLIOGRAPHY

490 See entries nos. 4, 12, 28, 33, 45, 48, 473, 503, 510, 514.

BIOGRAPHY AND CRITICISM

491 See entries nos. 126, 127, 146, 150, 173, 382, 890.

492 Bergman, Herbert. "David Belasco's Dramatic Theory." UNIVERSITY OF TEXAS STUDIES IN ENGLISH, 32 (1953), 110-22.

    Based on Belasco's numerous comments on drama and theatre, this essay concludes that Belasco found the theatre a place for emotional, inspirational entertainment and was not concerned with the dregs of life or intellectual probing.

493 [Dale, Alan]. "The Success of Belasco." COSMOPOLITAN, 44 (1908), 395-96.

    Praise for ingenuity and realism of Belasco's work.

David Belasco

494   Eaton, Walter Pritchard. THE AMERICAN STAGE OF TO-DAY. Boston: Small, Maynard, 1908.

   Contains an essay entitled "Kisses and David Belasco" (pp. 203-14): "Once it was a bed, now it is a kiss, that Mr. Belasco cannot get along without in his dramas."

495   _____. "Concerning David Belasco." AMERICAN, 75 (1913), 61-67.

   Eaton criticizes Belasco for subordinating play to action, details of lighting, and costume.

496   _____. "Madame Butterfly's Cocoon: A Sketch of David Belasco." AMERICAN SCHOLAR, 5 (1936), 172-82.

497   _____. PLAYS AND PLAYERS: LEAVES FROM A CRITIC'S SCRAPBOOK. Cincinnati: Stewart & Kidd, 1916.

   Essay on "Belasco and Hypnotism."

498   Frohman, Daniel. DANIEL FROHMAN PRESENTS. New York: Lee Furman, 1937.

   Numerous references to Belasco's plays and theatre activity.

499   Harris, H.A. "David Belasco, the Man and His Works." COSMOPOLITAN, 46 (1909), 755-64.

   General essay; gossipy.

500   Herron, Ima Honaker. THE SMALL TOWN IN AMERICAN DRAMA. See entry no. 140.

   Comments on rural plays (pp. 130-32, 146-47).

501   Huneker, James G. "David Belasco." OUTLOOK, 16 March 1921, pp. 418-22; rpt. in entry no. 384, pp. 29-39.

   A brief assessment of the man and his contribution to American drama with some nostalgic praise.

502   LaVerne, Sister Mary. "Belascoism." PLAYERS, 20 (1943), 6, 8, 17.

   A negative reaction to detailed realism.

503   Mantle, Burns. AMERICAN PLAYWRIGHTS OF TODAY. See entry no. 426.

   See "David Belasco," a review of his career (pp. 233-39). Mantle considers Belasco's contribution as a producer rather than as a dramatist.

David Belasco

504 Marker, Lise-Lone. DAVID BELASCO: NATURALISM IN THE AMERICAN THEATRE. Princeton, N.J.: Princeton University Press, 1975.

   Concerned with production techniques; valuable for Belasco's theories of drama. Bibliography.

505 Meserve, Walter J. AN OUTLINE HISTORY OF AMERICAN DRAMA. See entry no. 153.

   This volume contains numerous references and brief discussions relating Belasco to frontier and realistic drama and commenting on his several collaborators and his experimentation on stage.

506 Middleton, George. THESE THINGS ARE MINE. New York: Macmillan Co., 1947.

   Numerous references plus personal, anecdotal experience (pp. 273-90).

507 Moses, Montrose J. THE AMERICAN DRAMATIST. See entry no. 157.

   See "David Belasco and the Psychology of the Switchboard" (pp. 111-34).

508 _____. "David Belasco, Dramatist." BOOK NEWS MONTHLY, 26 (1908), 759-65.

509 Nathan, George Jean. MR. GEORGE JEAN NATHAN PRESENTS. New York: Knopf, 1917. Rpt. in entry no. 330, pp. 228-35.

   Admiration and condemnation in "Legend's End--David Belasco." Nathan concludes that through his "many counterfeits" Belasco did "ill" to American drama and theatre.

510 Quinn, Arthur Hobson. A HISTORY OF THE AMERICAN DRAMA FROM THE CIVIL WAR TO THE PRESENT DAY. See entry no. 164.

   "David Belasco and His Associates" (pp. 163-99) is a good review of Belasco's life and career as dramatist. Quinn notes that Belasco's "My Life Story," serialized in HEARST'S MAGAZINE beginning March 1914, is inaccurate.

511 Rahill, Frank. THE WORLD OF MELODRAMA. See entry no. 166.

   "Melodrama Comes of Age" (pp. 262-71) deal with plays of Belasco and Gillette.

David Belasco

512   Salem, James M. A GUIDE TO CRITICAL REVIEWS: PART I: AMERICAN DRAMA, 1909-1969. See entry no. 47.

       See pages 60-63 for references to Belasco productions.

513   Sievers, W. David. FREUD ON BROADWAY: A HISTORY OF PSYCHOANALYSIS AND THE AMERICAN DRAMA. See entry no. 169.

       See "David Belasco Discovers Sex" (pp. 41-45) a Freudian interpretation.

514   Timberlake, Craig. THE BISHOP OF BROADWAY: THE LIFE AND WORK OF DAVID BELASCO. New York: Library Publishers, 1954.

       Largely concerned with production details of Belasco's melodramas. Bibliography.

515   Winter, William. THE LIFE OF DAVID BELASCO. 2 vols. New York: Moffat, Yard, 1918.

       Standard biography. Completed by author's son, Jefferson Winter, after Winter's death.

516   Young, Stark. "Belascosity." NEW REPUBLIC, 19 December 1923, pp. 94-95.

       On excesses.

517   _____. "An Estimate of Belasco." NEW REPUBLIC, 17 June 1931, pp. 123-24.

       Defense of Belasco as a "kind of genius," a showman.

ROBERT MONTGOMERY BIRD (1806-54)

MAJOR PLAYS

THE CITY LOOKING GLASS, 1828.
PELOPIDAS, 1830.
THE GLADIATOR, 1831.
ORALLOOSSA, 1832.
THE BROKER OF BOGOTA, 1833.

PUBLISHED PLAYS

A. Individual Titles

518   THE CITY LOOKING GLASS. Ed. Arthur Hobson Quinn. New York: Printed for the Colophon, 1933.

      Contains a biographical introduction.

B. Collected Plays

519   THE COWLED LOVER & OTHER PLAYS BY ROBERT MONTGOMERY BIRD. Ed. Edward H. O'Neill. Vol. 12 of AMERICA'S LOST PLAYS. Ed. Barrett H. Clark. See entry no. 100.

      Includes THE COWLED LOVER, CARIDORF, NEWS OF THE NIGHT, 'TWAS ALL FOR THE BEST. Brief introduction to previously unpublished plays.

520   Foust, Clement E. THE LIFE AND DRAMATIC WORKS OF ROBERT MONTGOMERY BIRD. New York: Knickerbocker Press, 1919; rpt. New York: Burt Franklin, 1971.

      Includes PELOPIDAS, THE GLADIATOR, ORALLOOSSA, and THE BROKER OF BOGOTA. Useful bibliography.

Robert Montgomery Bird

C. Plays in Anthologies

521   THE BROKER OF BOGOTA. In REPRESENTATIVE AMERICAN PLAYS. Ed. Arthur H. Quinn, pp. 199-235. See entry no. 114.

   Contains brief biographical and critical introduction with bibliography.

522   THE GLADIATOR. In AMERICAN PLAYS. Ed. Allen G. Halline, pp. 153-98. See entry no. 105.

523   THE GLADIATOR. In DRAMAS FROM THE AMERICAN THEATRE, 1762-1909. Ed. Richard Moody, pp. 241-75. See entry no. 108.

   Contains substantial biographical and critical introduction, (pp. 229-40), and bibliography (pp. 857-58).

524   Harris, Richard. "From the Papers of R.M. Bird: The Last Scene from NEWS OF THE NIGHT." LIBRARY CHRONICLE UNIVERSITY OF PENNSYLVANIA, 24 (Winter 1958), 1-12.

   Provides lost scene to this early comedy, Act I, Scene ii. Speculation as to its use.

BIBLIOGRAPHY

525   See entries nos. 4, 12, 29, 33, 45, 48, 520, 521, 523, 530, 533, 541, 722.

BIOGRAPHY AND CRITICISM

526   See entries nos. 95, 150, 155, 157, 166, 173.

527   "Address, Written by Dr. R.M. Bird, and Delivered by Mrs. Maywood, at the Wood Complimentary Benefit." NATIONAL GAZETTE, 19 January 1836, p. 2.

528   Bird, Mary Mayer. LIFE OF ROBERT MONTGOMERY BIRD. Ed. E.C. Seymour Thompson. Philadelphia: University of Pennsylvania Library, 1945.

   A basic source. First published in the LIBRARY CHRONICLE UNIVERSITY OF PENNSYLVANIA, 12 (October 1944) through 13 (September 1945).

Robert Montgomery Bird

529   Bronson, Daniel R. "A Note on Robert Montgomery Bird's ORALLOOSSA." ENGLISH LANGUAGE NOTES, 9 (1971), 46-49.

   Author contends that the failure of the play is offset by the strength of the character.

530   Dahl, Curtis. ROBERT MONTGOMERY BIRD. New York: Twayne Publishers, 1963.

   Biographical and critical commentary. See particularly chapters 3-5. Bibliography.

531   "Dr. R.M. Bird, Dramatist and Novelist." PUBLIC LEDGER (Philadelphia), 5 April 1908.

532   Durang, Charles. "The Philadelphia Stage. From the Year 1749 to the Year 1855. Partly Compiled from the Papers of his Father, the Late John Durang; With Notes by the Editors (of the PHILADELPHIA SUNDAY DISPATCH)." Published serially in the PHILADELPHIA DISPATCH as follows: First Series, 1749-1821, beginning in the issue of 7 May 1854; Second Series, 1822-30, beginning 29 June 1856; Third Series, 1830-55, beginning 8 July 1860.

   For a good discussion of Bird's plays, see chapters 16 and 25.

533   Foust, Clement E. THE LIFE AND DRAMATIC WORKS OF ROBERT MONTGOMERY BIRD. See entry no. 520.

   A standard work. Part I (pp. 1-159) provides biographical and critical information. Useful bibliography.

534   _____. "A Little-known Philadelphia Author." PUBLIC LEDGER (Philadelphia), 28 December 1919.

535   Grimsted, David. MELODRAMA UNVEILED: AMERICAN THEATRE AND CULTURE, 1800-1850. See entry no. 135.

   Scattered comments plus minor interest in THE BROKER OF BOGOTA; see pages 167-70.

536   Harris, Richard A. "The Major Dramas of Robert Montgomery Bird: A Critical Analysis of Their Structure and Development." Ph.D. dissertation, Indiana University, 1966.

   Study of PELOPIDAS, THE GLADIATOR, ORALLOOSSA, and THE BROKER OF BOGOTA in terms of Aristotelian structure.

537   _____. "A Young Dramatist's Diary: THE SECRET RECORDS of R.M. Bird." LIBRARY CHRONICLE UNIVERSITY OF PENNSYLVANIA, 25 (Winter 1959), 8-24.

Robert Montgomery Bird

Reproduces Bird's comments on (1) a manuscript entitled "The Decline of Drama," (2) the background of GLADIATOR and BROKER, and (3) his attitude toward writing. These comments are in the diary entries of 27 August, 26 October, 14 December 1831, respectively.

538 Havens, Daniel F. THE COLUMBIAN MUSE OF COMEDY. See entry no. 139.

A thorough study of THE CITY LOOKING GLASS (pp. 78-100).

539 Meserve, Walter J. AN EMERGING ENTERTAINMENT: THE DRAMA OF THE AMERICAN PEOPLE TO 1828. See entry no. 152.

A discussion of Bird's early plays (pp. 297-301).

540 _____. AN OUTLINE HISTORY OF AMERICAN DRAMA. See entry no. 153.

Summary comment on pages 56-59, 67.

541 Quinn, Arthur Hobson. "Dramatic Works of Robert Montgomery Bird." NATION, 3 August 1916, pp. 108-09.

Brief description of library acquisitions.

542 _____. "Robert Montgomery Bird and the Rise of the Romantic Play." In A HISTORY OF THE AMERICAN DRAMA FROM THE BEGINNING TO THE CIVIL WAR, pp. 220-48. See entry no. 163.

Extremely laudatory evaluation of Bird's contribution to American drama, but important to any study.

543 _____, ed. THE LITERATURE OF THE AMERICAN PEOPLE. See entry no. 165.

For comments on Bird as dramatist, see pages 474-81.

544 Rees, James. DRAMATIC AUTHORS OF AMERICA. See entry no. 168.

For discussion of Bird's plays, see pages 29-34.

545 _____. THE LIFE OF EDWIN FORREST WITH REMINISCENCES AND PERSONAL RECOLLECTIONS. Philadelphia: T.B. Peterson, 1874.

Good commentary on Bird in Chapter 40.

546   Thompson, C. Seymour, ed. "Travelling with Robert Montgomery Bird." LIBRARY CHRONICLE UNIVERSITY OF PENNSYLVANIA, 7 (March 1939), 11-22; (June 1939), 34-50; (October-December 1939), 75-90; 8 (April 1940), 4-21.

> Letters from Bird while travelling in American Southwest and West and in England.

547   Wayne, John Lakmond. "The Writings of Robert Montgomery Bird." HOBBIES, 52 (1947), 128.

> Slight and general.

548   Wemyss, Francis C. TWENTY-SIX YEARS OF THE LIFE OF AN ACTOR AND MANAGER. 2 vols. New York: Burgess, Stringer, 1847.

> For comments on Bird's plays by contemporary actor, see Volume I, pages 111-13, 194 and Volume II, pages 239, 264.

549   Williams, Stanley T. THE SPANISH BACKGROUND OF AMERICAN LITERATURE. 2 vols. New Haven, Conn.: Yale University Press, 1955.

> Comments on Bird's two plays with South American settings.

GEORGE HENRY BOKER (1823-90)

MAJOR PLAYS

THE BETROTHAL, 1850.
THE WORLD A MASK, 1851.
LEONOR DE GUZMAN, 1853.
FRANCESCA DA RIMINI, 1855.
GLAUCUS, 1886.

PUBLISHED PLAYS

A. Individual Titles

550   ANNE BOLEYN. Philadelphia: A. Hart, 1850.

551   CALAYNOS. Philadelphia: E.H. Butler, 1848.

552   KONIGSMARK, THE LEGEND OF THE HOUNDS AND OTHER POEMS. Philadelphia: J.B. Lippincott, 1869.

553   NYDIA. Ed. Edward Sculley Bradley. Philadelphia: University of Pennsylvania Press, 1927.

B. Collected Plays

554   GLAUCUS AND OTHER PLAYS. Ed. Edward Sculley Bradley. Vol. 3 of AMERICA'S LOST PLAYS. Ed. Barrett H. Clark. See entry no. 100.

> Contains THE WORLD A MASK, THE BANKRUPT, GLAUCUS, plus introductions to each play.

555 PLAYS AND POEMS. 2 vols. Boston: Ticknor and Fields, 1856; rpt. Philadelphia: J.B. Lippincott, 1869, 1883, 1891; New York: AMS Press, 1967.

> Contains CALAYNOS, ANNE BOLEYN, THE BETROTHAL, THE WIDOW'S MARRIAGE, LEONOR DE GUZMAN, FRANCESCA DA RIMINI. An interesting review of the original publication appears in the NATIONAL ERA, 30 October 1856, pages 74-75.

C. Plays in Anthologies

556 FRANCESCA DA RIMINI. In AMERICAN PLAYS. Ed. Allan G. Halline, pp. 273-331. See entry no. 105.

557 FRANCESCA DA RIMINI. In THE BLACK CROOK AND OTHER NINETEENTH CENTURY AMERICAN PLAYS. Ed. Myron Matlow, pp. 97-200. See entry no. 104.

558 FRANCESCA DA RIMINI. In DRAMAS FROM THE AMERICAN THEATRE 1762-1909. Ed. Richard Moody, pp. 431-73. See entry no. 108.

559 FRANCESCA DA RIMINI. In REPRESENTATIVE AMERICAN PLAYS. Ed. Arthur Hobson Quinn, pp. 319-68. See entry no. 114.

560 FRANCESCA DA RIMINI. In REPRESENTATIVE AMERICAN PLAYS BY AMERICAN DRAMATISTS. Ed. Montrose J. Moses. III, 73-195. See entry no. 111.

BIBLIOGRAPHY

561 See entries nos. 4, 12, 29, 33, 34, 45, 48, 587.

562 Bradley, Edward Sculley. GEORGE HENRY BOKER, POET AND PATRIOT. Philadelphia: University of Pennsylvania Press, 1927.

> See Appendix I, "A Chronological List of the Writings of George Henry Boker" (pp. 343-49); and Appendix II, "Bibliographies" (pp. 350-55). See also entry no. 567.

563 Tayton, G.H. "Check-List to Writings by and about George H. Boker (1823-1890)." AMERICAN BOOK COLLECTOR, 5 (1934), 372-74.

George Henry Boker

BIOGRAPHY AND CRITICISM

564   See entries nos. 119, 120, 141, 143, 145, 150, 157, 173.

565   Barnes, James. "George Henry Boker." NASSAU LITERARY MAGAZINE, 46 (1891), 90.

566   Beatly, Richmond C. "Bayard Taylor and George H. Boker." AL, 6 (1934), 316-27.

> One letter concerned with THE BETROTHAL; general comments on dramas.

567   Bradley, Edward Sculley. GEORGE HENRY BOKER, POET AND PATRIOT. See entry no. 562.

> Standard and comprehensive critical biography.

568   _____. "George Henry Boker and Angie Hicks." AL, 8 (1936), 258-65.

> Personal reflections.

569   _____. "Poe and the New York Stage in 1855." AL, 9 (1937), 353-54.

> Bradley argues that Boker's THE BANKRUPT is indebted to Poe's detective stories and theory of "ratiocination."

570   Brewer, E. "Boker's Francesca da Rimini." AMERICAN, 5 (1883), 363.

> Brief notes on the character and the play.

571   Conrad, R.T. "Boker's LEONOR DE GUZMAN." GRAHAM'S, 44 (1854), 273-85.

> Early review. Author surveys contemporary stage and concludes that Boker is superior to English dramatists.

572   Flory, Claude R. "Boker, Barrett and the Francesca Theme in Drama." PLAYERS, 50 (1975), 58-61, 80.

> Thirteen notes on script Boker sent to Barrett in rehearsal suggest dramatist's interest in relations between characters and in stage realism. Flory considers FRANCESCA the best drama in English written between the works of Sheridan and Shaw.

George Henry Boker

573 Gallagher, Kent G. "The Tragedies of George Henry Boker: The Measure of American Romantic Drama." EMERSON SOCIETY QUARTERLY, 20 (1974), 187-215.

> Gallagher analyzes Boker's poetic canon as part of the stream of American romantic drama and concludes that he is mainly a dramatist of one play--FRANCESCA DA RIMINI.

574 Henderson, Archibald. "Rimini Story in Modern Drama." ARENA, 39 (1908), 142-48.

> Author considers Boker's plot one in which deception leads to marriage after a possible refusal to marriage is rejected.

575 Hubbell, Jay B. "Five Letters from George Henry Boker to William Gilmore Simms." PENNSYLVANIA MAGAZINE OF HISTORY AND BIOGRAPHY, 63 (1939), 66-71.

> Two letters written in 1869 explain Boker's view of the duties of the writer of historical drama.

576 _____. "George Henry Boker, Paul Hamilton Hayne, and Charles Warren Stoddard: Some Unpublished Letters." AL, 5 (1933), 146-65.

> Seven Boker letters indicate his attitude toward poetry. Hubbell also shows Hayne's view of Boker's plays.

577 Krutch, Joseph W. "George Henry Boker, A Little Known American Dramatist." SEWANEE REVIEW, 25 (1917), 457-68.

> A review of Boker's work, with particular emphasis upon FRANCESCA DA RIMINI and the development of character.

578 Lathrop, George P. "Authors at Home. George H. Boker in Walnut Street, Philadelphia." CRITIC, 9 (1888), 175-76.

579 _____. "Some Recollections of Boker." ATLANTIC MONTHLY, 65 (1896), 427-30.

> Obituary notice. Personal view of Boker as diplomat, dramatist, and poet; a vigorous writer and modest man who looked like Hawthorne.

580 Leland, Charles G. "Boker's Plays." SARTAIN'S UNION MAGAZINE OF LITERATURE AND ART, 8 (1851), 369-78.

> Extended criticism of ANNE BOLEYN, THE BETROTHAL, THE WORLD A MASK, and CALAYNOS; assumes that plays will give Boker a secure place among American authors.

George Henry Boker

581 _____. "George H. Boker." CRITIC, 13 (1890), 22.

    Brief comment at Boker's death.

582 _____. "Reminiscences of George Henry Boker." AMERICAN, 19 (1890), 392-404.

    Review essay published at Boker's death.

583 Meserve, Walter J. AN OUTLINE HISTORY OF AMERICAN DRAMA. See entry no. 153.

    For Boker as writer of poetic drama see pages 59-61.

584 Metcalf, John C. "An Old Romantic Triangle: Francesca da Rimini in Three Dramas." SEWANEE REVIEW, 29 (1921), 45-58.

    Mainly concerned with Boker's play.

585 Quinn, Arthur Hobson. "The Dramas of George Henry Boker." PMLA, 32 (1917), 233-66.

    An extensive survey of Boker's work; quotations from Boker manuscripts; comment on language.

586 _____. "George Henry Boker--Playwright and Patriot." SCRIBNER'S 73 (1923), 701-15.

    Based on material furnished by Mrs. George Boker. Emphasis upon FRANCESCA DA RIMINI among the plays.

587 _____. "George Henry Boker and the Later Romantic Tragedy." In A HISTORY OF THE AMERICAN DRAMA FROM THE BEGINNING TO THE CIVIL WAR, pp. 337-67. See entry no. 163.

    A good survey of Boker's contribution to American drama. Bibliography.

588 Sherr, Paul C. "George Henry Boker's FRANCESCA DA RIMINI, a Justification for the Literary Historian." PENNSYLVANIA HISTORY, 34 (1967), 361-71.

    An analysis of the play, showing that it reveals the author and his awareness of contemporary literary, social, and political matters.

589 Shuman, R.B. "A Note on George Boker's FRANCESCA DA RIMINI." AL, 31 (1960), 180-82.

    Quotes Boker letter indicating Boccaccio's commentaries as a source for FRANCESCA DA RIMINI.

George Henry Boker

590   Stoddard, Richard H. "Recollections of George Henry Boker." LIP-PINCOTT'S, 45 (1890), 856-67.

   Personal reminiscence at Boker's death.

591   Urban, Gertrude. "Paolo and Francesca in History and Literature." CRITIC, 40 (1902), 425-38.

   An assessment of importance through a historical review. Good illustrations.

592   Voelker, Paul D. "George Henry Boker's FRANCESCA DA RIMINI: An Interpretation and an Evaluation." ETJ, 24 (1972), 383-95.

   Author contends that Boker took the traditional conflict of love versus honor and used it as the basis for a criticism of the fraudulent nature of politics under an aristocratic system.

593   Winter, William. THE WALLET OF TIME. 2 vols. New York: Moffat Yard, 1913.

   Contemporary reaction to Boker's work in Volume I, pages 312-22.

594   Woods, Alan. "Producing Boker's FRANCESCA DA RIMINI." ETJ, 24 (1972), 396-401.

   Woods used play to suggest nineteenth-century acting and production styles.

595   Zanger, Jules. "Boker's FRANCESCA DA RIMINI: The Brothers' Tragedy." ETJ, 25 (1973), 410-19.

   A convincing argument that the play has no heroes or villains, only victims of fate and character, thus becoming the tragedy of Paolo and Lanciotto, "America's first high tragedy."

DION BOUCICAULT (1820-90)

MAJOR PLAYS

LONDON ASSURANCE, 1840.
THE POOR OF NEW YORK, 1857.
THE OCTOROON, 1859.
THE COLLEEN BAWN, 1860.
ARRAH-NA-POGUE, 1864.
FLYING SCUD, 1866.
THE SHAUGHRAUN, 1874.
THE JILT, 1885.

PUBLISHED PLAYS

A. Individual Titles

596   JESSIE BROWN; OR, THE RELIEF OF LUCKNOW. New York: Samuel French, 1858.

   This play is listed only as an example of the many plays for which acting editions were published in both New York and London. For a list of individual editions of Boucicault's plays with dates and publishers, see entry no. 640, Robert Hogan's DION BOUCICAULT, pages 125-34.

B. Collected Plays

597   THE DOLMAN PRESS BOUCICAULT. Ed. David Krause. Dublin: Dolmen Press, 1964.

   Contains THE COLLEEN BAWN and THE SHAUGHRAUN.

598   FORBIDDEN FRUIT & OTHER PLAYS. Ed. Allardyce Nicoll and F. Theodore Cloak. Vol. I of AMERICA'S LOST PLAYS. Ed. Barrett H. Clark. See entry no. 100.

Contains FORBIDDEN FRUIT, LOUIS XI, DOT, FLYING SCUD, MERCY DODD, ROBERT EMMET.

C. Plays in Anthologies

599   BELLE LAMAR. In PLAYS FOR THE COLLEGE THEATRE. Ed. Garrett H. Leverton, pp. 129-47. New York: Samuel French, 1937.

600   THE COLLEEN BAWN. In NINETEENTH CENTURY PLAYS. Ed. George Rowell, pp. 176-231. London: Oxford University Press, 1953.

601   FLYING SCUD. In FAVORITE AMERICAN PLAYS OF THE NINETEENTH CENTURY. Ed. Barrett H. Clark, pp. 129-201. See entry no. 101.

602   THE OCTOROON. In BEST PLAYS OF THE EARLY AMERICAN THEATRE. Eds. John Gassner with Mollie Gassner, pp. 185-215. See entry no. 104.

603   THE OCTOROON. In THE BLACK CROOK AND OTHER NINETEENTH-CENTURY AMERICAN PLAYS. Ed. Myron Matlaw, pp. 203-56. See entry no. 107.

604   THE OCTOROON. In REPRESENTATIVE AMERICAN PLAYS. Ed. Arthur Hobson Quinn, pp. 374-98. See entry no. 114.

605   THE OCTOROON. In SIX EARLY AMERICAN PLAYS, 1798-1900. Eds. William Coyle and Harry G. Damaser, pp. 163-202. See entry no. 102.

606   THE POOR OF NEW YORK. In THE CHARACTER OF MELODRAMA: AN EXAMINATION THROUGH DION BOUCICAULT'S "THE POOR OF NEW YORK" INCLUDING THE TEXT OF THE PLAY, pp. 60-101. By William Paul Steele. Orono: University of Maine Press, 1968.

NONDRAMATIC WORKS

607   "The Art of Dramatic Composition." NAR, 126 (1878), 40-52.
    Shows Boucicault's close adherence to the theories of Aristotle.

608   "At the Goethe Society." NAR, 148 (1889), 335-43.
    On theories of drama.

609   "Boucicault's Hints to Young Playwrights." CRITIC, 8 (1886), 155.

Dion Boucicault

610 "The Debut of a Dramatist." NAR, 148 (1889), 454-63.
   An interview with Charles Matthews that led to production of LONDON ASSURANCE.

611 "The Decline of the Drama." NAR, 125 (1877), 235-45.
   A discussion of the "contemporaneous" or "realistic" drama.

612 "Early Days of a Dramatist." NAR, 148 (1889), 584-93.
   A discussion of the difficulties of writing a second play after the success of LONDON ASSURANCE.

613 "The Future of American Drama." ARENA, 3 (1890), 641-52.
   Recognizes no "literary institution which could be called the American drama" but feels that American drama will eventually surpass that of other countries.

614 "Leaves from a Dramatist's Diary." NAR, 149 (1889), 228-36.
   Concern with copyright in America; proposes system to reward the dramatist.

615 "Letter." TIMES (London), 8 November 1861, p. 5.
   Defends THE OCTOROON and explains his reluctant revision to a happy ending.

616 "Mutilations of Shakespeare: The Poet Interviewed." NAR, 148 (1889), 266-68.

617 "My Pupils." NAR, 147 (1888), 435-40.

618 "Opera." NAR, 144 (1887), 341-48.
   Importance of music and color.

619 "Shakespeare's Influence on the Drama." NAR, 147 (1888), 680-85.

620 "Spots on the Sun." ARENA, 2 (1889), 131-39.
   Characterization in plays.

BIBLIOGRAPHY

621 See entries nos. 4, 12, 29, 33, 34, 45, 48, 640, 646, 649, 651-52, 655.

Dion Boucicault

BIOGRAPHY AND CRITICISM

622 See entries nos. 119, 135, 142, 143, 166, 371.

623 Archer, William. ENGLISH DRAMATISTS OF TO-DAY. London: Sampson Low, 1882.

> For comments on Boucicault, see pages 41-46.

624 "Boucicault's THE OCTOROON." ILLUSTRATED LONDON NEWS, 14 December 1861, p. 597.

> A review of the play with a detailed description of the fourth act providing a happy ending.

625 Dalton, Frank. "Small-change and Boucicault." DUBLIN, 1 (1923), 280-85.

> Early life of Boucicault and his effectiveness as a stage manager.

626 Daly, Joseph Francis. THE LIFE OF AUGUSTIN DALY. New York: Macmillan, 1917.

> Scattered references, some Boucicault letters, and an account of an attempted collaboration between Boucicault and Bret Harte.

627 Degen, John A. "How to End THE OCTOROON." ETJ, 27 (1975), 170-78.

> A discussion of the happy and tragic endings of play and Boucicault's bitterness about making the change to a happy ending.

628 "Dion Boucicault." CRITIC, 9 (1887), 145-46.

> Favorable comparison with contemporary dramatists.

629 "Dion Boucicault." SATURDAY REVIEW [English], 70 (1890), 323.

> Obituary essay.

630 Enkvist, Nils Erik. "THE OCTOROON and English Opinion of Slavery." AQ, 8 (1956), 166-70.

> Author traces negative reception of play in London (1861), until Boucicault provided a happy ending. Some inaccuracies.

Dion Boucicault

631 Faulkner, Seldon. "THE OCTOROON War." ETJ, 15 (1963), 33-38.

> Author points out that the legal battle between manager and stage director at Winter Garden Theatre over performance rights of play helped clarify copyright procedures.

632 Folland, Harold. "The Plays of Dion Boucicault." Ph.D. dissertation, Harvard University, 1940.

633 Frohman, Daniel. "Dion Boucicault." In his ENCORE. New York: L. Furman, 1937, pp. 97-105.

634 Gambone, Kenneth. "Boucicault's Contribution to Theatre." BALL STATE TEACHERS COLLEGE FORUM, 4 (1963), 73-78.

> Survey essay.

635 Harris, William E. "Dion Boucicault." BOSTON TRANSCRIPT, 19 January 1929.

> A good general essay with particular reference to THE OCTOROON.

636 Harrison, A. Cleveland. "Boucicault on Dramatic Character." SSConJ, 37, (1971), 73-83.

> Boucicault's theory of character compared with that of Aristotle.

637 _____. "Boucicault on Dramatic Action: His Confirmation of the POETICS." QJS, 56 (1970), 45-53.

> Five basic points relating Boucicault's theory to the POETICS.

638 _____. "Boucicault's Formula: Illusion Equals Pleasure." ETJ, 21 (1969), 299-309.

> A significant analysis of Boucicault's dramatic theory based on published essays. Objective was to bring pleasure.

639 _____. "The Dramatic Theories of Dion Boucicault: A Study of Statements on Dramaturgy in his Published Essays." Ph.D. dissertation, University of Kansas, 1967.

640 Hogan, Robert. DION BOUCICAULT. New York: Twayne, 1969.

> A substantive book-length study emphasizing the playwriting. Nothing on Boucicault's dramatic theory; no assessment of his place in English and American drama. Bibliography (pp. 125-34).

641   Hunter, Jack W. "Some Research Problems in a Study of THE CORSICAN BROTHERS." OSUTCB, No. 9 (1962), pp. 6-22.

   Explanation of the way the stage was trapped for this play.

642   Johnson, Albert. "The Birth of Dion Boucicault." MD, 11 (1968), 157-63.

   Compelling research to show birth date as 27 December 1820.

643   _____. "Fabulous Boucicault." THEATRE ARTS, 37 (1953), 26-30, 90-93.

   Concerned with Boucicault the man, particularly with reference to his work in theatre.

644   Kaplan, Sidney. "THE OCTOROON: Early History of the Drama of Miscegenation." JOURNAL OF NEGRO EDUCATION, 20 (1951), 547-57.

   Criticism of Boucicault in contemporary reaction to abolition play.

645   Kenney, Charles Lamb. THE CAREER OF BOUCICAULT. New York: Graphic Co., n.d.

   Generally accepted as written by life-long friend but attributed to Boucicault by his third wife.

646   Krause, David. "The Theatre of Dion Boucicault, A Short View of His Life and Art." In THE DOLMEN PRESS BOUCICAULT. Ed. Krause, pp. 9-47. See entry no. 597.

647   Meserve, Walter J. AN OUTLINE HISTORY OF AMERICAN DRAMA. See entry no. 153.

   For comments on Boucicault see pages 93-94, 98-102, 174-76, 203.

648   Morris, Clara. "A Memory of Dion Boucicault." COSMOPOLITAN, 38 (1905), 273-78.

   Reminiscence of Boucicault visiting her dressing room.

649   Moses, Montrose J. "The Prolific Dion Boucicault." In his THE AMERICAN DRAMATIST, pp. 146-70. See entry no. 157.

650   "Mr. Boucicault and Mr. Barnum." SATURDAY REVIEW (London), 61 (1886), 607-08.

   Concerned with spectacle.

Dion Boucicault

651 Nicoll, Allardyce. A HISTORY OF ENGLISH DRAMA, 1660-1900: VOL. IV, EARLY NINETEENTH CENTURY DRAMA, 1800-1850. Cambridge: Cambridge University Press, 1955.

> For a discussion of Boucicault's early works, see pages 188-90; for list of early plays, see pages 269-70.

652 _____. A HISTORY OF ENGLISH DRAMA, 1660-1900: VOL. V, LATE NINETEENTH CENTURY DRAMA, 1850-1900. Cambridge: Cambridge University Press, 1959.

> For a general assessment of Boucicault's contribution, see pages 84-94; for a list of later plays, see pages 267-69, 779.

653 Orr, Lynn Earl. "Dion Boucicault and the Nineteenth Century Theatre: A Biography." Ph.D. dissertation, Louisiana State University, 1952.

654 Peffer, Susan. "Dion Boucicault." LETTERS, 1-2 (August 1929), 7-18.

> A discussion of Boucicault's appeal to Americans, his sense of humanity, and his Irish characters.

655 Quinn, Arthur Hobson. "The Influence of Dion Boucicault." In his A HISTORY OF THE AMERICAN DRAMA FROM THE BEGINNING TO THE CIVIL WAR, pp. 368-92. See entry no. 163.

> An assessment of Boucicault's contribution to American drama.

656 Rahill, Frank. THE WORLD OF MELODRAMA. See entry no. 166.

> Numerous references to Boucicault, especially pages 182-92.

657 _____. "Dion Boucicault and Royalty Payments for Playwrights." THEATRE ARTS, 23 (1939), 807-13.

> Reviews Boucicault's fight for royalty payments for playwrights.

658 Scott, Clement. THE DRAMA OF YESTERDAY AND TO-DAY. 2 vols. London: Macmillan, 1899.

> Quotes Boucicault's preface to LONDON ASSURANCE and gives account of origin of the play (I, 92-109).

659 Steele, William Paul. THE CHARACTER OF MELODRAMA: AN EXAMINATION THROUGH DION BOUCICAULT'S "THE POOR OF NEW YORK" INCLUDING THE TEXT OF THE PLAY. See entry no. 606.

> Poorly devised study; weak scholarship.

660 Thompson, Vance. "Dion Boucicault." In FAMOUS AMERICAN ACTORS OF TO-DAY. Ed. F.E. Mckay and Charles E.L. Wingate. New York: Thomas Y. Crowell & Co., 1896, pp. 81-89.

    A belittling and strongly, negative view of Boucicault; points out defects and errors in facts.

661 Tolson, Julius H. "Dion Boucicault: A Biography." Ph.D. dissertation, University of Pennsylvania, 1951.

    A detailed discussion of the plays.

662 Walsh, Townsend. THE CAREER OF DION BOUCICAULT. New York: Dunlap Society, 1915.

    First major work on Boucicault. Significant in spite of errors.

663 Wheeler, A.C. "Dion Boucicault." ARENA, 3 (1890), 47-60.

    Praise for Boucicault as a showman, a conjuror, who fitted the drama to the demands of society and brought the romanticisim of Hugo and Dumas to "our time."

664 Wingfield, Lewis. "Realism behind the Footlights." FORTNIGHTLY REVIEW, 1 April 1884, pp. 472-81.

    On Boucicault's contribution to stage realism.

665 Winter, William. OTHER DAYS. New York: Moffat, Yard, 1908.

    For Winter's caustic view of Boucicault, see pages 124-51.

JOHN BROUGHAM (1810-80)

MAJOR PLAYS

METAMORA; OR, THE LAST OF THE POLLYWOGS, 1847.
PO-CA-HON-TAS; OR, THE GENTLE SAVAGE, 1855.
THE IRISH YANKEE, 1856 (pub.).
ROMANCE AND REALITY, 1856 (pub).
TEMPTATION; OR, THE IRISH EMIGRANT, 1856 (pub).
COLUMBUS EL FILIBUSTERO, 1857 (pub.).
MUCH ADO ABOUT A MERCHANT OF VENICE, 1869 (pub).

PUBLISHED PLAYS

A. Individual Titles

> See annotation for entry no. 666; and see entry no. 671.

B. Collected Plays

666   BROUGHAM'S DRAMATIC WORKS; CONSISTING OF A COLLECTION OF DRAMAS, COMEDIES AND FARCES BY JOHN BROUGHAM. New York: Samuel French, c. 1856.

> Includes a three-page "Biographical Notice" by a personal friend, R. Shelton MacKenzie, who emphasizes Brougham's youth and young manhood before he achieved fame in the theatre. Volume 1 (only volume published): GAME OF LIFE, LOVE AND MURDER, DAVID COPPERFIELD, TEMPTATION, GAME OF LOVE, PO-CA-HON-TAS, DOMBEY AND SON, ROMANCE AND REALITY.
>
> Brougham wrote over 125 plays, many of which were published individually and variously in French's Modern Standard Drama, in French's Minor Drama, in acting editions in both of the French series, and in Dick's Standard Plays from London.

C. Plays in Anthologies

667   THE DUKE'S MOTTO; OR, I AM HERE! Ed. Eugene R. Page. Vol. 14 of AMERICA'S LOST PLAYS. Ed. Barrett H. Clark. See entry no. 100.

668   PO-CA-HON-TAS. In AMERICAN DRAMA. Vol. 20 of THE DRAMA. Ed. Alfred Bates, pp. 153-95. See entry no. 96.

669   PO-CA-HON-TAS. Eds. Walter J. Meserve and William Reardon. In AMERICA'S LOST PLAYS. Ed. Barrett H. Clark. XXI, pp. 117-55. See entry no. 100.

670   PO-CA-HON-TAS. In DRAMAS FROM THE AMERICAN THEATRE, 1762-1909. Ed. Richard Moody, pp. 403-21. See entry no. 108.

BIBLIOGRAPHY

671   See entries nos. 4, 12, 29, 33, 45, 48, 675, 684.

BIOGRAPHY AND CRITICISM

672   See entries nos. 135, 141, 145, 146, 150, 151, 153, 155, 157, 164.

673   "The Drama." LITERARY WORLD, 12 May 1848, p. 417.

        Assessment of Brougham's ROMANCE AND REALITY; compares Brougham to John Buckstone the British playwright.

674   Eaton, Walter Pritchard. "John Brougham." In DAB. Ed. Allen Johnson. New York: Charles Scribner's Sons, 1929. III, 95-96.

675   Hawes, David S. "John Brougham as American Playwright and Man of the Theatre." Ph.D. dissertation, Stanford University, 1953.

        The most complete study of Brougham's work in the theatre as playwright, actor, and manager.

676   _____. "John Brougham as a Playwright." ETJ, 9 (1957), 184-93.

        A survey of Brougham's plays to indicate his contribution to various forms and styles of American drama; describes him as actor's playwright.

John Brougham

677 _____. "Much Ado about John Brougham and Jim Fisk." MASJ, 8 (Spring 1967), 73-89.

> A study of the short-lived partnership of Brougham and Fisk in early 1869 and the play, MUCH ADO ABOUT THE MERCHANT OF VENICE, which may have helped terminate the friendship and Brougham's Theatre in New York.

678 Hutton, Laurence. "The American Burlesque." HARPER'S MONTHLY, 81 (1890), 58-74.

> On actors who specialized in burlesque; much on Brougham.

679 _____. PLAYS AND PLAYERS. See entry no. 147.

> Numerous references to Brougham's work.

680 Keese, W.L. A GROUP OF COMEDIANS. New York: Dunlap Society, 1901.

> For a commentary on the work of John Brougham, see pages 43-80.

681 Matthews, Brander, and Laurence Hutton, eds. ACTORS AND ACTRESSES OF GREAT BRITAIN AND THE UNITED STATES. 5 vols. New York: Cassell and Co., 1886.

> For an extended commentary surveying Brougham's activity in the theatre, see IV, 273-96.

682 [Oakes, James]. "Letter from Acorn." SPIRIT OF THE TIMES, 12 June 1858, p. 205.

> Good commentary on COLUMBUS and Brougham.

683 Pallard, Anna. "John Brougham." DRAMATIC MAGAZINE, 7 June 1880, pp. 121-29.

> Concern for Brougham as comic actor and writer of comedy.

684 Ryan, Pat M., Jr. "John Brougham: The Gentle Satirist." BNYPL, 63 (1959), 619-40.

> On Brougham's general accomplishments. "A critique, with a handlist and census." Most valuable for the census.

685 "Theatre." DAILY TIMES (New York), 24 December 1855, p. 4.

> A perceptive review of PO-CA-HON-TAS, which was playing at Wallack's Theatre, and Brougham's talent for writing burlesque.

John Brougham

686 "Things Theatrical." SPIRIT OF THE TIMES, 9 January 1858, p. 576.

Review of COLUMBUS EL FILIBUSTERO with quotations from the play.

687 "Things Theatrical." SPIRIT OF THE TIMES, 13 October 1860, p. 440.

A review of PLAYING WITH FIRE that comments on Brougham's general contribution to American drama.

688 Whitton, Joseph. WAGS OF THE STAGE. Philadelphia: George H. Rigby, 1902.

A few interesting anecdotes on the man and actor in "John Brougham" (pp. 12-18).

689 Winter, William. "Supplementary Memoir." In LIFE, STORIES AND POEMS OF JOHN BROUGHAM. Ed. William Winter. Boston: James R. Osgood, 1881, pp. 97-114.

A good source for information about Brougham. Personal comments on Brougham's development as a playwright, which he overvalues; incorrect in listing total number of Brougham's plays. Divided into four parts:

- I. 1. "Autobiography of John Brougham. A Fragment." Four brief chapters on his boyhood and student days.

    2. "Synopsis of Brougham's Career. By Himself." An inaccurate sketch written at Winter's request in 1868.

    3. "A Talk about the Past." Felix G. Defontaine's interview with Brougham, published in New York HERALD, 26 August 1877. Mainly on Brougham's American career but not always accurate.

    4. "Extracts from Brougham's Diaries." Selections from 1853, 1854, 1878, 1879, 1880. Interesting and of value to researchers.

    5. "Brougham's Will."

- II. "Supplementary Memoir." Essentially two articles on Brougham by Winter plus some items relating to Brougham.

- III. "Brougham and his Club Life." An essay by Noah Brooks concerned with Brougham's activities in the Lotus Club in New York.

- IV. "Brougham's Selected Writing." Poems and short stories selected by Winter.

JOHN DALY BURK (1776?-1808)

MAJOR PLAYS

BUNKER-HILL; OR, THE DEATH OF GENERAL WARREN, 1797.
FEMALE PATRIOTISM, 1798.
BETHLEM GABOR, 1807.

PUBLISHED PLAYS

A. Individual Titles

690   BETHLEM GABOR. Petersburg, Va.: Somerwell & Conrad, 1807.

691   BUNKER-HILL. New York: T. Greenleaf, 1797.

692   BUNKER-HILL. Baltimore: R.D. Ryder, 1808.

693   BUNKER-HILL. New York: D. Longworth, 1817.

694   BUNKER-HILL. Ed. Brander Matthews. Ser. 1, Vol. 15. New York: Dunlap Society, 1891.
        Good introduction.

695   FEMALE PATRIOTISM. New York: M. Hurtin, 1798.

B. Plays in Anthologies

696   Bunker-Hill. In DRAMAS FROM THE AMERICAN THEATRE, 1762-1909. Ed. Richard Moody, pp. 70-86. See entry no. 108.

John Daly Burk

BIBLIOGRAPHY

697   See entries nos. 4, 12, 29, 45, 48, 702, 703.

BIOGRAPHY AND CRITICISM

698   See entries nos. 135, 150, 151, 153, 155, 157, 173.

699   Campbell, Charles, ed. SOME MATERIALS TO SERVE FOR A BRIEF MEMOIR OF JOHN DALY BURK, AUTHOR OF A HISTORY OF VIRGINIA. Albany, N.Y.: J. Munsell, 1868.

700   Clapp, William W., Jr. A RECORD OF THE BOSTON STAGE. See entry no. 123.

> For comments on BUNKER-HILL and Burk, see pages 51-55; Clapp's information is not always correct.

701   Gallagher, Kent G. THE FOREIGNER IN EARLY AMERICAN DRAMA. See entry no. 133.

> For discussion of FEMALE PATRIOTISM, see pages 48-51.

702   Meserve, Walter J. AN EMERGING ENTERTAINMENT: THE DRAMA OF THE AMERICAN PEOPLE TO 1828. See entry no. 152.

> For an evaluation of Burk's contribution to American drama, see pages 119-25.

703   Quinn, Arthur Hobson. A HISTORY OF THE AMERICAN DRAMA FROM THE BEGINNING TO THE CIVIL WAR. See entry no. 163.

> For commentary on FEMALE PATRIOTISM, see pages 117-19.

704   Shulim, Joseph I. "John Daly Burk, Playwright of Libertarianism: From 1796 to 1807." BNYPL, 65 (1961), 451-63.

> In clashing worlds of conservatism and libertarianism, Shulim sees libertarianism of BUNKER-HILL and FEMALE PATRIOTISM diminishing in BETHLEM GABOR.

705   Wyatt, Edward A. "John Daly Burk: Patriot-Playwright-Historian." SOUTHERN SKETCHES. No. 7, 1st ser. Charlottesville, Va.: Historical Society, 1936.

> A basic source.

BARTLEY CAMPBELL (1843-88)

MAJOR PLAYS

PERIL, 1871.
THE VIRGINIAN, 1874.
THE GALLEY SLAVE, 1879.
MY PARTNER, 1879.
SIBERIA, 1882.
THE WHITE SLAVE, 1882.

PUBLISHED PLAYS

A. Individual Titles

706   GRAND HISTORICAL ALLEGORY OF AMERICA. Pittsburgh: Samuel A. Barr, 1871.

707   LITTLE SUNSHINE. New York: Samuel French, n.d.

B. Collected Plays

708   THE WHITE SLAVE AND OTHER PLAYS BY BARTLEY CAMPBELL. Ed. Napier Wilt. Vol. 19 of AMERICA'S LOST PLAYS. Ed. Barrett H. Clark. See entry no. 100.

> Contains THE VIRGINIAN, MY PARTNER, THE GALLEY SLAVE, FAIRFAX, THE WHITE SLAVE.

BIBLIOGRAPHY

709   See entries nos. 4, 12, 29, 48, 715, 719.

Bartley Campbell

BIOGRAPHY AND CRITICISM

710   See entries nos. 141, 145, 150, 151, 153, 173, 370.

711   "American Dramatic Authors." DRAMATIC MAGAZINE, (1880), pp. 244-50.

   An essay in appreciation of Campbell's work.

712   Frenz, Horst. "Bartley Campbell's 'My Partner' in Berlin." GERMAN QUARTERLY, 17 (1944), 32-35.

   A discussion of the translation and reception of the play in Berlin.

713   Frohman, Daniel. DANIEL FROHMAN PRESENTS: AN AUTOBIOGRAPHY. New York: Claude Kendall and Willoughby Sharp, 1935.

   For two anecdotes concerning Campbell, see pages 54-56.

714   Montgomery, George E. "Bartley Campbell." THEATRE, 14 June 1886, pp. 348-49.

   Short biographical comment plus quotations from Campbell, particularly on MY PARTNER.

715   Quinn, Arthur Hobson. A HISTORY OF THE AMERICAN DRAMA FROM THE CIVIL WAR TO THE PRESENT DAY. See entry no. 164.

   For a discussion of the dramatist and his works, see pages 118-24; for a list of his plays, see pages 328-29.

716   Rahill, Frank. THE WORLD OF MELODRAMA. See entry no. 166.

   Scattered references to Campbell.

717   Strang, Lewis C. PLAYERS AND PLAYS OF THE LAST QUARTER CENTURY. See entry no. 170.

   For a discussion of MY PARTNER and list of plays, see Volume II, pages 130-33.

718   Wheeler, A.C. [Nym Crinkle]. Obituary. NEW YORK DRAMATIC MIRROR, 4 August 1888, p. 13.

719   THE WHITE SLAVE AND OTHER PLAYS BY BARTLEY CAMPBELL. Ed. Napier Wilt. Vol. 19 of AMERICA'S LOST PLAYS. Ed. Barrett H. Clark. See entry no. 100.

   A short, well-documented biographical sketch with a list of Campbell's plays, including production information and a number of contemporary reviews. A substantive work.

SAMUEL CLEMENS (1835-1910)

MAJOR PLAYS

AH SIN (with Bret Harte), 1877.
COLONEL SELLERS AS A SCIENTIST (with W.D. Howells), 1883.
THE DEATH DISK, 1883.

PUBLISHED PLAYS

A. Plays in Anthologies

720   COLONEL SELLERS AS A SCIENTIST. In THE COMPLETE PLAYS OF W.D. HOWELLS. Ed. Walter J. Meserve, pp. 209-41. New York: New York University Press, 1960.

BIBLIOGRAPHY

721   See entries nos. 4, 12, 29, 48, 720.

722   Kirby, David K., comp. "Samuel L. Clemens." In AMERICAN FICTION TO 1900: A GUIDE TO INFORMATION SOURCES. Ed. David K. Kirby. Detroit: Gale Research Co., 1975, pp. 59-62.

>   A basic bibliographical guide with listings by works, letters, bibliography, journals, biography.

BIOGRAPHY AND CRITICISM

723   Gilder, Rodman. "Mark Twain Detested the Theatre." THEATRE ARTS, 28 (1944), 109-16.

>   Gilder quotes Howells on Mark Twain's attitude but is unconvincing in argument. Weak, errors of fact.

Samuel Clemens

724   Matthews, Brander. PLAYWRIGHTS ON PLAYMAKING. New York: Charles Scribner's Sons, 1923.

        Scattered anecdotes concerning Mark Twain (pp. 161-65).

725   Meserve, Walter J. "'Colonel Sellers as a Scientist,' A Play by Mark Twain and W.D. Howells." MD, 1 (1958), 151-56. Rpt. in THE COMPLETE PLAYS OF W.D. HOWELLS, pp. 205-41; see entry no. 720.

        A detailed discussion of the creation of this play and the attempts of the authors to have it produced.

726   Ryan, Pat M., Jr. "Mark Twain: Frontier Theatre Critic." ARIZONA QUARTERLY, 16 (1960), 197-209.

        From Mark Twain correspondence Ryan excerpts colorful comments on Edwin Forrest, Adah I. Menken, THE BLACK CROOK, and other theatre-related subjects.

727   Stronks, James B. "Mark Twain's Boston Stage Debut as Seen by Hamlin Garland." NEQ, 36 (1963), 85-86.

        A brief note on Twain's acting-reading in the Twain-Cable lecture performance, Boston, 13 November 1884.

728   Walker, Phillip. "Mark Twain, Playwright." ETJ, 8 (1956), 185-93.

        With reference to seven plays that Mark Twain wrote either alone or with others, Walker concludes that Twain should have chosen better collaborators.

729   Wiggins, Robert A. "Mark Twain and the Drama." AL, 25 (1953), 279-86.

        Author suggests some of Mark Twain's connections with theatre. Some erroneous information, weak and insubstantial.

AUGUSTIN DALY (1838-99)

MAJOR PLAYS

LEAH, THE FORSAKEN, 1862.
UNDER THE GASLIGHT, 1867.
FROU FROU, 1870.
MAN AND WIFE, 1870.
HORIZON, 1871.
DIVORCE, 1871.
THE BIG BONANZA, 1875.

PUBLISHED PLAYS

A. Collected Plays

730   MAN AND WIFE & OTHER PLAYS. Ed. Catherine Sturtevant. Vol. 20 of AMERICA'S LOST PLAYS. Ed. Barrett H. Clark. See entry no. 100.

        Contains MAN AND WIFE, DIVORCE, THE BIG BONANZA, PIQUE, NEEDLES AND PINS. An introduction to each play with a list of Daly's plays.

B. Plays in Anthologies

731   HORIZON. In AMERICAN PLAYS. Ed. Allan G. Halline, pp. 333-75. See entry no. 105.

732   UNDER THE GASLIGHT. In HISS THE VILLAIN. Ed. Michael Booth, pp. 272-341. See entry no. 97.

Augustin Daly

NONDRAMATIC WORKS

733 "The American Dramatist." NAR, 142 (1886), 485-92.

> Refers to many plays and declares that American drama exists to present native character and contemporary fashions and follies. Strong statement.

734 "Mr. Augustin Daly's Views." In "American Playwrights on the American Drama." See entry no. 422.

> Statement on theory and attitudes.

BIBLIOGRAPHY

735 See entries nos. 4, 12, 29, 30, 33, 34, 45, 48, 756.

BIOGRAPHY AND CRITICISM

736 See entries nos. 137, 141, 143, 145, 147, 150, 166.

737 "Augustin Daly--Career Sketched." NEW YORK TIMES, 22 April 1886, p. 16.

738 "Augustin Daly--Early Career." NEW YORK TIMES, 25 April 1884, p. 3.

739 Coleman, A.I. "Augustin Daly: An Appreciation." CRITIC, 35 (1899), 719-20.

> Brief and different view from Joseph Daly's longer approach.

740 Daly, Joseph. "Augustin Daly's First Stage Production." LITERARY DIGEST, 24 November 1917, pp. 78-79.

> Excerpt from THE LIFE OF AUGUSTIN DALY.

741 _____. THE LIFE OF AUGUSTIN DALY. New York: Macmillan, 1917.

> Standard biography by Daly's brother. A detailed and valuable account in spite of intense sympathy and occasional inaccuracy.

Augustin Daly

742 [Dithmar, Edward A.]. MEMORIES OF DALY'S THEATRES. New York: Privately printed, 1896.

> A series of essays, sympathetic to Daly's life and work. Mainly concerned with theatre management and the acting of Daly's plays. Includes an essay entitled "Augustin Daly" by John Talbot Smith. Well illustrated.

743 Felhein, Marvin. "Daly's Ghost and Rake of Avon." THEATRE ARTS, 40 (1956), 66-68.

> An excerpt from THE THEATRE OF AUGUSTIN DALY.

744 _____. THE THEATRE OF AUGUSTIN DALY. Cambridge, Mass.: Harvard University Press, 1956.

> An excellent study of Daly's life and his plays. No bibliography.

745 Hall, Margaret. "Personal Recollections of Augustin Daly." THEATRE, 5 (1905), 150, 174, 188, 213.

> Slight value; a few interesting sidelights.

746 Hapgood, Norman. THE STAGE IN AMERICA, 1897-1900. See entry no. 136.

> Scattered references to Daly opinions and his work.

747 Herron, Ima Honaker. THE SMALL TOWN IN AMERICAN DRAMA. See entry no. 140.

> References to Daly's plays, particularly HORIZON (pp. 136-38).

748 Kobbe, Gustav. "Augustin Daly and His Life-Work." COSMOPOLITAN, 27 (1899), 405-18.

> Good study of Daly in his theatre.

749 Koster, Donald Nelson. THE THEME OF DIVORCE IN AMERICAN DRAMA, 1871-1939. See entry no. 388.

> For a discussion of Daly's DIVORCE, see pages 42-47.

750 Lathrop, George Parsons. "An American School of Dramatic Art. II. The Inside Working of the Theatre." CENTURY, 56 (1898), 265-75.

> In a discussion of Daly's theatre practice, Lathrop presents a strong defense of his methods of adapting plays.

Augustin Daly

751   "Leah." HARPER'S WEEKLY, 7 March 1863, p. 146.

       A penetrating review of the play as social commentary.

752   Meserve, Walter J. AN OUTLINE HISTORY OF AMERICAN DRAMA. See entry no. 153.

       Author comments on Daly's realism (pp. 135-39), social comedy (pp. 147-50), melodrama (pp. 176-77); also other references.

753   Morris, Clara. "Recollections of the Stage and Its People." MCCLURE'S, 16 (1901), 201-14.

       Little value, but some insight into Daly's personal demeanor.

754   _____. STAGE CONFIDENCES. Boston: Lothrop, 1902.

       See Chapter III, "In Connection with DIVORCE and Daly's."

755   Moses, Montrose J. THE AMERICAN DRAMATIST. See entry no. 157.

       Mainly concerned with Daly's adaptations and relations with other dramatists--Harte, Howells, James, Mark Twain.

756   Quinn, Arthur Hobson. "Augustin Daly, Conservative Artist of the Theatre." In his A HISTORY OF THE AMERICAN DRAMA FROM THE CIVIL WAR TO THE PRESENT DAY. I, 1-38. See entry no. 164.

       A good summary and evaluation of Daly's plays.

757   Strang, Lewis C. PLAYERS AND PLAYS OF THE LAST QUARTER CENTURY. See entry no. 170.

       Numerous references to Daly's plays (in particular, II, 124-28, 204-07).

758   Towse, J. Ranken. "An American School of Dramatic Art. I. A Critical Review of Daly's Theatre." CENTURY 56 (1898), 261-64.

       Passing reference to a number of American plays.

759   Wayne, Palma. "Mr. Daly." THEATRE ARTS, 38 (1954), 67-69, 93-96.

       Revealing comments on Daly as man and theatre director by a member of his troupe.

760   White, Matthew. "Landmarks of Mr. Daly's Career and His Work for the American Stage." MUNSEY'S 21 (1899), 745.

       Summary of Daly's accomplishments.

Augustin Daly

761 Wilson, Garff B. THREE HUNDRED YEARS OF AMERICAN DRAMA AND THEATRE. See entry no. 173.

> Comments on Daly as playwright (pp. 215-17); other references on theatrical management.

762 Winter, William. "Memories of the Players--Augustin Daly." COLLIERS, 26 April 1913, pp. 19-20, 26.

> Character sketch which documents career; sympathetic but relatively balanced view.

WILLIAM DUNLAP (1766-1839)

MAJOR PLAYS

THE FATHER; OR, AMERICAN SHANDYISM, 1789.
    Later called THE FATHER OF AN ONLY CHILD.
DARBY'S RETURN, 1789.
THE FATAL DECEPTION; OR, THE PROGRESS OF GUILT, 1794.
    Published as LEICESTER in Dunlap's WORKS (entry no. 782).
FONTAINVILLE ABBEY, 1795.
THE ARCHERS; OR, MOUNTAINEERS OF SWITZERLAND, 1796.
Adapted Kotzebue's THE STRANGER, 1798.
ANDRÉ, 1798.
Adapted Kotzebue's PIZARRO IN PERU; OR, THE DEATH OF ROLLA, 1800.
Adapted Zschokke's ABAELLINO, THE GREAT BANDIT, 1801.
THE GLORY OF COLUMBIA--HER YEOMANRY, 1803.
Adapted Pixérécourt's THE WIFE OF TWO HUSBANDS, 1804.
YANKEE CHRONOLOGY, 1812.
A TRIP TO NIAGARA; OR, TRAVELLERS IN AMERICA, 1828.

PUBLISHED PLAYS

A. Individual Titles

763   ABAELLINO, THE GREAT BANDIT. New York: D. Longworth, 1802.

764   ANDRÉ. New York: T. & J. Swords, 1798.

765   ANDRÉ. Ed. Brander Matthews. Ser. 1, Vol. 4. New York: Dunlap Society, 1887.

766   THE ARCHERS; OR, MOUNTAINEERS OF SWITZERLAND. New York: T. & J. Swords, 1796.

William Dunlap

767 DARBY'S RETURN. New York: Hodge, Allen & Campbell, 1789.

768 THE FATHER; OR, AMERICAN SHANDYISM. New York: Hodge, Allen & Campbell, 1789.

769 THE FATHER; OR, AMERICAN SHANDYISM. Ed. T.J. McKee. Ser. 1, Vol. 2. New York: Dunlap Society, 1887.

770 FRATERNAL DISCORD. New York: D. Longworth, 1809.

771 THE ITALIAN FATHER. New York: D. Longworth, 1810.

772 LOVER'S VOWS. New York: D. Longworth, 1814.

773 PIZARRO IN PERU; OR, THE DEATH OF ROLLA. New York: Printed for the author, 1800.

774 RIBBEMONT; OR, THE FEUDAL BARON. New York: D. Longworth, 1803.

775 TELL TRUTH AND SHAME THE DEVIL. New York: T. & J. Swords, 1797.

776 A TRIP TO NIAGARA; OR, TRAVELLERS IN AMERICA. New York: E.B. Clayton, 1830.

777 THE VIRGIN OF THE SUN. New York: Printed for the author, 1800.

778 THE VOICE OF NATURE. New York: D. Longworth, 1803.

779 THE WIFE OF TWO HUSBANDS. New York: D. Longworth, 1804.

780 THE WILD GOOSE CHASE. New York: Printed for the author, 1800.

781 YANKEE CHRONOLOGY; OR, HUZZA FOR THE CONSTITUTION! New York: D. Longworth, 1812.

B. Collected Plays

782 THE DRAMATIC WORKS OF WILLIAM DUNLAP. 3 vols. Philadelphia: T. and G. Palmer, 1806-16.

Volume I contains THE FATHER OF AN ONLY CHILD, LEICESTER, FONTAINVILLE ABBEY, DARBY'S RETURN. Volume II: THE VOICE OF NATURE, FRATERNAL DISCORD, THE ITALIAN FATHER, THE GOOD NEIGHBOR. Volume III: THE WIFE OF TWO HUSBANDS, ABAELLINO, THE GREAT BANDIT, LOVERS' VOWS, PETER THE GREAT.

All plays were printed by Longworth in 1807.

783   FALSE SHAME and THIRTY YEARS. Ed. Oral Sumner Coad. In AMERICA'S LOST PLAYS. Ed. Barrett H. Clark. II. See entry no. 100.

784   FOUR PLAYS BY WILLIAM DUNLAP, 1789-1812. Ed. Julian Mates. New York: Scholars' Facsimiles and Reprints, 1976.

Contains THE FATHER OF AN ONLY CHILD, LEICESTER, THE ITALIAN FATHER, YANKEE CHRONOLOGY.

C. Plays in Anthologies

785   ANDRÉ. In SIX EARLY AMERICAN PLAYS, 1798-1900. Eds. William Coyle and Harry G. Damaser, pp. 8-46. See entry no. 102.

786   ANDRÉ. In AMERICAN PLAYS. Ed. Allan G. Halline, pp. 41-74. See entry no. 105.

787   ANDRÉ. In REPRESENTATIVE PLAYS BY AMERICAN DRAMATISTS. Ed. Montrose J. Moses, I, pp. 499-564. See entry no. 111.

788   ANDRÉ. In REPRESENTATIVE AMERICAN PLAYS. Ed. Arthur Hobson Quinn, pp. 83-107. See entry no. 114.

789   DARBY'S RETURN. In WASHINGTON AND THE THEATRE. Ed. P.L. Ford, pp. 2-14. Ser. 2, Vol. 8. New York: Dunlap Society, 1899.

790   DARBY'S RETURN. Eds. Walter J. Meserve and William Reardon, pp. 103-13. In AMERICA'S LOST PLAYS. Ed. Barrett H. Clark. XXI. See entry no. 100.

791   FATHER OF AN ONLY CHILD. In AMERICAN DRAMA. Vol. 19 of THE DRAMA. Ed. Alfred Bates, pp. 59-63. See entry no. 96.

A scene only.

792   A TRIP TO NIAGARA. In DRAMAS FROM THE AMERICAN THEATRE, 1762-1909. Ed. Richard Moody, pp. 175-97.

William Dunlap

NONDRAMATIC WORKS

793   DIARY OF WILLIAM DUNLAP. Ed. Dorothy C. Barck. 3 vols. New York: New York Historical Society, 1930; rpt. in COLLECTIONS OF THE NEW YORK HISTORICAL SOCIETY, vols. 62-64, 1929-31; rpt. as DIARY OF A DRAMATIST, 1766-1839. New York: Blom, 1969.

794   HISTORY OF THE AMERICAN THEATRE. 2 vols. New York: J. & J. Harper, 1832; rpt. 2 vols. in 1. New York: Burt Franklin, 1963.

>The reprint also contains John Hodgkinson's "A Narrative of His Connection with the Old American Company 1792-1797," first printed in New York by J. Oram, 1797.

BIBLIOGRAPHY

795   See entries nos. 4, 12, 29, 33, 34, 45, 48, 806, 808, 816.

796   Wegelin, Oscar. A BIBLIOGRAPHICAL CHECKLIST OF THE PLAYS AND MISCELLANEOUS WRITINGS OF WILLIAM DUNLAP. New York: Charles F. Heartman, 1916.

>Superseded by Blanck and Coad (entries nos. 12, 806), but still valuable.

BIOGRAPHY AND CRITICISM

797   See entries nos. 133, 141, 150, 151, 153, 155, 157, 173.

798   "American Actors and Dramatic Authors." SPIRIT OF THE TIMES, 7 March 1840, p. 12.

>Writer notes lack of attention paid to American drama and comments on Dunlap as earliest playwright.

799   Argetsinger, Gerold. "Dunlaps ANDRÉ: The Beginning of American Tragedy." PLAYERS, 49 (1974), 60-64.

>A superficial discussion with little comment on tragedy.

800   Behrman, Alfred. "Kotzebue on the American Stage." ARCADIA, 4 (1969), 274-84.

>A chronological discussion, beginning with Dunlap's production of THE STRANGER, of Kotzebue's success, influence, and decline in America.

William Dunlap

801   Bowman, Mary R. "Dunlap and the 'Theatrical Register' of the NEW YORK MAGAZINE." STUDIES IN PHILOLOGY, 24 (1927), 413-25.

      A good essay suggesting that Dunlap functioned as the magazine's anonymous theatre critic, November 1794 to April 1796, writing eleven essays.

802   Brooks, Van Wyck. "William Dunlap and His Circle." In his THE WORLD OF WASHINGTON IRVING. New York: E.P. Dutton, 1944, pp. 152-75.

      Well-written review and summary of accomplishments.

803   Canary, Robert H. WILLIAM DUNLAP. New York: Twayne, 1970

      An informative and well-written general study limited by the Twayne series approach. Lists separate publications of major plays; provides slight but annotated bibliography.

804   _____. "William Dunlap and the Search for an American Audience." MASJ, 4 (Spring 1963), 45-51.

      Canary answers the question why Dunlap is important as a critic, an artist, and a theatre person. Well written.

805   Coad, Oral Sumner. "The Dunlap Diaries at Yale." STUDIES IN PHILOLOGY, 24 (1927), 403-12.

      Coad describes the six volumes of manuscript diary and discusses newly found details.

806   _____. WILLIAM DUNLAP: A STUDY OF HIS LIFE AND WORKS AND OF HIS PLACE IN CONTEMPORARY CULTURE. New York: Dunlap Society, 1917; rpt. New York: Russell & Russell, 1962.

      A basic biographical and critical text on Dunlap with good bibliography.

807   _____. "William Dunlap: New Jersey Artist." PROCEEDINGS OF THE NEW JERSEY HISTORICAL SOCIETY, 83 (1965), 238-63.

      A discussion of Dunlap's range as a painter.

808   Cronin, James F. THE DIARY OF ELIHU HUBBARD SMITH. Philadelphia: American Philosophical Society, 1973.

      Comments by Smith, a close friend of Dunlap, relative to Dunlap's activities in the theatre.

William Dunlap

809   Grimsted, David. "The Corruption of an Enlightened Age." In his MELODRAMA UNVEILED: AMERICAN THEATRE & CULTURE, 1800-1850, pp. 1-21. See entry no. 135.

        An analysis of Dunlap's melodramas.

810   Grinchuk, Robert A. "The Plays of William Dunlap. A Study of Dramatic Failure and the Shift in Popular Taste, 1795-1805." Ph.D. dissertation, University of Minnesota, 1972.

811   McGinnis, William C. WILLIAM DUNLAP. Perth Amboy, N.J.: City of Perth Amboy, 1956.

        A local view of Perth Amboy's "most illustrious citizen."

812   Matlaw, Myron. "MENSCHENHASS UND REUE in English." SYMPOSIUM, 14 (1960), 129-34.

        An account of Dunlap's version of Kotzebue's drama.

813   Meserve, Walter J. AN EMERGING ENTERTAINMENT: THE DRAMA OF THE AMERICAN PEOPLE TO 1828. See entry no. 152.

        For the contribution of Dunlap to a developing American drama, see pages 102-15.

814   Moramarco, Fred. "The Early Drama Criticism of William Dunlap." AL, 40 (1968), 9-14.

        A careful analysis of the essays in the NEW YORK MAGAZINE ("Theatrical Register") to show that Dunlap could have been the author.

815   Philbrick, Norman. "The Spy as Hero: An Examination of ANDRÉ by William Dunlap." In STUDIES IN THEATRE AND DRAMA: ESSAYS IN HONOR OF HUBERT C. HEFFNER. Ed. Oscar G. Brockett. The Hague: Mouton, 1972, pp. 97-119.

        A thorough discussion of the historical background and details attendant to the play's production and reception.

816   Quinn, Arthur Hobson. "William Dunlap, Playwright and Producer." In his A HISTORY OF THE AMERICAN DRAMA FROM THE BEGINNING TO THE CIVIL WAR, pp. 74-112. See entry no. 163.

        A good discussion of Dunlap's plays and theatre activity.

817   "Review [of William Dunlap's DARBY'S RETURN from the GAZETTE OF THE UNITED STATES, 28 November 1789]. In THE AMERICAN THEATRE AS SEEN BY ITS CRITICS, 1752-1934. Eds. Montrose J. Moses and John Mason Brown, pp. 26-27. See entry no. 330.

William Dunlap

818 "Review" [of William Dunlap's THE FATHER from the GAZETTE OF THE UNITED STATES, 9 September 1789]. In THE AMERICAN THEATRE AS SEEN BY ITS CRITICS, 1752-1934. Eds. Montrose J. Moses and John Mason Brown, p. 26. See entry no. 330.

819 Wegelin, Oscar. WILLIAM DUNLAP AND HIS WRITINGS. New York: Privately printed, 1904.

    Slight but interesting as early scholarship on Dunlap.

820 Woolsey, T.S. "The American Vasari." YALE REVIEW, 3 (1914), 778-89.

    Author attempts to reintroduce Dunlap as painter and historian and concentrates on his HISTORY OF THE RISE AND PROGRESS OF THE ARTS OF DESIGN IN THE UNITED STATES.

821 Wyld, Lionel D. "A Farce on Erie Water." NEW YORK FOLKLORE QUARTERLY, 17 (1961), 59-62.

    Concerned with A TRIP TO NIAGARA.

CLYDE FITCH (1865-1909)

MAJOR PLAYS

BEAU BRUMMEL, 1890.
NATHAN HALE, 1899.
BARBARA FRIETCHIE, 1899.
THE CLIMBERS, 1901.
CAPTAIN JINKS OF THE HORSE MARINES, 1901.
THE GIRL WITH THE GREEN EYES, 1902.
THE TRUTH, 1907.
THE CITY, 1909.

PUBLISHED PLAYS

A. Individual Titles

822   BARBARA FRIETCHIE. New York: Life Publishing Co., 1900.

823   CAPTAIN JINKS OF THE HORSE MARINES. New York: Doubleday, Page, 1902.

824   NATHAN HALE. New York: R.H. Russell, 1899.

B. Collected Plays

825   MEMORIAL EDITION OF THE PLAYS OF CLYDE FITCH. Eds. Montrose J. Moses and Virginia Gerson. 4 vols. Boston: Little, Brown, 1915.

    Volume I: BEAU BRUMMELL, LOVER'S LANE, NATHAN HALE; Volume II: BARBARA FRIETCHIE, CAPTAIN JINKS OF THE HORSE MARINES, THE CLIMBERS; Volume III: THE STUBBORNNESS OF GERALDINE, THE GIRL WITH THE GREEN EYES, HER OWN WAY; Volume IV: THE WOMAN IN

Clyde Fitch

THE CASE, THE TRUTH, THE CITY. These plays are also available in Samuel French editions.

C. Plays in Anthologies

826   THE CITY. In DRAMAS FROM THE AMERICAN THEATRE, 1762-1909. Ed. Richard Moody, pp. 821-54. See entry no. 108.

827   THE CITY. In REPRESENTATIVE AMERICAN DRAMAS: NATIONAL AND LOCAL. Ed. Montrose J. Moses, pp. 151-88. See entry no. 109.

828   THE GIRL WITH THE GREEN EYES. In REPRESENTATIVE AMERICAN PLAYS. Ed. Arthur Hobson Quinn, pp. 642-74. See entry no. 114.

   This play appears only in editions of this collection published after 1930.

829   HER GREAT MATCH. In REPRESENTATIVE AMERICAN PLAYS. Ed. Arthur Hobson Quinn, pp. 665-707. See entry no. 114.

   This play appears only in editions of this collection published prior to 1930 and subtitled "1767-1923."

830   THE MOTH AND THE FLAME. In REPRESENTATIVE PLAYS BY AMERICAN DRAMATISTS. Ed. Montrose J. Moses. III, 521-96. See entry no. 110.

NONDRAMATIC WORKS

831   "The Play and the Public." SMART SET, 14 (1904), 97-100.

BIBLIOGRAPHY

832   See entries nos. 4, 12, 29, 30, 33, 34, 45, 48, 840, 850, 854.

833   Lowe, John A. "A Reading List of Clyde Fitch." BULLETIN OF BIBLIOGRAPHY, 7 (1912), 304.

BIOGRAPHY AND CRITICISM

834   See entries nos. 119, 120, 141, 151, 165, 426, 1347.

Clyde Fitch

835   "The American Stage Loses Clyde Fitch." THEATRE, 10 (1909), 112.
>An obituary.

836   Atkinson, Brooks. BROADWAY. New York: Macmillan, 1970.
>Numerous references, especially pages 51-59.

837   Bell, Archie. THE CLYDE FITCH I KNEW. New York: Broadway Publishing Co., 1909.
>The standard biography, written with affection and containing some valuable personal insights.

838   Bernbaum, Martin. "Clyde Fitch, an Appreciation." INDEPENDENT, 15 July 1909, pp. 123-31.

839   Clark, Barrett H. A STUDY OF THE MODERN DRAMA. New York: D. Appleton and Co., 1925, 1928.
>An assessment of Fitch with biographical details and quotations (pp. 375-80).

840   CLYDE FITCH AND HIS LETTERS. Eds. Montrose J. Moses and Virginia Gerson. Boston: Little, Brown 1924.
>Contains a complete list of Fitch's plays and other writings.

841   Eaton, Walter Pritchard. "The Dramatist as Man of Letters: The Case of Clyde Fitch." SCRIBNER'S, 46 (1910), 490-97; rpt. in AT THE NEW THEATRE AND OTHERS by Eaton. Boston: Small Maynard, 1910; and rpt. in THE AMERICAN THEATRE AS SEEN BY ITS CRITICS, 1752-1934. Eds. Montrose J. Moses and John Mason Brown, pp. 171-75. See entry no. 330.
>>Eaton finds it necessary to make concessions for Fitch, who held the "literary dramatist" in contempt, and sees Fitch's best plays as truthful comments on life and, therefore, judges them to be literature.

842   "The Evolution of Clyde Fitch." CURRENT LITERATURE, 47 (1909), 316-17.

843   "The Fatal Modesty of Clyde Fitch." CURRENT LITERATURE, 47 (1909), 552-54.

844   Hapgood, Norman. THE STAGE IN AMERICA, 1897-1900. See entry no. 136.
>For commentary on NATHAN HALE and BARBARA FRIETCHIE, see pages 85-91.

Clyde Fitch

845 Hartman, John Geoffrey. THE DEVELOPMENT OF AMERICAN SOCIAL COMEDY, 1787-1931. See entry no. 137.

    Views American social comedy as established with the plays of Clyde Fitch.

846 Herron, Ima Honaker. THE SMALL TOWN IN AMERICAN DRAMA. See entry no. 140.

    Discussion of several Fitch plays (pp. 155-59).

847 Masters, Robert W. "Clyde Fitch. A Playwright of His Time." Ph.D. dissertation, Northwestern University, 1942.

848 Mayorga, Margaret G. A SHORT HISTORY OF THE AMERICAN DRAMA. See entry no. 150.

    Discussion of BEAU BRUMMEL and THE TRUTH (pp. 202-12); comments on other plays.

849 Meserve, Walter J. AN OUTLINE HISTORY OF AMERICAN DRAMA. See entry no. 153.

    Comments on Fitch's social comedy (pp. 155-59); also other references.

850 Moses, Montrose J. "Concerning Clyde Fitch and the Local Scene." In his THE AMERICAN DRAMATIST, pp. 309-28. See entry no. 157.

    Biographical commentary and clear assessment of Fitch's plays, with brief bibliography.

851 Murray, James J. "The Contribution of Clyde Fitch to the American Theatre." Ph.D. dissertation, Boston University, 1942.

852 Patterson, Ada. "How a Rapid-Fire Dramatist Writes His Plays." THEATRE, 7 (1907), 14-16.

    A revealing essay with statements by Fitch on his methods.

853 Phelps, Willion Lyon. "Clyde Fitch." In his ESSAYS ON MODERN DRAMATISTS. New York: Macmillan, 1921, pp. 142-78.

    An appreciative assessment.

854 Quinn, Arthur Hobson. "Clyde Fitch and the Development of Social Comedy." In his A HISTORY OF THE AMERICAN DRAMA FROM THE CIVIL WAR TO THE PRESENT DAY. I, 265-96. See entry no. 164.

    Biographical information and substantial critical evaluation of his plays.

Clyde Fitch

855 Salem, James M., comp. A GUIDE TO CRITICAL REVIEWS: PART I: AMERICAN DRAMA, 1909-1969. See entry no. 46.

    For reviews of Fitch's plays, see pages 145-47.

856 SOME CORRESPONDENCE AND SIX CONVERSATIONS. New York: Stone & Kimball, 1896; Chicago: Herbert S. Stone, 1900.

    Some affected wit in fictional letters. Conversations reveal Fitch's ability to create dialogue.

857 Steele, Willis. "Clyde Fitch as Collaborator." THEATRE, 10 (1909), 176-78.

    Steele and Fitch collaborated on WOLFVILLE, 1905.

858 Strang, Lewis C. PLAYERS AND PLAYS OF THE LAST QUARTER CENTURY. See entry no. 170.

    For a general discussion of Fitch, see Volume II, pages 167-83.

859 Wilson, Garff B. THREE HUNDRED YEARS OF AMERICAN DRAMA AND THEATRE. See entry no. 173.

    Contains a commentary on THE CITY, called Fitch's "play of ideas" (pp. 235-40).

WILLIAM GILLETTE (1855-1937)

MAJOR PLAYS

THE PRIVATE SECRETARY, 1884.
HELD BY THE ENEMY, 1886.
TOO MUCH JOHNSON, 1894.
SECRET SERVICE, 1896.
SHERLOCK HOLMES, 1899.

PUBLISHED PLAYS

A. Individual Titles

860   ELECTRICITY. DRAMA, 3 (November 1913), 13-123.

861   ESMERALDA. CENTURY, n.s. 1 (1882), 513-31.

B. Plays in Anthologies

862   AMONG THIEVES. In ONE-ACT PLAYS FOR STAGE AND STUDY. 2nd ser. Ed. W.P. Eaton. New York: S. French, 1925, pp. 247-67.

863   THE RED OWL. In ONE-ACT PLAYS FOR STAGE AND STUDY. 1st ser. Ed. Augustus Thomas. New York: S. French, 1924, pp. 48-80.

864   SECRET SERVICE. In THE BEST PLAYS OF 1894-99. Eds. John Chapman and Garrison P. Sherwood, pp. 36-49. See entry no. 99.

       An abbreviated version with commentary.

865   SECRET SERVICE. In BEST PLAYS OF THE EARLY AMERICAN THEATRE. Eds. John Gassner and Mollie Gassner, pp. 277-360. See entry no. 104.

William Gillette

866   SECRET SERVICE. In REPRESENTATIVE AMERICAN PLAYS. Ed. Arthur Hobson Quinn, pp. 550-620. See entry no. 114.

NONDRAMATIC WORKS

867   "Gillette at Last Capitulates to an Interview." NEW YORK TIMES, 1 November 1914, p. 8.

> Mainly on acting but some opinions on contemporary drama.

868   "How to Write a Play." In PAPERS ON PLAYWRITING. Ed. Brander Matthews. New York: Dramatic Museum of Columbia University, 1916.

> Gillette's approach to playwriting in which he stresses "invention," "the required knowledge of life," and a "study of the habits and tastes" of people and audiences.

869   "Mr. William Gillette Surveys the Field." In "American Playwrights on the American Drama." See entry no. 422.

> Gillette's comments on contemporary drama in America.

BIBLIOGRAPHY

870   See entries nos. 4, 12, 29, 30, 34, 45, 46, 370, 877, 889.

BIOGRAPHY AND CRITICISM

871   See entries nos. 136, 150, 151, 153, 173, 426, 839, 975.

872   [Beaumont, Fletcher.]. "William Gillette's Warplay, SECRET SERVICE." GODEY'S, 134 (1897), 73-79.

> A critical review of his play, particular reference to plot; concern for Gillette's place among American dramatists.

873   Brock, H.I. "Sherlock Holmes Returns to the Stage." NEW YORK TIMES MAGAZINE, 10 November 1929, pp. 14, 20.

> A rambling discussion of Gillett's personality, acting, and playwriting.

874   Burton, Richard. "William Gillette." DRAMA, 3 (November 1913), 5-11.

> Burton uses a review of ELECTRICITY as basis for vague and general discussion of Gillette's plays.

William Gillette

875 _____. "William Gillette--An American Playwright." BOOK BUYER, 16 (1898), 26-30.

    Biographical sketch of Gillette's youth and career to 1898.

876 Clark, Barrett H. THE BRITISH AND AMERICAN DRAMA OF TO-DAY. Cincinnati: Stewart & Kidd, 1921.

    For biographical notes and guide to a study of HELD BY THE ENEMY, see pages 243-44.

877 Cook, Doris E. SHERLOCK HOLMES AND MUCH MORE: OR SOME OF THE FACTS ABOUT WILLIAM GILLETTE. Hartford: Connecticut Historical Society, 1970.

    As subtitle indicates, author uses a scattered but interesting approach. No assessment of plays but good use of unpublished letters, collections.

878 Frenz, Horst, and Louis W. Campbell. "William Gillette on the London Stage." QUEEN'S QUARTERLY, 52 (1945), 443-57.

    Reaction to Gillette's plays by London critics.

879 Hamilton, Clayton. "Plays, Home-made and Imported." BOOKMAN 33 (1911), 594-607.

    Essay includes an analysis of Gillette's plays and his place in the developing American drama.

880 _____. "William Gillette, Theatrical Craftsman." COLLIER'S, 18 December 1915, pp. 9, 23.

    A good appraisal of Gillette's theory of playwriting.

881 Hapgood, Norman. THE STAGE IN AMERICA, 1897-1900. See entry no. 136.

    Comment on Gillette's two major works (pp. 61-79).

882 Howells, W.D. "Life in Letters." HARPER'S WEEKLY, 30 January 1897, pp. 106-07.

    A commentary on Gillette's SECRET SERVICE.

883 Lynch, Gertrude. "The Real William Gillette." THEATRE, 13 (1911), 123-25.

    A personal view of the man and actor.

884 Macfarlane, Peter Clark. "The Magic of William Gillette." EVERYBODY'S MAGAZINE, 32 (1915), 257-68.

    A brief discussion for the popular audience.

William Gillette

885 McGraw, Rex T. "The Role of the Villain in Civil War Melodramas." Ph.D. dissertation, Indiana University, 1966.

> Dissertation includes discussion of HELD BY THE ENEMY (pp. 333-37) and SECRET SERVICE (pp. 177-81).

886 Moses, Montrose J. THE AMERICAN DRAMATIST. See entry no. 157.

> Sketchy review of Gillette's work (pp. 164-68).

887 _____. "The American Dramatist: William Gillette." INDEPENDENT, 61 (1906), 735-43.

> Basic biographical information.

888 Nichols, Harold J. "William Gillette: Innovator in Melodrama." THEATRE ANNUAL, 31 (1975), 7-15.

> Explains Gillette's techniques in writing melodrama.

889 Quinn, Arthur Hobson. "William Gillette and the Realism of Action." In his A HISTORY OF THE AMERICAN DRAMA FROM THE CIVIL WAR TO THE PRESENT DAY, pp. 212-38. See entry no. 164.

> Outlines and assesses both his acting and playwriting careers.

890 Rahill, Frank. "Melodrama Comes of Age." In his THE WORLD OF MELODRAMA, pp. 262-71. See entry no. 166.

> The melodrama of Gillette and Belasco.

891 Schuttler, Georg W. "Sherlock Holmes as Hamlet?" TS, 18 (1977), 72-85.

> A detailed discussion of Gillette's planned adaptation of HAMLET with himself in the title role.

892 Scott, Clement. "Held by the Enemy." THEATRE (London), 2 April 1887, pp. 281-83.

> A review by a major English critic.

893 Shafer, Yvonne. "A Sherlock Holmes of the Past: William Gillette's Later Years." PLAYERS, 46 (1971), 229-35.

> A brief outline of Gillette's career and an assessment of his later years. Weak evidence; many quotations with footnotes.

894 Sherk, H. Denis. "William Gillette: His Life and Works." Ph.D. dissertation, Pennsylvania State University, 1961.

A comprehensive study that includes some suspect biographical material; detailed analysis only for SECRET SERVICE and SHERLOCK HOLMES.

895 Stone, P.M. "Mr. William Gillette." SHERLOCK HOLMES JOURNAL, 4 (1960), 115-18.

A history of Gillette's Sherlock Holmes; see similar comment by Stone, "William Hooker Gillette." BAKER STREET JOURNAL, n.s. 3 (1954), supp.

896 White, Matthew, Jr. "The Stage." MUNSEY'S, 45 (1911), 273-86.

A discussion of Gillette's rewriting of SECRET SERVICE after its initial failure.

THOMAS GODFREY (1736-63)

MAJOR PLAYS

THE PRINCE OF PARTHIA, 1759.

PUBLISHED PLAYS

A. Individual Titles

897   THE PRINCE OF PARTHIA. In JUVENILE POEMS ON VARIOUS SUBJECTS WITH THE PRINCE OF PARTHIA, A TRAGEDY, pp. 95-130. Introd. Nathaniel Evans. Philadelphia: Henry Miller, 1765.

898   THE PRINCE OF PARTHIA. Ed. Archibald Henderson. Boston: Little, Brown, 1917.
       Valuable introduction.

B. Plays in Anthologies

899   THE PRINCE OF PARTHIA. In REPRESENTATIVE PLAYS BY AMERICAN DRAMATISTS. Ed. Montrose J. Moses. I, 19-108. See entry no. 111.

900   THE PRINCE OF PARTHIA. In REPRESENTATIVE AMERICAN PLAYS. Ed. Arthur Hobson Quinn, pp. 5-42. See entry no. 114.

BIBLIOGRAPHY

901   See entries nos. 4, 12, 29, 33, 45, 48, 912.

Thomas Godfrey

BIOGRAPHY AND CRITICISM

902   See entries nos. 120, 141, 157, 173.

903   Carlson, C.L. "A Further Note on Thomas Godfrey in England." AL, 9 (1937), 73-76.

904   _____. "Thomas Godfrey in England." AL, 7 (1935), 302-09.

        Reception of poems by English critics.

905   Gegenheimer, Albert F. "Thomas Godfrey: Protegé of William Smith." PENNSYLVANIA HISTORY, 9 (1942), 233-51; 10 (1943), 26-43.

        First part on life, education, and poems; second part on poems, with one-page comment on play.

906   George, Dorothy. "More Evidence on an Early Theatrical Withdrawal." AmN&Q, 2 (October 1942), 100-01.

        An unclear note which quotes a letter signed "S" (R.P. Smith?), dated 18 September 1826, stating that THE PRINCE OF PARTHIA was never performed.

907   Henderson, Archibald. "Thomas Godfrey, American Dramatist: Carolina Days." EVERYWOMAN'S MAGAZINE, 1 (August 1917), 19-24.

        Godfrey lived, 1759-63, in Wilmington, North Carolina.

908   Mayorga, Margaret G. A SHORT HISTORY OF THE AMERICAN DRAMA. See entry no. 150.

        Brief commentary on THE PRINCE OF PARTHIA (pp. 30-32).

909   Meserve, Walter J. AN EMERGING ENTERTAINMENT: THE DRAMA OF THE AMERICAN PEOPLE TO 1828. See entry no. 152.

        A discussion of Godfrey's contribution to American drama and analysis of THE PRINCE OF PARTHIA (pp. 47-51).

910   _____. AN OUTLINE HISTORY OF AMERICAN DRAMA. See entry no. 153.

        A plot summary and brief discussion of THE PRINCE OF PARTHIA (pp. 9-10).

911   Pollock, Thomas C. "Rowe's TAMERLANE and THE PRINCE OF PARTHIA." AL, 6 (1934), 158-62.

        A comparison to suggest influence of Rowe's play. Minor importance.

Thomas Godfrey

912   Quinn, Arthur Hobson. A HISTORY OF THE AMERICAN DRAMA FROM THE BEGINNING TO THE CIVIL WAR. See entry no. 163.

    A good commentary on THE PRINCE OF PARTHIA with quotations from the play (pp. 17, 21-27).

913   Seilhamer, George O. HISTORY OF THE AMERICAN THEATRE. 3 vols. Philadelphia: Globe Printing House, 1888-91.

    A discussion of Godfrey and THE PRINCE OF PARTHIA (I, 185-95).

914   Smith, William. "Thomas Godfrey." AMERICAN MAGAZINE, (1758), 602-04.

    An account by Godfrey's sponsor.

915   Tyler, Moses Coit, A HISTORY OF AMERICAN LITERATURE DURING COLONIAL TIMES. 2 vols. New York: G.P. Putnam Sons, 1879-81.

    A critical evaluation of Godfrey's work (II, 244-51).

916   Wolf, H.B. "Thomas Godfrey: Eighteenth Century Chaucerian." AL, 12 (1941), 486-90.

    Author comments on Chaucer as Godfrey's "spiritual master" and also mentions the strong influence of William Smith on Godfrey.

EDWARD HARRIGAN (1844-1911)

MAJOR PLAYS

OLD LAVENDER, 1877.
THE MULLIGAN GUARD BALL, 1879.
THE MULLIGAN GUARD NOMINEE, 1880.
CORDELIA'S ASPIRATIONS, 1883.
THE LEATHER PATCH, 1886.
WADDY GOOGAN, 1888.
REILLY AND THE FOUR HUNDRED, 1890.

PUBLISHED PLAYS

A. Plays in Anthologies

917   THE MULLIGAN GUARD BALL. In DRAMAS FROM THE AMERICAN THEATRE, 1762-1909. Ed. Richard Moody, pp. 535-65. See entry no. 108.

> The play is introduced with a balanced discussion of Harrigan's career and theories.

NONDRAMATIC WORKS

918   "Mr. Edward Harrigan Speaks." In "American Playwrights on the American Drama." See entry no. 422.

> A clear statement of Harrigan's theory of playwriting.

BIBLIOGRAPHY

919   See entries nos. 4, 12, 29, 33, 34, 45, 48, 938, 941.

Edward Harrigan

BIOGRAPHY AND CRITICISM

920   See entries nos. 140, 141, 150, 151, 153, 173.

921   "The Amusement Season." THEATRE, 3 May 1886, p. 193.
> A comment on the public enthusiasm for Harrigan's work.

922   Blake, W.S. "Edward Harrigan." In FAMOUS AMERICAN ACTORS OF TO-DAY. Eds. Frederic Edward McKay and Charles E.L. Wingate. New York: Thomas Y. Crowell, 1896, pp. 395-99.
> A brief but perceptive comment on Harrigan as actor and playwright.

923   "Career." NEW YORK DRAMATIC MIRROR, 14 June 1911, pp. 12-14.
> A brief survey of his career at Harrigan's death.

924   "Career and Death of Edward Harrigan." THEATRE, 14 (1911), 14.
> Obituary notice.

925   Davis, Richard Harding. "Edward Harrigan and the East Side." HARPER'S WEEKLY, 21 March 1891, p. 210.
> A review of REILLY AND THE 400 with detailed comments on the characters and their sources.

926   Eaton, Walter Pritchard. THE ACTOR'S HERITAGE. Boston: Atlantic Monthly Press, 1924.
> Brief but perceptive comments on Harrigan and Tony Hart (pp. 154, 214).

927   "Edward Harrigan." NEW YORK TIMES, 7 June 1911, p. 9.
> General and laudatory obituary notice.

928   "The Eloquence of Rags." NEW YORK WORLD, 18 November 1888, p. 5.
> An explanation of Dan Collyer's costume in OLD LAVENDER.

929   "Harrigan's Thirty-fifth Street Theatre." NEW YORK TIMES, 5 December 1890, p. 3.
> Although mainly on the theatre, this essay includes a statement on Harrigan's theory of actor-audience relations.

Edward Harrigan

930   Howells, William Dean. "Editor's Study." HARPER'S 73 (1886), 314-19; rpt. in THE AMERICAN THEATRE AS SEEN BY ITS CRITICS, 1752-1934. Eds. Montrose J. Moses and John Mason Brown, pp. 132-35. See entry no. 330.

> Concerned with realism in the drama, Howells enthusiastically endorses Harrigan's work and calls him the "American Goldoni."

931   _____. "Life and Letters." HARPER'S WEEKLY, 10 October 1896, pp. 997-98.

> Further praise of Harrigan by a major American critic.

932   Hutton, Laurence. CURIOSITIES OF THE AMERICAN STAGE. See entry no. 146.

> A brief comment on American audiences and Harrigan's plays (pp. 52-53).

933   "Interview with Harrigan." THEATRE, 31 March 1888, p. 157.

> Under the general heading "Entre Nous" (pp. 155-58), the reviewer quotes from an interview in the NEW YORK HERALD of the previous Sunday.

934   Kahn, E.J., Jr. THE MERRY PARTNERS: THE AGE AND STAGE OF HARRIGAN AND HART. New York: Random House, 1955.

> The only book-length study of Harrigan's work and period, marred by an uncritical approach and a complete lack of references and bibliography. Reprint of NEW YORKER material (see entry no. 935).

935   _____. "Profiles." NEW YORKER, 19 March 1955, pp. 42-64.; 26 March 1955, pp. 39-65; 2 April 1955, pp. 45-63; 9 April 1955, pp. 41-75.

> A series of essays on Harrigan, Tony Hart, and Irish theatre in New York during the last part of the nineteenth century.

936   Montgomery, G.E. "American Play-writer III, Edward Harrigan." THEATRE, 5 July 1886, pp. 397-98.

> Author praises Harrigan's "odd and out-of-the-way composition" and compares his work to the "logical sequence of Zola's novels."

937   Moody, Richard. "Edward Harrigan." MODERN DRAMA, 19 (1976), 319-25.

> A substantive modern assessment of Harrigan's playwriting.

Edward Harrigan

938   Moses, Montrose J. THE AMERICAN DRAMATIST. See entry no. 157.

       Moses sees Harrigan as a delineator of a special type of American comedy and one of the distinct figures in the late nineteenth-century drama (pp. 278-85).

939   _____. "Edward Harrigan." THEATRE ARTS, 10 (1926), 176-88.

       Moses calls Harrigan's plays a graphic record of contemporary life; includes scene from SQUATTER SOVEREIGNTY (pp. 185-88).

940   "Our Gallery of Players." ILLUSTRATED AMERICAN, 25 February 1893, pp. 240-42.

       A short biographical sketch with a portrait; general praise of Harrigan.

941   Quinn, Arthur Hobson. A HISTORY OF THE AMERICAN DRAMA FROM THE CIVIL WAR TO THE PRESENT DAY. See entry no. 164.

       A discussion of Harrigan's plays and their place in a developing American drama (pp. 82-96).

942   _____. "The Perennial Humor of the American Stage." YALE REVIEW, 16 (1927), 553-66.

       Mainly on Harrigan and Charles Hoyt. A discussion of the basic characteristics of their humor.

943   Spillane, Daniel. "Looking Backward." THEATRE, 13 July 1889, p. 362.

       Spillane comments on the plays of Denman Thompson, Harrigan, and Charles Hoyt.

944   Strang, Lewis C. PLAYERS AND PLAYS OF THE LAST QUARTER CENTURY. See entry no. 170.

       A commentary which tends to stress negative reaction (II, 130, 135-38.).

945   "Where American Drama Began." LITERARY DIGEST, 1 July 1911, pp. 20-21.

       On realistic drama with an emphasis upon the work of Harrigan and Hoyt.

JAMES A. HERNE (1839-1901)

MAJOR PLAYS

WITHIN AN INCH OF HIS LIFE (with Belasco), 1879.
THE MINUTE MEN OF 1774-75, 1886.
DRIFTING APART, 1888.
MARGARET FLEMING, 1890.
SHORE ACRES, 1892.
THE REVEREND GRIFFITH DAVENPORT, 1899.
SAG HARBOR, 1899.

PUBLISHED PLAYS

A. Collected Plays

946   THE EARLY PLAYS OF JAMES A. HERNE. Ed. Arthur H. Quinn. Vol. 7 of AMERICA'S LOST PLAYS. Ed. Barrett H. Clark. See entry no. 100.

> Contains WITHIN AN INCH OF HIS LIFE, THE MINUTE MEN OF 1774-1775, DRIFTING APART, THE REVEREND GRIFFITH DAVENPORT (Act IV only).

947   SHORE ACRES AND OTHER PLAYS BY JAMES A. HERNE. Ed. Mrs. James A. Herne. New York: S. French, 1928.

> Contains SHORE ACRES, SAG HARBOR, HEARTS OF OAK.

B. Plays in Anthologies

948   MARGARET FLEMING. In THE BLACK CROOK AND OTHER NINE-TEENTH CENTURY AMERICAN PLAYS. Ed. Myron Matlaw, pp. 455-510. See entry no. 107.

James A. Herne

949 MARGARET FLEMING. In REPRESENTATIVE AMERICAN PLAYS. Ed. Arthur Hobson Quinn, pp. 519-44. See entry no. 114.

950 MARGARET FLEMING. In SIX EARLY AMERICAN PLAYS, 1798-1900. Eds. William Coyle and Harry G. Damaser, pp. 273-313. See entry no. 102.

951 [THE REVEREND GRIFFITH DAVENPORT]. "Act III of 'Griffith Davenport,' with a Preparatory Note by Arthur Hobson Quinn and a Commentary by Julie A. Herne." AL, 24 (1952), 330-51.

>A very brief comment by Quinn; Julie, Herne's daughter, explains the purpose of act.

952 SHORE ACRES. In AMERICAN DRAMA. Ed. Alan S. Downer, pp. 48-105. See entry no. 100.

953 SHORE ACRES. In DRAMAS FROM THE AMERICAN THEATRE, 1762-1909. Ed. Richard Moody, pp. 672-720. See entry no. 108.

NONDRAMATIC WORKS

954 "Art for Truth's Sake in the Drama." ARENA, 17 (1897), 361-70; rpt. in AMERICAN DRAMA AND ITS CRITICS. Ed. Alan S. Downer, pp. 1-9 (see entry no. 384); rpt. in part in DISCUSSIONS OF MODERN AMERICAN DRAMA. Ed. Walter J. Meserve. Boston: D.C. Heath, 1965, pp. 127-28.

>Herne's credo concerning a realistic and truthful drama in contemporary society.

955 "Old Stock Days in the Theatre." ARENA, 6 (1892), 401-16.

>Essay contains some of Herne's reminiscences on theatre practices of the past.

BIBLIOGRAPHY

956 See entries nos. 4, 12, 29, 30, 33, 34, 45, 48, 967, 976, 987, 989, 994.

957 Perry, John. "Selected Bibliography on James A. Herne." BULLETIN OF BIBLIOGRAPHY, 31 (1974), 50, 53.

>Brief and selective, some inaccuracies.

James A. Herne

BIOGRAPHY AND CRITICISM

958   See entries nos. 119, 141, 145, 151, 170, 173, 1347.

959   Bucks, Dorothy S., and A.H. Nethercot. "Ibsen and Herne's MARGARET FLEMING: A Study of the Early Ibsen Movement in America." AL, 17 (1946), 311-33.

   Authors show the similarity between MARGARET FLEMING and GHOSTS and DOLL'S HOUSE and conclude that Herne's work was a consequence of discovery of Ibsen, not an independent creation.

960   _____. "A Reply to Professor Quinn." AL, 19 (1947), 177-80.

   Authors respond to an article by A.H. Quinn (see entry no. 993) that the memory of Herne's daughter, Julie, was not as reliable as contemporary evidence and still contend that Ibsen influenced Herne.

961   Clark, Barrett H. THE BRITISH AND AMERICAN DRAMA OF TO-DAY. See entry no. 876.

   An evaluation of Herne (pp. 228-32).

962   Corbin, John. "Drama." HARPER'S WEEKLY, 11 February 1899, p. 139; 4 March 1899, p. 217.

   Sympathetic and perceptive comments on THE REVEREND GRIFFITH DAVENPORT.

963   Dithmar, Edward A. "James A. Herne's MARGARET FLEMING." NEW YORK TIMES, 10 December 1891, p. 5; rpt. in THE AMERICAN THEATRE AS SEEN BY ITS CRITICS, 1752-1934. Eds. Montrose J. Moses and John Mason Brown, pp. 142-47. See entry no. 330. Also rpt. in THEATRE AND DRAMA IN THE MAKING. Eds. John Gassner and Ralph G. Allen. Boston: Houghton Mifflin, 1964, pp. 956-60.

   Dithmar terms the play the "quintessence of the commonplace."

964   "Drifting Apart; or, The Fisherman's Child." NEW YORK TIMES, 20 August 1941, p. 16.

   A modern review.

965   Edwards, Herbert J. "Herne, Garland, and Henry George." AL, 28 (1956), 359-67.

   On the basis of a relationship created during the writing of

SHORE ACRES, Edwards concludes that Herne's views on land speculation came from his own experience and that George had "little direct influence on his dramas."

966 _____. "Howells and Herne." AL, 22 (1951), 432-41.

Edwards chronicles Howells' reactions to Herne's plays and their planned work on dramatization of SILAS LAPHAM. He points out that Howells was the first important critic to understand what Herne was doing.

967 Edwards, Herbert J., and Julie A. Herne. JAMES A. HERNE: THE RISE OF REALISM IN THE AMERICAN DRAMA. Orono: University of Maine Press, 1964.

A general study of Herne and his work, based on his daughter's notes. Generally laudatory, it includes a bibliography.

968 Flower, B.O. "An Epoch-Marking Drama." ARENA, 4 (1891), 247-49.

Flower asserts that MARGARET FLEMING advances a beginning for American realism in thought and action.

969 _____. "Mask or Mirror; The Vital Difference between Artificiality and Veritism on the Stage." ARENA, 8 (1893), 304-13.

Essay explains Flower's concept of realism as rebellion against melodrama, with particular praise for SHORE ACRES.

970 Garland, Hamlin. "Mr. and Mrs. James A. Herne." ARENA, 4 (1891), 543-60.

A study of Herne's plays with particular emphasis upon the new theatrical aspects in MARGARET FLEMING.

971 _____. "On the Road with James A. Herne." CENTURY, 88 (1914), 573-81).

Praises of DRIFTING APART.

972 Garland, Hamlin, J.J. Enneking, and B.O. Flower. "An Appreciation: James A. Herne, Actor, Dramatist and Man." ARENA, 26 (1901), 282-91.

These three essays appear as eulogies at Herne's death. Garland's essay, "His Sincerity as a Playwright," emphasized Herne's high ideals; Enneking focused on idealism and realism in "Mr. Herne As I Knew Him;" Flower considered the influences upon him and Herne's success in "The Man and His Work."

James A. Herne

973 Garrison, L. McK. "Herne's MARGARET FLEMING." NATION, 14 May 1891, pp. 399-400.

> A perceptive view of performance in Chickering Hall.

974 Gillespie, Patti P. "James A. Herne: A Reassessment." PLAYERS, 51 (1975), 66-71.

> Author sees Herne's lack of "artistry of execution" as the basis of weak contribution to American drama; an evaluation on the basis of dramatic structure.

975 Hapgood, Norman. THE STAGE IN AMERICA: 1897-1900. See entry no. 746.

> Chapter II (pp. 61-79) treats "Our Two Ablest Dramatists"-- William Gillette and Herne.

976 Hatlen, Theodore. "The Development of James A. Herne as an Exponent of Realism in American Drama." Ph.D. dissertation, Stanford University, 1950.

> A chronological study of Herne's plays suggesting his development from melodrama to realism. Valuable.

977 _____. "MARGARET FLEMING and the Boston Independent Theatre." ETJ, 8 (1956), 17-21.

> Author argues that play stimulated thought of independent theatre in America.

978 Herne, Chrystal. "Some Memories of My Father." GREEN BOOK, 6 (1909), pp. 744-49.

979 Herron, Ima Honaker. THE SMALL TOWN IN AMERICAN DRAMA. See entry no. 140.

> For a careful discussion of several of Herne's plays as they fit into the thesis of this work see particularly pages 78-81, 179-86.

980 Howells, W.D. "Editor's Study." HARPER'S MONTHLY, 81 (1890), 153-54.

> Howells finds DRIFTING APART not completely satisfying but praises its naturalness.

981 _____. "Editor's Study." HARPER'S MONTHLY, 83 (1891), 476-79.

> Howells criticizes the preaching in MARGARET FLEMING but lauds the play, which he finds particularly American.

James A. Herne

982 _____. "A New Kind of Play." LITERATURE, 31 March 1899, pp. 256-66.

> Howells praises Herne's work, especially MARGARET FLEMING and finds GRIFFITH DAVENPORT best play of season.

983 "MARGARET FLEMING." CRITIC, 18 December 1891, pp. 352-53.

984 Meserve, Walter J. AN OUTLINE HISTORY OF AMERICAN DRAMA. See entry no. 153.

> For comments on Herne's realism, see pages 143-47; also other references.

985 Morton, Frederich. "James A. Herne." THEATRE ARTS, 24 (1940), 899-902.

> Morton argues, poorly, that Herne's influence was more important than his plays; he emphasizes SHORE ACRES which he considers to be Herne's best effort.

986 Moses, Montrose J. "James A. Herne and the Realistic Drama." BOOK NEWS MONTHLY, 26 (1908), 917-24.

> Part of a series on "Contemporary Drama and Dramatists, VII." Previews Moses' later assessment.

987 _____. "James A. Herne and the Realistic Drama." In his THE AMERICAN DRAMATIST, pp. 90-110. See entry no. 157.

> A study of Herne's contribution to American theatre and drama. Bibliography (pp. 109-110).

988 "Our Gallery of Players. CXXVII--James A. Herne." ILLUSTRATED AMERICAN, 20 January 1894, p. 60.

> A portrait and brief theatrical biography.

989 Perry, John. JAMES A HERNE, THE AMERICAN IBSEN. Chicago: Nelson-Hall, 1978.

> A study of Herne's life and accomplishments with reference to his friends, influences upon him, and the social and theatrical activities of his time. There is little analysis of the plays as theatre or literature, but despite a discursive style the book reads easily and has good notes.

990 Pizer, Donald. "An 1890 Account of MARGARET FLEMING." AL, 47 (1955), 264-67.

Pizer reprints "Mr. Herne's New Play" by Hamlin Garland, a review that first appeared in the BOSTON EVENING TRANSCRIPT, 8 July 1890, page 6. At that time the play had a different third act setting and radically different climactic action.

991 _____. "The Radical Drama in Boston, 1889-1891." NEQ, 31 (1958), 361-74.

Pizer considers Garland's A MEMBER OF THE THIRD HOUSE and Herne's MARGARET FLEMING and SHORE ACRES as concerned with social and moral problems which were not usually presented in the theatre at this time.

992 Poggi, Jack. THEATRE IN AMERICA, THE IMPACT OF ECONOMIC FORCES, 1870-1967. Ithaca, N.Y.: Cornell University Press, 1968.

A brief comment (pp. 102-04) on Herne's difficulties in getting MARGARET FLEMING on the stage.

993 Quinn, Arthur Hobson. "Ibsen and Herne--Theory and Fact." AL, 19 (1947), 171-77.

Quotes Julie Herne, Herne's daughter, to refute article by Bucks and Nethercot (see entry 959); for rebuttal by Bucks and Nethercot, see entry 960.

994 _____. "James A. Herne and the Realism of Characters." In his A HISTORY OF THE AMERICAN DRAMA FROM THE CIVIL WAR TO THE PRESENT DAY. I, 125-62. See entry no. 164.

A detailed criticism of Herne's plays.

995 _____, ed. THE LITERATURE OF THE AMERICAN PEOPLE. See entry no. 165.

Devotes pages 803-06 to Herne, his life, and his plays.

996 Robinson, Alice M. "James A. Herne and His 'Theatre Libre' in Boston." PLAYERS, 48 (1973), 202-09.

A good comment on the experiment in Chickering Hall, also subsequent productions of MARGARET FLEMING, Herne's relationship with Garland, and the idea for the Independent Theatre. Good study.

997 Saraceni, Gene A. "Herne and the Single Tax: An Early Plea for an Actor's Union." ETJ, 26 (1974), 315-25.

Saraceni relates Herne's politics to his concern for actors.

James A. Herne

998 Strang, Lewis C. "James A. Herne." In his FAMOUS ACTORS OF THE DAY IN AMERICA. Boston: L.C. Page, 1900, pp. 18-35.

>Concerned mainly with GRIFFITH DAVENPORT.

999 Tiempo, Marco. "James A. Herne in GRIFFITH DAVENPORT." ARENA, 22 (1899), 375-82.

>Author emphasizes realistic acting and playwriting for faithful interpretation of American life.

1000 Waggoner, Hyatt A. "The Growth of a Realist: James A. Herne." NEQ, 15 (1942), 62-73.

>Concerned with the influences upon Herne, particularly science and realism, Waggoner states that Herne matured before becoming aware of other naturalists.

1001 Willey, Malcolm. "James A. Herne's SAG HARBOR." LONG ISLAND FORUM, 2 (1948), 5-11.

>A stage history of the play with liberal quotes from newspaper critics and letters from Sag Harbor residents supporting truthfulness of the production.

1002 Wilson, J.H. "The Independent Theatre in Boston." HARPER'S WEEKLY, 7 November 1891, pp. 874-75.

>A description of MARGARET FLEMING production in Boston.

BRONSON HOWARD (1842-1908)

MAJOR PLAYS

SARATOGA, 1870.
THE BANKER'S DAUGHTER, 1878.
YOUNG MRS. WINTHROP, 1882.
ONE OF OUR GIRLS, 1885.
THE HENRIETTA, 1887.
SHENANDOAH, 1888.
ARISTOCRACY, 1892.

PUBLISHED PLAYS

A number of Howard's plays were privately printed during his lifetime.

A. Collected Plays

1003 THE BANKER'S DAUGHTER & OTHER PLAYS. Ed. Allan G. Halline. Vol. 10 of AMERICA'S LOST PLAYS. Ed. Barrett H. Clark. See entry no. 100.

> Contains HURRICANES, OLD LOVE LETTERS, THE BANKER'S DAUGHTER, BARON RUDOLPH, KNAVE AND QUEEN, ONE OF OUR GIRLS. Good bibliography of plays, works, and criticisms.

B. Plays in Anthologies

1004 THE BANKER'S DAUGHTER. In FAVORITE AMERICAN PLAYS OF THE NINETEENTH CENTURY. Ed. Barrett H. Clark, pp. 203-55. See entry no. 101.

Bronson Howard

1005 THE HENRIETTA. In AMERICAN PLAYS. Ed. Allan G. Halline, pp. 407-53. See entry no. 105.

1006 SHENANDOAH. In THE BLACK CROOK AND OTHER NINETEENTH-CENTURY AMERICAN PLAYS. Ed. Myron Matlaw, pp. 377-452. See entry no. 107.

1007 SHENANDOAH. In DRAMAS FROM THE AMERICAN THEATRE, 1762-1909. Ed. Richard Moody, pp. 575-609. See entry no. 108.

1008 SHENANDOAH. In REPRESENTATIVE AMERICAN PLAYS. Ed. Arthur Hobson Quinn, pp. 478-512. See entry no. 114.

1009 SHENANDOAH. In REPRESENTATIVE PLAYS BY AMERICAN DRAMATISTS. Ed. Montrose J. Moses, III, 355-445. See entry no. 111.

NONDRAMATIC WORKS

1010 "The American Drama." SUNDAY MAGAZINE (New York), 7 October 1906; rpt. in REPRESENTATIVE PLAYS BY AMERICAN DRAMATISTS. Ed. Montrose J. Moses, III, 364-70. See entry no. 111.

> A survey assessment of American dramatists and their critics since 1890 with attention to the influences of Ibsen and the general public.

1011 THE AUTOBIOGRAPHY OF A PLAY. Introd. Augustus Thomas. New York: Dramatic Museum of Columbia University, 1914. Rpt. in A LIBRARY OF AMERICAN LITERATURE FROM THE EARLIEST SETTLEMENT TO THE PRESENT TIME. Comp. Edmund Clarence Stedman and Ellen Mackay Hutchinson. New York: Charles L. Webster, 1889, pp. 121-27.

> First given as a lecture before the Shakespeare Club at Harvard College in March 1886 and repeated for the Nineteenth Century Club in New York, December 1889. Included in IN MEMORIAM (see entry no. 1033). A discussion of the creation and development of THE BANKER'S DAUGHTER with attention to Howard's theory of "The Laws of Dramatic Composition." Volume contains excellent notes by Brander Matthews.

1012 "Mr. Bronson Howard Illustrates and Defines." In "American Playwrights on the American Drama." See entry no. 422.

1013 "Our Schools for the Stage." CENTURY, 61 (1900), 25-37.

> Concerned with the "art of acting" and the theatre as a profession.

1014 "Trash on the Stage and the Lost Dramatists of America." In IN ME-MORIAM, BRONSON HOWARD, pp. 115. See entry no. 1033.

> In this lecture Howard indicates his practical views of the theatre, and expresses an optimistic view of American drama, which must come from professional dramatists rather than literary men.

BIBLIOGRAPHY

1015 See entries nos. 4, 12, 29, 33, 34, 45, 48, 1003, 1043.

BIOGRAPHY AND CRITICISM

1016 See entries nos. 141, 145, 150, 151, 170, 173, 370, 376.

1017 Archer, William. ENGLISH DRAMATISTS OF TODAY. London: Sampson Low, Marston, Searle & Rivington, 1882, pp. 209-10.

> Brief comment indicating Howard's reputation in England and the changes that may occur when American plays are transferred to English circumstance.

1018 Bloomfield, Maxwell. "Mirror for Businessmen: Bronson Howard's Melodramas, 1870-1890." MASJ, 5 (Fall 1964), 38-49.

> Author shows Howard's sentimental approach as a social critic to businessmen and their families; concludes that his plays are a "unique introduction to the Golden Age of Big Business."

1019 Boyle, Charles John. "Bronson Howard and the Popular Temper of the Gilded Age." Ph.D. dissertation, University of Wisconsin, 1957.

1020 Briscoe, Johnson. "The Pioneer American Dramatist." GREEN BOOK, 11 (1914), 749-56.

> A concern for the new development in American drama of which Howard is a leader.

1021 Clapp, J.B., and E.F. Edgett. PLAYS OF THE PRESENT. New York: Dunlap Society Publications, 1902.

> Theatre notices for ARISTOCRACY, THE HENRIETTA, SARATOGA, and SHENANDOAH.

1022 Clark, Barrett H. THE BRITISH AND AMERICAN DRAMA OF TO-DAY. See entry no. 876.

> A good account of Howard's work (pp. 219-27).

Bronson Howard

1023 _____. A STUDY OF THE MODERN DRAMA. See entry no. 839.

     Biographical information and critical comment with particular analysis of YOUNG MRS. WINTHROP (pp. 361-68).

1024 Dithmar, Edward A. "Bronson Howard's SHENANDOAH." NEW YORK TIMES, 10 September 1889; rpt. in THE AMERICAN THEATRE AS SEEN BY ITS CRITICS, 1752-1934. Eds. Montrose J. Moses and John Mason Brown, pp. 140-42. See entry no. 330.

1025 Felheim, Marvin. "Bronson Howard, 'Literary Attaché.'" AMERICAN LITERARY REALISM, 2 (1969), 174.

     A discussion of Howard's method of revision and his limited productivity.

1026 Ford, James L. "THE BANKER'S DAUGHTER." MUNSEY'S 34 (1905), 199-202.

     A favorable review of the play plus a brief survey of Howard's career.

1027 Ferrer, Lloyd A. "Bronson Howard: Dean of American Dramatists." Ph.D. dissertation, University of Iowa, 1971.

1028 Halline, Allan G. "Bronson Howard's THE AMATEUR BENEFIT." AL, 14 (1942), 74-76.

     A description of a typescript of a play found in the Library of Congress; not considered important. See Marshall's corrections to this study (entry no. 1035).

1029 Hamilton, Clayton. "Bronson Howard." BOOKMAN, 28 (1908), 55-56.

     A sensible assessment of an important but not superior dramatist who helped establish a comedy of manners and a drama of American life.

1030 Howells, W.D. "Editor's Study." HARPER'S MONTHLY, 73 (1886), 316.

     A review of ONE OF OUR GIRLS.

1031 _____. "Editor's Study." HARPER'S MONTHLY, 81 (1890), 152-157.

     A review of SHENANDOAH and comment on Howard.

1032 _____. "Editor's Study." HARPER'S MONTHLY, 133 (1916), 146-49.

     Essay contains Howells' final estimate of Howard with comments on American drama.

1033 IN MEMORIAM, BRONSON HOWARD. ADDRESSES DELIVERED AT THE MEMORIAL MEETING, OCTOBER 18, 1908, AT THE LYCEUM THEATRE. New York: Privately printed by the American Dramatists' Club, 1910.

> An important collection of essays that contains "An Appreciation" by Brander Matthews; "A Brief Biography" by Harry P. Mawson; "Among His Books" by John Ernest Warren; and two previously published lectures by Howard, "The Autobiography of a Play" (see entry no. 1006); and "Trash on the Stage and the Lost Dramatists of America" (see entry no. 1013). Inaccurate list of Howard's plays.

1034 Mabie, Hamilton W. "American Plays, Old and New." See entry no. 390.

> In a survey of contemporary dramatists, Mabie discusses Howard's plays on American business.

1035 Marshall, Thomas F. "Performances of Bronson Howard's THE AMATEUR BENEFIT." AL, 14 (1942), 311-12.

> Marshall supplements and corrects Halline's essay on the play produced as FOUR IN A GREEN ROOM (see entry no. 1028).

1036 Matthews, Brander. "Bronson Howard." NAR, 188 (1908), 504-13.

> A personal appreciation of Howard's "long and honorable" career with detailed comments on his plays. Includes letter from Howard insisting upon separation of drama from literature. Perceptive assessment.

1037 _____. "Bronson Howard." In his GATEWAYS TO LITERATURE, AND OTHER ESSAYS. New York: C. Scribner's Sons, 1912, pp. 279-96.

> A survey appreciation.

1038 _____, ed. PAPERS ON PLAYMAKING. New York: Hill and Wang, 1957.

> A commentary on THE BANKER'S DAUGHTER (pp. 25-42).

1039 Meserve, Walter J. AN OUTLINE HISTORY OF AMERICAN DRAMA. See entry no. 153.

> A brief survey of Howard's major contributions to American Drama (pp. 150-53).

1040 Montgomery, G.E. "Bronson Howard." THEATRE, 2 August 1886, pp. 469-70.

Part IV of a series entitled "Living American Dramatists." Mainly praises Howard for having reputation in London and New York.

1041 Moses, Montrose J. "Bronson Howard: Dean of the American Drama." In his THE AMERICAN DRAMATIST, pp. 73-89. See entry no. 157.

> Moses outlines Howards "significant position" as a playwright and theoretician and the man who founded the Dramatists' Club. Essay appeared first in SUNDAY MAGAZINE (New York), 7 October 1906.

1042 "The Plays of Bronson Howard." CENTURY, 3 (1883), 465-66.

> A brief but positive attitude toward Howard's originality, dramatic skill, use of dialogue, and general success in theatre.

1043 Quinn, Arthur Hobson. "Bronson Howard and the Establishment of Professional Playwriting." In his A HISTORY OF THE AMERICAN DRAMA FROM THE CIVIL WAR TO THE PRESENT DAY. I, 39-65. See entry no. 164.

> Quinn traces Howard's career with particular attention to THE BANKER'S DAUGHTER and includes a five-page quotation from "The Autobiography of a Play."

1044 Thomas, Augustus. "Bronson Howard." PROCEEDINGS OF THE AMERICAN ACADEMY OF ARTS AND LETTERS, 10 (November 1917), 56-57.

> A brief appreciation.

1045 Touse, J. Rankin. "Bronson Howard." BOOK BUYER, 16 (1893), 113-17.

> Writes comments on Howard's development as playwright but is not always accurate in biographical information.

1046 _____. "The Works of Bronson Howard." BOOKMAN, 10 (1899), 195.

> A brief reference to Howard's plays, of which he considers THE HENRIETTA the best.

WILLIAM DEAN HOWELLS (1837-1920)

MAJOR PLAYS

A COUNTERFEIT PRESENTMENT, 1877.
YORICK'S LOVE, 1878.
THE GARROTERS, 1885.
THE MOUSE TRAP, 1886.
FIVE O'CLOCK TEA, 1887.
THE UNEXPECTED GUESTS, 1893.

PUBLISHED PLAYS

A. Individual Titles

1047   THE ALBANY DEPOT. HARPER'S WEEKLY, 14 December 1889, pp. 989, supp. 1005-08; New York: Harper & Bros., 1892; Edinburgh: David Douglas, 1897; New York: Samuel French, 1921.

1048   BRIDE ROSES. HARPER'S MONTHLY, 37 (1893), 424-30; Boston: Houghton Mifflin, 1900.

1049   A COUNTERFEIT PRESENTMENT. ATLANTIC MONTHLY, 40 (1977), 148-61, 296-305, 448-60; Boston: James R. Osgood; Ticknor, 1877; Boston: Houghton Mifflin, 1880, 1905.

1050   THE ELEVATOR. HARPER'S MONTHLY, 70 (1884), 111-15; Boston: James R. Osgood; Ticknor, 1885; Boston: Houghton Mifflin, 1896, 1913.

1051   EVENING DRESS. COSMOPOLITAN, 13 (May 1892), 116-27; New York: Harper & Bros., 1893; Edinburgh: David Douglas, 1897; New York: Samuel French, 1921.

William Dean Howells

1052   FIVE O'CLOCK TEA. HARPER'S MONTHLY, 76 (1887), 86-96; New York: Harper & Bros., 1894; Edinburgh: David Douglas, 1897; New York: Samuel French, 1921.

1053   THE GARROTERS. HARPER'S MONTHLY, 72 (1885), 146-62; New York: Harper & Bros., 1886, 1894; Edinburgh: David Douglas, 1897; New York: Samuel French, 1921.

1054   HER OPINION OF HIS STORY. HARPER'S BAZAAR, 13 (1907), 429-37.

1055   THE IMPOSSIBLE, A MYSTERY PLAY. HARPER'S MONTHLY, 122 (1910), 116-25.

1056   AN INDIAN GIVER. HARPER'S MONTHLY, 94 (1897), 235-52; Boston: Houghton Mifflin, 1900.

1057   A LETTER OF INTRODUCTION. HARPER'S MONTHLY, 84 (1892), 243-56; New York: Harper & Bros., 1892; Edinburgh: David Douglas, 1897; New York: Samuel French, 1921.

1058   A LIKELY STORY. HARPER'S MONTHLY, 77 (1888), 26-38; New York: Harper & Bros., 1894; Edinburgh: David Douglas, 1897; New York: Samuel French, 1921.

1059   A MASTERPIECE OF DIPLOMACY. HARPER'S MONTHLY, 88 (1894), 371-85; CINCINNATI MEDICAL JOURNAL, 9 (1894), 79-92.

1060   THE MOTHER AND THE FATHER. HARPER'S MONTHLY, 100 (1900), 869-74; New York: Harper & Bros., 1909.

1061   THE MOUSE TRAP. HARPER'S MONTHLY, 74 (1886), 64-75; New York: Harper & Bros., 1894; Edinburgh: David Douglas, 1897; New York: Samuel French, 1921.

1062   THE NIGHT BEFORE CHRISTMAS. HARPER'S MONTHLY, 120 (1910), 207-16; in THE DAUGHTER OF THE STORAGE. New York: Harper & Bros., 1916, pp. 319-52.

1063   OUT OF THE QUESTION. ATLANTIC MONTHLY, 39 (1877), 195-208, 317-29, 447-61; Boston: James R. Osgood; Ticknor, 1877; Boston: Houghton Mifflin, 1905; in OUT OF THE QUESTION AND AT THE SIGN OF THE SAVAGE. Edinburgh: David Douglas, 1882.

1064 THE PARLOR CAR. ATLANTIC MONTHLY, 38 (1876), 290-300; Boston: James R. Osgood; Ticknor, 1876; Boston: Houghton Mifflin, 1889, 1901.

1065 PARTING FRIENDS. HARPER'S MONTHLY, 121 (1910), 670-77; New York: Harper & Bros., 1911; New York: Samuel French, 1921.

1066 A PREVIOUS ENGAGEMENT. HARPER'S MONTHLY, 92 (1895), 29-44; New York: Harper & Bros., 1897; New York: Samuel French, 1921.

1067 THE REGISTER. HARPER'S MONTHLY, 68 (1883), 70-86; Boston: James R. Osgood & Co., 1884; Boston: Ticknor, n.d.; Boston: Houghton Mifflin, 1899, 1903.

1068 ROOM FORTY-FIVE. FRANK LESLIE'S, 49 (December 1899), 132-148; Boston: Houghton Mifflin, 1900.

1069 SAMSON. New York: Charles D. Koppel, 1889.

1070 SAVED. HARPER'S WEEKLY, 26 December 1908, pp. 22-24.

1071 A SEA CHANGE; OR, LOVE'S STOWAWAY. Boston: James R. Osgood, 1884.

1072 SELF-SACRIFICE. HARPER'S MONTHLY, 122 (1911), 748-57; in THE DAUGHTER OF THE STORAGE. New York: Harper & Bros., 1916, pp. 283-316.

1073 THE SLEEPING CAR. HARPER'S CHRISTMAS (1882), 6-7; Boston: James R. Osgood; Ticknor, 1883; Houghton Mifflin, 1911; see entry no. 1097.

1074 THE SMOKING CAR. FRANK LESLIE'S, 47 (December 1898), 183-99; Boston: Houghton Mifflin, 1900.

1075 A TRUE HERO. HARPER'S MONTHLY, 119 (1909), 866-75.

1076 THE UNEXPECTED GUESTS. HARPER'S MONTHLY, 86 (1893), 211-25; New York: Harper & Bros., 1893; Edinburgh: David Douglas, 1897; New York: Samuel French, 1921.

B. Collected Plays

1077 THE COMPLETE PLAYS OF W.D. HOWELLS. Ed. and introd. Walter J. Meserve. New York: New York University Press, 1960.

William Dean Howells

Volume includes the texts of thirty-six plays, including one fragment, with a detailed description of the writing, production, and publication history of each play plus an annotated bibliography of the plays.

1078   A COUNTERFEIT PRESENTMENT AND THE PARLOR CAR. Edinburgh: David Douglas, 1882.

1079   MINOR DRAMAS. 2 vols. Edinburgh: David Douglas, 1907.

Volume I: THE PARLOR CAR, THE SLEEPING CAR, THE REGISTER, THE ELEVATOR, THE GARROTERS, THE MOUSE TRAP, FIVE O'CLOCK TEA, A LIKELY STORY, THE ALBANY DEPOT.

Volume II: A LETTER OF INTRODUCTION, THE UNEXPECTED GUESTS, EVENING DRESS, ROOM FORTY-FIVE, A PREVIOUS ENGAGEMENT, A MASTERPIECE OF DIPLOMACY, BRIDE ROSES, AN INDIAN GIVER, THE SMOKING CAR, HER OPINION OF HIS STORY.

1080   THE MOUSE TRAP AND OTHER FARCES. New York: Harper & Bros., 1889.

Contains THE GARROTERS, FIVE O'CLOCK TEA. THE MOUSE TRAP, A LIKELY STORY.

1081   THE PARLOR CAR AND THE SLEEPING CAR. Boston: Houghton Mifflin, 1918.

1082   THE SLEEPING CAR AND OTHER FARCES. Boston: Houghton Mifflin, 1889.

Contains THE PARLOR CAR, THE SLEEPING CAR, THE REGISTER, THE ELEVATOR.

C. Plays in Anthologies

1083   A LETTER OF INTRODUCTION. In DRAMAS FROM THE AMERICAN THEATRE, 1762-1909. Ed. Richard Moody, pp. 618-28. See entry no. 108.

1084   THE MOUSE TRAP. In BEST PLAYS OF THE EARLY AMERICAN THEATRE. Eds. John Gassner and Mollie Gassner, pp. 262-76. See entry no. 104.

NONDRAMATIC WORKS

1085   "The Ibsen Influence." HARPER'S WEEKLY, 27 April 1895, p. 390.

Prophesies great acceptance of Ibsenism, the "master who has more to say to our generation in the theatre than any other."

1086 "A Second Apparition of Ghosts." LITERATURE, 16 June 1899, pp. 529-30.

Sees artistry and social value in play.

1087 "A Question of Propriety." LITERATURE, 7 July 1899, p. 609.

Argues that public reaction to Ibsen's GHOSTS arises from American unfamiliarity with subject.

BIBLIOGRAPHY

1088 See entries nos. 4, 12, 29, 30, 31, 32, 33, 45, 48, 1077, 1097, 1106.

1089 Kirby, David K., comp. "William Dean Howells." In AMERICAN FICTION TO 1900: A GUIDE TO INFORMATION SOURCES. Ed. Kirby, pp. 146-48. See entry no. 722.

A basic bibliography of works, letters, bibliography, journals, biography.

BIOGRAPHY AND CRITICISM

1090 See entries nos. 137, 140, 150, 151, 157, 173.

1091 [Drake, Frank C.]. "William Dean Howells Helped This Young Man Write a Play." LITERARY DIGEST, 19 June 1920, pp. 56-58.

An unsigned reprint of Drake's essay in the NEW YORK HERALD, 30 May 1920, entitled "W.D. Howells' Kindly Help to a Young Writer a Score of Years Ago." Concerned with the dramatization of A HAZARD OF NEW FORTUNES.

1092 Dube, Anthony. "William Dean Howells' Theory and Practice of Drama." Ph.D. dissertation, Texas Tech College, 1967.

Howells' theory of drama seen as based largely on his concept of realism.

1093 Edwards, Herbert. "The Dramatization of The Rise of SILAS LAPHAM." NEQ, 30 (1957), 235-43.

Unaware of different versions of the dramatization in the Harvard Library, Edwards bases his study upon inadequate information.

1094   _____. "Howells and Herne." AL, 22 (1951), 432-41.

        Edwards is concerned in part with a proposed dramatization of SILAS LAPHAM.

1095   Hutton, Laurence. "Literary Notes." HARPER'S MONTHLY, 86 (1893), Supp. 3, 3.

        Comment on A LETTER OF INTRODUCTION.

1096   _____. "Literary Notes." HARPER'S MONTHLY, 94 (1897), Supp. I, 818.

        Comment on A PREVIOUS ENGAGEMENT.

1097   Kirk, Clara Marburg, and Rudolph Kirk. WILLIAM DEAN HOWELLS. New York: American Book Co., 1950; rev. ed., New York: Hill and Wang, 1961.

        A section in the introduction entitled "Dramatic Interlude" (pp. xciv-xcix) concludes that Howells did not take the drama seriously. Volume includes an excellent bibliography and the text of THE SLEEPING CAR.

1098   LIFE IN LETTERS OF WILLIAM DEAN HOWELLS. Ed. Mildred Howells. New York: Doubleday Press, 1928.

1099   Matthews, Brander. "Bret Harte and Mr. Howells as Dramatists." LIBRARY TABLE, 13 September 1877, p. 174.

        A brief comment on Howells' early stage success; rpt. in THE AMERICAN DRAMA AS SEEN BY ITS CRITICS, 1752-1934. Eds. Montrose J. Moses and John Mason Brown, pp. 147-48. See entry no. 330.

1100   _____. "Mr. Howells as a Critic." FORUM, 32 (1902), 636-38.

        Matthews sees Howells as "a man of a large nature and a transparent sincerity, liberal in his appreciation, loyal to his convictions, and little hampered by mere academic restructions."

1101   Meserve, Walter J. "'Colonel Sellers As a Scientist,' A Play by Mark Twain and W.D. Howells." MD, 1 (1958), 151-56.

        A detailed discussion of the creation of this play and the attempts of the authors to have it produced.

1102   _____. AN OUTLINE HISTORY OF AMERICAN DRAMA. See entry no. 153.

Volume includes discussions of Howells' realism, pages 140-43; social comedy, pages 238-41; and poetic drama, pages 192-93.

1103 _____. "The Plays of William Dean Howells." HOWELLS SENTINEL, No. 3 (1957), pp. 3-4.

A brief review of Howells' work as a dramatist.

1104 _____. "William Dean Howells and the Drama." Ph.D. dissertation, University of Washington, 1952.

1105 Perry, Thomas Sargent. "William Dean Howells." CENTURY, n.s. 1 (1888), 680-85.

Perry sees Howells' plays as light and delightful dramatic sketches.

1106 Quinn, Arthur Hobson. A HISTORY OF THE AMERICAN DRAMA FROM THE CIVIL WAR TO THE PRESENT DAY. See entry no. 164.

For a discussion of Howells' works, see pages 68-81.

1107 Shaw, Bernard. DRAMATIC OPINIONS AND ESSAYS. 2 vols. New York: Brentano's, 1925.

For Shaw's passing praise for A DANGEROUS RUFFIAN, the English title for THE GARROTERS, see Volume 1, pages 266-67.

1108 Tarkington, Booth. "Mr. Howells." HARPER'S MONTHLY, 141 (1920), 346-50.

Tarkington comments on the popularity of Howells' farces.

1109 Wagenknecht, Edward. WILLIAM DEAN HOWELLS, THE FRIENDLY EYE. New York: Oxford University Press, 1969.

Author makes reference to several of Howells' plays.

1110 "William Dean Howells." NAR, 212 (1920), 1-16.

Tributes to Howells on his seventy-fifth birthday dinner, 9 May 1912; includes Howells' assessment of the accomplishments of American drama.

CHARLES H. HOYT (1859-1900)

MAJOR PLAYS

A BUNCH OF KEYS, 1883.
A TEXAS STEER, 1890.
A TRIP TO CHINATOWN, 1891.
A TEMPERANCE TOWN, 1893.
A MILK WHITE FLAG, 1894.
A RUNAWAY COLT, 1895.

PUBLISHED PLAYS

A. Collected Plays

1111   FIVE PLAYS BY CHARLES HOYT. Ed. Douglas L. Hunt. Vol. 9 of AMERICA'S LOST PLAYS. Ed. Barrett H. Clark. See entry no. 100.

      Contains A BUNCH OF KEYS, A MIDNIGHT BELL, A TRIP TO CHINATOWN, A TEMPERANCE TOWN, A MILK WHITE FLAG.

B. Plays in Anthologies

1112   A TEMPERANCE TOWN. In DRAMAS FROM THE AMERICAN THEATRE, 1762-1909. Ed. Richard Moody, pp. 635-58. See entry no. 108.

1113   A TEXAS STEER. In REPRESENTATIVE AMERICAN DRAMAS, NATIONAL AND LOCAL. Ed. Montrose J. Moses, pp. 8-45. See entry no. 109.

1114   A TRIP TO CHINATOWN. In FAVORITE AMERICAN PLAYS OF THE NINETEENTH CENTURY. Ed. Barrett H. Clark, pp. 309-52. See entry no. 101.

BIBLIOGRAPHY

1115   See entries nos. 4, 12, 29, 45, 48, 108, 1123, 1127.

BIOGRAPHY AND CRITICISM

1116   See entries nos. 145, 150, 151, 382, 426, 942, 943.

1117   Brownell, Atherton. "Charles H. Hoyt." BOSTONIAN, 3 (January 1896), 386.

        Biographical.

1118   Hapgood, Norman. THE STAGE IN AMERICA, 1897-1900. See entry no. 136.

        A comment on "Broad American Humor" in Hoyt's A DAY AND A NIGHT IN NEW YORK (pp. 92-111).

1119   Herron, Ima Honaker. THE SMALL TOWN IN AMERICAN DRAMA. See entry no. 140.

        Numerous references to Hoyt's work as it reflects the writer's thesis. See particularly pages 138-40, 187-91.

1120   Howells, W.D. "Editor's Study." HARPER'S MONTHLY, 79 (1889), n.v., 317-18.

        On Denman Thompson and Charles Hoyt.

1121   _____. "Life and Letters." HARPER'S WEEKLY, 28 December 1895, p. 1236.

        A prudish reaction to A RUNAWAY COLT.

1122   Hunt, Douglas L. "Charles H. Hoyt: Playwright-Manager." THEATRE ANNUAL (1942), pp. 42-50.

        A discussion of Hoyt's work as writer-manager-producer, particularly during the 1883-1900 period. Most detailed analysis of A TRIP TO CHINATOWN.

1123   _____. THE LIFE AND WORK OF CHARLES H. HOYT. Nashville, Tenn.: Privately printed, 1945.

        A forty-page summary of his Ph.D. dissertation, Vanderbilt University, 1942. This is the most complete study to date of Hoyt's work and includes a good bibliography.

Charles H. Hoyt

1124 Meserve, Walter J. AN OUTLINE HISTORY OF AMERICAN DRAMA. See entry no. 153.

> A brief comment, mainly on A TEXAS STEER (pp. 190-91).

1125 Moses, Montrose J. THE AMERICAN DRAMATIST. Rev. ed. See entry no. 157.

> A brief note plus a partial list of plays and quotations from Hoyt's Preface to A BRASS MONKEY (pp. 286-87).

1126 Pearson, Harlan C. "Charles H. Hoyt." GRANITE MONTHLY, 17 (1894), 143-49.

> A good source for biographical information.

1127 Quinn, Arthur Hobson. A HISTORY OF THE AMERICAN DRAMA FROM THE CIVIL WAR TO THE PRESENT DAY. See entry no. 164.

> An assessment of Hoyt's contribution to American drama (pp. 96-104).

1128 _____. "The Perennial Humor of the American Stage." See entry no. 942.

> On Hoyt and Harrigan.

1129 Thomas, Augustus. THE PRINT OF MY REMEMBERANCE. New York: Scribner's Sons, 1922.

> Some personal reflections and comments on productions by a contemporary.

1130 _____. "Where American Drama Began." See entry no. 945.

> On the realistic drama of America with major attention to Hoyt and Harrigan.

HENRY JAMES (1843-1916)

MAJOR PLAYS

DAISY MILLER, 1882.
THE AMERICAN, 1890.
TENANTS, 1890.
DISENGAGED, 1892(?).
GUY DOMVILLE, 1893.
THE HIGH BID, 1907.
THE OTHER HOUSE, 1908.
THE OUTCRY, 1909.

PUBLISHED PLAYS

A. Collected Plays

1131　THE COMPLETE PLAYS OF HENRY JAMES. Ed. Leon Edel. Philadelphia: J.B. Lippincott, 1949.

>   Contains an essay entitled "Henry James: The Dramatic Years" (also published separately in Paris as HENRY JAMES: LES ANNÉES DRAMATIQUES) and the following plays: PYRAMUS AND THISBE, STILL WATERS, A CHANGE AT HEART, DAISY MILLER, THE AMERICAN, fragment of a new fourth act for THE AMERICAN, TENANTS, DISENGAGED, THE REPROBATE, GUY DOMVILLE, SUMMERSOFT, THE HIGH BID, rough outline for three acts founded on THE CHAPERON, THE SALOON, THE OTHER HOUSE, THE OUTCRY, and MONOLOGUE.

1132　THEATRICALS, TWO COMEDIES. London: Osgood, McInvain, 1894.

>   Includes TENANTS and DISENGAGED.

Henry James

1133   THEATRICALS: SECOND SERIES. New York: Harper & Brothers, 1895.
Includes THE ALBUM and THE REPROBATE.

NONDRAMATIC WORKS

1134   "Notes on the Theatres: New York, 1875." NATION, 11 March 1895, pp. 178-79. Rpt. in THE AMERICAN THEATRE AS SEEN BY ITS CRITICS, 1752-1934. Eds. Montrose J. Moses and John Mason Brown, pp. 122-26. See entry no. 330. Rpt. in Henry James's THE SCENIC ART: NOTES ON ACTING AND DRAMA, 1872-1901. Ed. Allan Wade, pp. 22-27 (New Brunswick, N.J.: Rutgers University Press, 1948).

BIBLIOGRAPHY

1135   See entries nos. 4, 12, 29, 30, 31, 32, 33, 45, 46, 1154.

1136   Kirby, David K., comp. "Henry James." In AMERICAN FICTION TO 1900: A GUIDE TO INFORMATION SOURCES. Ed. Kirby, pp. 163-64. See entry no. 722.

1137   Long, Robert Emmet, comp. "Adaptations of Henry James' Fiction for Drama, Opera, and Films; With a Checklist of New York Theatre Critics' Reviews." AMERICAN LITERARY REALISM, 4 (1971), 268-78.
List includes thirteen plays, two operas, and four films.

BIOGRAPHY AND CRITICISM

1138   See entries nos. 140, 153, 164, 165.

1139   Dupee, F.W. "Henry James and the Play." NATION, 8 July 1950, pp. 40-42.
Stimulated by Edel's collection (see entry no. 1131), Dupee discusses James's plays and playwriting in terms of his novels and short stories.

1140   Durham, F.H. "Henry James' Dramatization of his Novels." BULLETIN CITADEL, 6 (1942), 51-64.
A survey of the novels James adapted for the stage.

1141   Edel, Leon. "Henry James and THE OUTCRY." UNIVERSITY OF TORONTO QUARTERLY, 18 (1949), 340-46.

An expanded version of the introduction to THE OUTCRY that appeared in THE COMPLETE PLAYS (entry no. 1131).

1142   Egan, Michael. HENRY JAMES: THE IBSEN YEARS. New York: Barnes & Noble, 1972.

A brief study of James's interest and activity in the theatre and Ibsen's influence upon his work.

1143   Fergusson, Francis. "James' Idea of Dramatic Form." KENYON REVIEW, 5 (1943), 495-507. Rpt. in AMERICAN DRAMA AND ITS CRITICS. Ed. Alan S. Downer, pp. 177-87. See entry no. 384.

An excellent essay on James's concept of drama. Contends that theatre of the 1880s and the dramatic form demanded by producers and audiences thwarted James's success.

1144   Forbes, Elizabeth L. "Dramatic Lustrum: Study of the Effect of Henry James' Theatrical Experience on His Later Novels." NEQ, 11 (1938), 108-20.

Beginning with THE AWKWARD AGE, Forbes argues that "through the practice" of drama, James "perfected the novel."

1145   Hatcher, Joe B. "Shaw the Reviewer and James' GUY DOMVILLE." MD, 14 (1971), 331-34.

Hatcher briefly reiterates Shaw's explanation of the audience's bad manners and his admiration of James's attempt to write a meaningful play.

1146   "Henry James' Failure as a Dramatist Expressed by a London Critic." CURRENT OPINION, 63 (1917), 247.

Author sees James's power as a novelist contributing to his failure in the theatre and quotes from John F. Hope's caustic review of THE OUTCRY in the London NEW AGE.

1147   Kenton, Edna. "The 'Plays' of Henry James." THEATRE ARTS, 12 (1928), 347-52.

Kenton argues for James's success in "private playwriting," and has no sympathy for sentimental critics of James's career in theatre.

1148   Kirby, David K. "Henry James' THE OTHER HOUSE: From Novel to Play." MARKHAM REVIEW, 3 (1972), 49-53.

A good analysis, comparing and contrasting the different versions.

Henry James

1149 McElderry, Bruce R., Jr. "Henry James' Neglected Thriller: THE OTHER HOUSE." ARIZONA QUARTERLY, 8 (1952), 328-32.

> A rather indignant questioning as to why other James's novels and plays have been produced in theatres and not this excellent melodrama.

1150 Matthews, Brander. PLAYWRIGHTS ON PLAYMAKING. New York: Charles Scribner's Sons, 1923.

> Some scattered comments on James as a critic (pp. 189-203).

1151 Mendelsohn, Michael J. "'Drop a Tear . . .': Henry James Dramatizes DAISY MILLER." 7 (1964), 60-64.

> A good discussion of James's willingness and inept efforts to employ theatrical tricks in dramatizing a novel with the hope of securing a stage success.

1152 Popkin, Henry. "Pretender to the Drama." THEATRE ARTS, 33 (1949), 32-35, 91.

> A review of James's plays and his art as that of a novelist who wrote for a "special kind of theatre, the theatre of his reader's imagination."

1153 _____. "The Two Theatres of Henry James." NEQ, 24, (1951), 69-83.

> Popkin uses THE AMERICAN to illustrate (1) the commercial stage and (2) the theatre of his mind's eye, that "centre of consciousness" which was his ideal theatre.

1154 Stafford, William T., ed. "James' DAISY MILLER: The Story, The Play, The Critics." New York: Scribner's Research Anthologies, 1963.

> Stafford prints both play and story and provides study guide with contemporary reactions and fifteen later essays.

1155 Staub, August W. "The Well-Made Failures of Henry James." SSJ, 27 (1961), 91-101.

> Author notes James's inability to judge his audiences, his unhealthy theatrical philosophy, and his refusal to learn from other playwrights.

1156 Steer, Helen Vane. "Henry James on Stage: A Study of Henry James' Plays, and of Dramatizations by Other Writers Based on Works by James." Ph.D. dissertation, Louisiana State University, 1967.

1157 Wade, Allan. "Henry James as a Dramatic Critic." THEATRE ARTS, 27 (1943), 735-40.

    Author praises James's standards of criticism with reference to his London comments of plays, actors, the scenic art.

1158 Walbrook, H.H. "Henry James and the Theatre." LONDON MERCURY, 20 (1929), 612-16.

    James' experiences in theatre.

1159 Wyld, L.D. "Drama vs. the Theatre in Henry James." FOUR QUARTERS, 7 (1958), 17-23.

    A good essay on James as closet dramatist, who felt that "an acted play is a novel intensified."

JAMES MORRISON STEELE MacKAYE (1842-94)

MAJOR PLAYS

ROSE MICHEL, 1875.
WON AT LAST, 1877.
HAZEL KIRKE, 1879.
PAUL KAUVAR, 1887.
AN ARRANT KNAVE, 1889.
THE WORLD FINDER, 1894.

PUBLISHED PLAYS

A. Individual Titles

1160   A FOOL'S ERRAND. Ed. Dean H. Keller. Metuchen, N.J.: Scarecrow Press, 1969.

        Written in collaboration with Allen W. Tourgee.

B. Collected Plays

1161   AN ARRANT KNAVE & OTHER PLAYS. Ed. Percy MacKaye. Vol. 11 of AMERICA'S LOST PLAYS. Ed. Barrett H. Clark. See entry no. 100.

        Contains ROSE MICHEL, WON AT LAST, IN SPITE OF ALL, AN ARRANT KNAVE.

C. Plays in Anthologies

1162   HAZEL KIRKE. In REPRESENTATIVE AMERICAN PLAYS. Ed. Arthur Hobson Quinn, pp. 439-71. See entry no. 114.

James Morrison Steele MacKaye

1163   PAUL KAUVAR. In REPRESENTATIVE PLAYS BY AMERICAN DRAMATISTS. Ed. Montrose J. Moses. III, 235-354. See entry no. 111.

NONDRAMATIC WORKS

1164   "Steele MacKaye." In "American Playwrights on the American Drama." See entry no. 422.

> Largely concerned with stage settings that MacKaye regarded as "the most pleasing feature" of contemporary American drama.

BIBLIOGRAPHY

1165   See entries nos. 4, 12, 29, 33, 45, 48, 1161, 1178, 1180.

BIOGRAPHY AND CRITICISM

1166   See entries nos. 141, 145, 150, 151, 173, 370.

1167   C.G.S. "Artists, Idealists and Steele MacKaye." MASK, 14 (1928), 22-23.

> An experimenter but less an artist than idealist who lacked a powerful vision.

1168   Curry, Wade. "Steele MacKaye: Producer and Director." ETJ, 18 (1966), 210-15.

> A good study to read with EPOCH (see entry no. 1173). Includes biographical material and descriptions of photographs in Dartmouth College's MacKaye Collection.

1169   Dickinson, T.H. "Epic of the World Finder." VIRGINIA QUARTERLY REVIEW, 4 (1928), 275-78.

> A review of EPOCH to which the critic adds his appreciation of MacKaye.

1170   Eaton, Walter P. "Steele MacKaye, or The Dreamer Delivered." THEATRE ARTS, 11 (1927), 827-37.

> An essay review of EPOCH, listing MacKaye's accomplishments and concluding that success in the theatre requires money.

James Morrison Steele MacKaye

1171 Grover, Osgood Edwin. ANNALS OF AN ERA: PERCY MACKAYE AND THE MACKAYE FAMILY, 1826-1932. Washington, D.C.: Pioneer Press, 1932.

> A useful catalog of material in MacKaye Collection at Dartmouth College plus commentary, mainly on Percy MacKaye, Steele MacKaye's son.

1172 Mackaye, Arthur Loring. "The Biography of Steele MacKaye." LOS ANGELES TIMES, 23 October 1927.

> A positive review of EPOCH by half-brother of author.

1173 MacKaye, Percy. EPOCH: THE LIFE OF STEELE MACKAYE, GENIUS OF THE THEATRE, IN RELATION TO HIS TIMES AND CONTEMPORARIES. 2 vols. New York: Boni and Liveright, 1927.

> An extensive and indispensible work for any study of MacKaye. It is, however, an enthusiastic homage to a father by his son and clearly lacks critical balance.

1174 _____. "Steele MacKaye, Dynamic Artist of the American Theatre, an Outline of this Life-Work." DRAMA, 1 (November 1911), 138-61; 2 February 1912), 153-73.

> MacKaye's sympathetic view of his father as a teacher, organizer, actor, dramatist, and director. Uses newspaper accounts and frequently quotes his father.

1175 Meserve, Walter J. AN OUTLINE HISTORY OF AMERICAN DRAMA. See entry no. 153.

> A discussion of HAZEL KIRKE (pp. 137-39).

1176 Moody, Richard. AMERICA TAKES THE STAGE. See entry no. 155.

> Moody points out MacKaye's tendencies toward romanticism, particularly in spectacle (pp. 228-32).

1177 Moses, Montrose J. THE AMERICAN DRAMATIST. See entry no. 157.

> Mainly concerned (pp. 333-45) with MacKaye as a man of the theatre but notes his various playwriting ventures and his success with HAZEL KIRKE.

1178 Quinn, Arthur Hobson. A HISTORY OF AMERICAN DRAMA FROM THE CIVIL WAR TO THE PRESENT DAY. See entry no. 164.

> Passing reference to MacKaye's plays and life in the theatre (I, 126-27).

James Morrison Steele MacKaye

1179 Spillane, Daniel. "Paul Kauvar." THEATRE MAGAZINE, 16 January 1888, p. 25.

    Author defends playwright and play against adverse criticism.

1180 "Steele MacKaye." ENCICLOPEDIA DELLO SPETTACOLO. Rome: Casa Ed. le Maschere, 1954-62. VIII, 349-50.

    A good account with bibliography. In Italian.

1181 "Steele MacKaye Dead." NEW YORK TIMES, 26 February 1894, pp. 1-2.

    Inaccurate and patronizing obituary.

1182 Wheeler, A.C. [Nym Crinkle]. "Steele MacKaye's PAUL KAUVAR." WORLD, 19 February 1888; rpt. in THE AMERICAN THEATRE AS SEEN BY ITS CRITICS, 1752-1934. Eds. Montrose J. Moses and John Mason Brown, pp. 135-40. See entry no. 330.

    On MacKaye as actor and playwright.

ROBERT MUNFORD (ca. 1737-83)

MAJOR PLAYS

THE CANDIDATES, 1770-71(?).
THE PATRIOTS, 1777-79.

PUBLISHED PLAYS

A. Individual Titles

1183 [THE CANDIDATES]. "Robert Munford's THE CANDIDATES; or, The Humours of a Virginia Election." WILLIAM AND MARY QUARTERLY, 3rd Ser. 5 (1948), 217-57.

    Edited with an introduction by Jay B. Hubbell and Douglas Adair.

1184 [THE PATRIOTS]. "Robert Munford's THE PATRIOTS." WILLIAM AND MARY QUARTERLY, 3rd Ser. 6 (1949), 437-502.

    Edited with an introduction by Courtlandt Canby.

B. Collected Plays

1185 A COLLECTION OF PLAYS AND POEMS, BY THE LATE COLONEL ROBERT MUNFORD, OF MECKLENBURG, IN THE STATE OF VIRGINIA. Petersburg, Va.: N.p., 1798.

    Contains THE CANDIDATES and THE PATRIOTS.

C. Plays in Anthologies

1186 THE CANDIDATES. In DRAMAS FROM THE AMERICAN THEATRE, 1752-1909. Ed. Richard Moody, pp. 11-26. See entry no. 108.

    Substantial introduction.

1187 THE PATRIOTS. In TRUMPETS SOUNDING: PROPAGANDA PLAYS OF THE AMERICAN REVOLUTION. Ed. Norman Philbrick, pp. 265-337. See entry no. 113.

BIBLIOGRAPHY

1188 See entries nos. 4, 12, 29, 48, 1193.

BIOGRAPHY AND CRITICISM

1189 See entries nos. 133, 140, 150, 151, 153, 155, 173.

1190 Baine, Rodney M. ROBERT MUNFORD, AMERICA'S FIRST COMIC DRAMATIST. Athens: University of Georgia Press, 1967.

> The only book-length study. Baine is better as an historian-biographer than as a critic of drama, but he discusses each of the plays and corrects past errors of fact.

1191 Lynn, Kenneth. MARK TWAIN AND SOUTHWESTERN HUMOR. Boston: Little, Brown, 1959.

> Chapter 3, "The Politics of a Literary Movement," considers Munford's contribution to the traditional humor of the Southwest before Mark Twain.

1192 Meserve, Walter J. AN EMERGING ENTERTAINMENT: THE DRAMA OF THE AMERICAN PEOPLE TO 1828. See entry no. 152.

> A discussion of Munford's plays and their place in the development of American drama (pp. 85-89).

1193 Quinn, Arthur Hobson. A HISTORY OF THE AMERICAN DRAMA FROM THE BEGINNING TO THE CIVIL WAR. See entry no. 163.

> A discussion of Munford's two plays (pp. 54-56).

MORDECAI M. NOAH (1785-1851)

MAJOR PLAYS

THE WANDERING BOYS, 1812, 1815.
SHE WOULD BE A SOLDIER, 1819.
THE SIEGE OF TRIPOLI, 1820.
THE GRECIAN CAPTIVE, 1822.

PUBLISHED PLAYS

A. Individual Titles

1194 THE FORTRESS OF SORRENTO. New York: D. Longworth, 1808.

1195 THE GRECIAN CAPTIVE. New York: E.M. Murden, 1822.

1196 MARION; OR, THE HERO OF LAKE GEORGE. New York: E.M. Murden, 1822.

1197 SHE WOULD BE A SOLDIER. New York: Longworth's Dramatic Repository, 1819.

1198 THE WANDERING BOYS. Boston: Richardson and Lord, 1821.

B. Plays in Anthologies

1199 SHE WOULD BE A SOLDIER. In DRAMAS FROM THE AMERICAN THEATRE, 1762-1909. Ed. Richard Moody, pp. 123-42. See entry no. 108.

1200 SHE WOULD BE A SOLDIER. In REPRESENTATIVE PLAYS BY AMERICAN DRAMATISTS. Ed. Montrose J. Moses. I, 629-78. See entry no. 111.

NONDRAMATIC WORKS

1201 GLEANINGS FROM A GATHERED HARVEST. New York: C. Wells, 1845; H. Long & Brothers, 1847.

    Later published as A LITERARY BIOGRAPHY OF MORDECAI MANUEL NOAH with an introduction by G.A. Kohut (Baltimore: N.p., 1897).

BIBLIOGRAPHY

1202 See entries nos. 4, 12, 29, 45, 48, 1210.

BIOGRAPHY AND CRITICISM

1203 See entries nos. 133, 135, 139, 143, 151, 153, 155, 234.

1204 Dunlap, William. HISTORY OF THE AMERICAN THEATRE. See entry no. 131.

    Contains a long letter from Noah describing his playwriting activity (II, 316-24).

1205 Goldberg, Isaac. MAJOR NOAH: AMERICAN-JEWISH PIONEER. Philadelphia: Jewish Publication Society of America, 1936; New York: Knopf, 1937.

    Standard biography of the man and his work; Chapter VIII includes discussions entitled "Footlights," and "Dramaturge D'occasion."

1206 Lockwood, Samuel. "Major M.M. Noah." LIPPINCOTT'S, 1 (1868), 665-70.

    A verbose eulogy, dealing with Noah's religion and politics plus a brief note stating that Noah was a "dramatist (or rather playwright)."

1207 Makover, Abraham B. MORDECAI M. NOAH--HIS LIFE AND WORK. New York: Bloch Publishing Co., 1917.

    Slight volume (96 p.) with emphasis on Jewish aspects of life and work; little relevance to the drama.

1208 Mayorga, Margaret G. A SHORT HISTORY OF THE AMERICAN DRAMA. See entry no. 150.

    A discussion of SHE WOULD BE A SOLDIER (pp. 83-85).

Mordecai M. Noah

1209 Meserve, Walter J. AN EMERGING ENTERTAINMENT: THE DRAMA OF THE AMERICAN PEOPLE TO 1828. See entry no. 152.

> An analysis of major plays with the emphasis upon their part in a growing American drama and Noah's admitted amateur standing (pp. 207-08, 253-56).

1210 Quinn, Arthur Hobson. A HISTORY OF THE AMERICAN DRAMA FROM THE BEGINNING TO THE CIVIL WAR. See entry no. 163.

> Commentary on Noah's war plays; discusses the background of his adaptations and gives production information (pp. 151-53, 193-94).

1211 Smith, Sol. THEATRICAL MANAGEMENT IN THE WEST AND SOUTH FOR THIRTY YEARS. New York: Harper & Brothers, 1868.

> Includes a letter (p. 205) from Noah to Smith with Smith's comment; Smith and Noah were old friends.

1212 Spitz, Leon. "Pioneers of the American Theatre." AMERICAN HEBREW, 8 September 1950, pp. 75, 78-79, 82.

1213 Wilson, Garff B. THREE HUNDRED YEARS OF AMERICAN DRAMA AND THEATRE. See entry no. 173.

> A brief comment on SHE WOULD BE A SOLDIER (pp. 110-11).

1214 Wolf, S. MORDECAI MANUEL NOAH. Philadelphia: n.p., 1897.

> Early biography.

JOHN HOWARD PAYNE (1791-1852)

MAJOR PLAYS

THE MAID AND THE MAGPIE, 1815.
THE TRAGEDY OF BRUTUS, 1818.
THÉRÈSE, THE ORPHAN OF GENEVA, 1821.
CLARI; OR THE MAID OF MILAN, 1823.
CHARLES THE SECOND, 1824.
RICHELIEU, 1826.

PUBLISHED PLAYS

A. Individual Titles

Payne's plays appeared in innumerable editions and issues; the following are selective.

1215   ACCUSATION. London: C. Chapple, 1817; Boston: West, Richardson & Lord, 1818.

1216   ADELINE. New York: E.M. Murden, 1822; London: J. Tabby, 1827.

1217   ALI PACHA. London: J. Cumberland, n.d., 1826; New York: E.M. Murden, 1823.

1218   THE BOARDING SCHOOL. New York: N.p., 1841.

1219   BRUTUS. London: Richard White; John Cumberland; T. Rodwell, 1818; New York: D. Longworth, 1819, 1821; Baltimore: J. Robinson, 1819.

John Howard Payne

1220   CHARLES THE SECOND. London: Longman, Hurst, Rees, Orme, Brown, and Green, 1824; J. Cumberland; Thomas Dolby, 1825; New York: French, n.d.; W. Taylor & Co., 18?; Philadelphia: Neal & MacKenzie, 1829.

1221   CLARI. London: John Miller; New York: Circulating Library and Dramatic Depository, 1823.

1222   JULIA. New York: D. Longworth, 1806.

1223   LOVERS' VOWS. New York: D. Longworth; Baltimore: Geo. Dobbin and Murphy, 1809.

1224   RICHELIEU. New York: E. Murden, 1826.

1225   THÉRÈSE. London: J. Tabby; New York: Thomas Longworth; Murden and Thomsen, 1821.

B. Collected Plays

1226   THE LAST DUEL IN SPAIN & OTHER PLAYS. Ed. Codman Hislop and W.R. Richardson. Vol. 6 of AMERICA'S LOST PLAYS. Ed. Barrett H. Clark. See entry no. 100.

       Contains THE LAST DUEL IN SPAIN, WOMAN'S REVENGE, THE ITALIAN BRIDE, ROMULUS, THE SHEPHERD KING, THE BLACK MAN. Slight introduction.

1227   TRIAL WITHOUT JURY & OTHER PLAYS. Ed. Codman Hislop and W.R. Richardson. Vol. 5 of AMERICA'S LOST PLAYS. Ed. Barrett H. Clark. See entry no. 100.

       Contains TRIAL WITHOUT JURY; OR, THE MAGPIE AND THE MAID, MOUNT SAVAGE, THE BOARDING SCHOOLS, THE TWO SONS-IN-LAW, MAZEPPA, THE SPANISH HUSBAND. Brief introduction.

C. Plays in Anthologies

1228   BRUTUS. In NEW YORK DRAMA, A CHOICE COLLECTION OF TRAGEDIES, COMEDIES, FARCES, COMEDIETTAS, ETC. I, no. 5, 1-15. See entry no. 112.

1229   BRUTUS. In REPRESENTATIVE PLAYS BY AMERICAN DRAMATISTS. Ed. Montrose J. Moses, II, 87-175. See entry no. 111.

John Howard Payne

1230 CHARLES II. In BEST PLAYS OF THE EARLY AMERICAN THEATRE. Eds. John Gassner and Mollie Gassner, pp. 73-96. See entry no. 104.

> Listed as written by Payne-Irving.

1231 CHARLES THE SECOND. In NEW YORK DRAMA, A CHOICE COLLECTION OF TRAGEDIES, COMEDIES, FARCES, COMEDIETTAS, ETC. II, no. 19, 1-13. See entry no. 112.

1232 CHARLES THE SECOND. In REPRESENTATIVE AMERICAN PLAYS. Ed. Arthur Hobson Quinn, pp. 145-64. See entry no. 114.

1233 THÉRÈSE, THE ORPHAN OF GENEVA. In AMERICAN DRAMA. Vol. 19 of THE DRAMA. Ed. Alfred Bates, pp. 149-94. See entry no. 96.

BIBLIOGRAPHY

1234 See entries nos. 4, 29, 33, 45, 48, 1247, 1259, 1261, 1265.

1235 Heartman, C.F., and H.B. Weiss. "John Howard Payne: A Bibliography." AMERICAN BOOK COLLECTOR, 3 (1933), 55-57, 181-84, 224-28, 305-07; 4 (1933), 27-29, 78-82.

BIOGRAPHY AND CRITICISM

1236 See entries nos. 119, 133, 140, 141, 145, 150, 151, 155, 173.

1237 Bass, Althea. "From the Notebook of John Howard Payne." FRONTIER & MIDLAND, 14 (1934), 139-46.

> Bass is concerned with journals Payne edited and the one he proposed to edit, JAM JEHAN NIMA, after he returned to America.

1238 Blakeley, Sidney H. "John Howard Payne's THESPIAN MIRROR, New York's First Theatrical Magazine." STUDIES IN PHILOLOGY, 46 (1949), 577-607.

> A thorough study of Payne's editorship; generous quotations.

1239 Boulter, E. Merton. "John Howard Payne's Visit to Georgia." GEORGIA HISTORICAL QUARTERLY, 46 (1962), 333-76.

> Biographical.

John Howard Payne

1240   Brainard, Charles H. JOHN HOWARD PAYNE, A BIOGRAPHICAL SKETCH OF THE AUTHOR OF "HOME, SWEET HOME" WITH A NARRATIVE OF THE REMOVAL OF HIS REMAINS FROM TUNIS TO WASHINGTON. Boston: Cupples, Upham; Washington, D.C.: George A. Coolidge, 1885.

> Sketchy, anecdotal and brief; seventy pages.

1241   Chiles, Rosa P. "John Howard Payne, American Poet, Actor, Playwright, Consul and Author of 'Home, Sweet Home.'" COLUMBIA HISTORICAL SOCIETY RECORDS, 31-32 (1930), 209-97.

> A general biographical approach.

1242   DeBaillou, Clemens, ed. JOHN HOWARD PAYNE TO HIS COUNTRYMEN. Athens: University of Georgia Press, 1961.

> Payne's Cherokee interests with explanatory introduction by editor.

1243   Fay, Theodore Sedgwick. "A Sketch of the Life of John Howard Payne." NEW YORK MIRROR, 24 November 1832, pp. 161-63; 1 December 1832, pp. 169-73.

> Valuable contemporary account reprinted as A SKETCH OF THE LIFE OF JOHN HOWARD PAYNE (Boston: N.p., 1833).

1244   Gilbert, Vedder Morris. "The Stage Career of John Howard Payne, Author of "Home, Sweet Home." NORTHWEST OHIO QUARTERLY, 23 (Winter 1950-51), 59-74.

> General review of Payne's acting. Good bibliography.

1245   Grimsted, David. MELODRAMA UNVEILED. AMERICAN THEATRE AND CULTURE, 1800-1850. See entry no. 135.

> Numerous references to Payne's work.

1246   Hanson, Willis T., Jr. THE EARLY LIFE OF JOHN HOWARD PAYNE WITH CONTEMPORARY LETTERS HERETOFORE UNPUBLISHED. Boston: Bibliophile Society, 1913.

> Concerned with Payne's editing, his time at Union College, and his acting career in America; ends in 1813. Excerpts from the THESPIAN MIRROR, a journal which Payne edited.

1247   Harrison, Gabriel. JOHN HOWARD PAYNE, DRAMATIST, POET, ACTOR, AND AUTHOR OF "HOME, SWEET HOME!" HIS LIFE AND WRITINGS. Rev. ed. Philadelphia: J.B. Lippincott, 1885.

> An early but still valuable biography. Reprints Payne's JUVENILE POEMS.

John Howard Payne

1248 Hutton, Laurence. "John Howard Payne, the Actor." MAGAZINE OF AMERICAN HISTORY, 9 (1883), 335-39.

> Sketchy comment on Payne as actor, judging him "careless and indifferent," and his tours in America and England.

1249 Leary, Lewis, and Arlin Turner. "John Howard Payne in New Orleans." LOUISIANA HISTORICAL QUARTERLY, 31 (1948), 110-22.

> Biographical.

1250 Luquer, Thatcher, T. Payne. "Correspondence of Washington Irving and John Howard Payne." SCRIBNER'S, 48 (1910), 461-82, 597-616.

> The first publication of this Irving-Payne correspondence with a comment on their collaboration by Payne's grandnephew. Most correspondence is from Irving to Payne.

1251 _____. "When Payne Wrote 'Home, Sweet Home!': Letters from Paris, 1822-1823." SCRIBNER'S, 58 (1915), 742-54.

1252 _____. "Writing a Play in a Debtor's Prison." SCRIBNER'S, 69 (1921), 66-81, 237-46.

> Diary excerpts edited by Luquer; detailed daily notes by Payne.

1253 MacDougall, A.R. "John Howard Payne (1791-1852)." AMERICANA, 33 (1939), 463-75.

> Biographical; quotations from diaries and letters; written as WPA Writers' Project.

1254 MEMOIRS OF JOHN HOWARD PAYNE, THE AMERICAN ROSCIUS: WITH CRITICISMS OF HIS ACTING, IN VARIOUS THEATRES OF AMERICA, ENGLAND AND IRELAND. London: N.p., 1815.

> On early life of Payne; chiefly a reprint of articles, especially Fay's accounts in the NEW YORK MIRROR (see entry no. 1243).

1255 Meserve, Walter J. AN EMERGING ENTERTAINMENT: THE DRAMA OF THE AMERICAN PEOPLE TO 1828. See entry no. 152.

> An assessment of Payne's contribution to a developing American drama (pp. 280-90).

1256 _____. AN OUTLINE HISTORY OF AMERICAN DRAMA. See entry no. 153.

> General comments; analysis of BRUTUS (pp. 54-56).

John Howard Payne

1257 Morris, Muriel. "Mary Shelley and John Howard Payne." LONDON MERCURY, 22 (1930), 443-50.

> Concerned with details of their romance.

1258 Moses, Montrose J. THE AMERICAN DRAMATIST. See entry no. 157.

> A general survey of acting and playwriting (pp. 122-29).

1259 Overmeyer, Grace. AMERICA'S FIRST HAMLET. New York: New York University Press, 1957.

> A biography. Bibliography. Good manuscript sources.

1260 _____. "The Baltimore Mobs and John Howard Payne." MARYLAND HISTORICAL MAGAZINE, 18 (1963), 54-61.

> Concerned with Payne's acting experiences in Baltimore.

1261 Quinn, Arthur Hobson. "John Howard Payne and the Foreign Plays, 1805-1825." In his A HISTORY OF THE AMERICAN DRAMA FROM THE BEGINNING TO THE CIVIL WAR, pp. 163-87. See entry no. 163.

> Life and work; particularly good analysis of BRUTUS.

1262 Saxon, Arthur H. "John Howard Payne, Playwright with a System." THEATRE NOTES, 24 (1969-70), 79-84.

> A discussion of Payne as an adapter of plays with commentary on his connections with British theatre, 1813-32.

1263 Skloot, Robert. "John Howard Payne: The Early Years." SYMPOSIUM (Union College), 5 (Summer 1966), 12-15.

> Writing with affection for Union College which Payne attended, Skloot discusses Payne's years prior to 1813.

1264 Stearns, B.M. "John Howard Payne as an Editor." AL, 5 (1933), 215-28.

> An assessment of this aspect of Payne's career.

1265 Trinka, Zdena. HOME, SWEET HOME. New York: International Book Publishers, 1942.

> The story of Payne's trip to and his life in North Africa. Little on playwriting. Bibliography.

1266 Wegelin, Oscar. THE WRITINGS OF JOHN HOWARD PAYNE. Greenwich, Conn.: Literary Collector Press, n.d.; rpt. from LITERARY COLLECTOR, March 1905.

1267 Wilkins, Thurman. "John Howard Payne: Friend of the Cherokees."
COLUMBIA LIBRARY COLUMNS, 12 November 1962), 3-11.

    Documentation of Payne's support of Cherokees.

ANNA CORA MOWATT RITCHIE (1819-70)

MAJOR PLAYS

FASHION, 1845.
ARMAND, THE CHILD OF THE PEOPLE, 1847.

PUBLISHED PLAYS

A. Individual Titles

1268   ARMAND; OR, THE PEER AND THE PEASANT. London: W. Newberry, 1849.

1269   FASHION. London: W. Newberry, 1850.

1270   FASHION. New York: S. French, 1854.

B. Collected Plays

1271   ARMAND; OR, THE PEER AND THE PEASANT and FASHION. Boston: Ticknor, Reed, and Fields, 1855.

C. Plays in Anthologies

1272   FASHION. In AMERICAN PLAYS. Ed. Allan G. Halline, pp. 231-12. See entry no. 105.

1273   FASHION. In THE BLACK CROOK AND OTHER NINETEENTH-CENTURY AMERICAN PLAYS. Ed. Myron Matlaw, pp. 27-93. See entry no. 107.

Anna Cora Mowatt Ritchie

1274   FASHION. In DRAMAS FROM THE AMERICAN THEATRE, 1762-1909. Ed. Richard Moody, pp. 317-47. See entry no. 105.

1275   FASHION. In REPRESENTATIVE AMERICAN PLAYS. Ed. Arthur Hobson Quinn, pp. 281-312. See entry no. 114.

1276   FASHION. In REPRESENTATIVE PLAYS BY AMERICAN DRAMATISTS. Ed. Montrose J. Moses, II, 521-601. See entry no. 111.

1277   FASHION. In SIX EARLY AMERICAN PLAYS: 1798-1890. Eds. William Coyle and Harry G. Damaser, pp. 105-54. See entry no. 102.

NONDRAMATIC WORKS

1278   AUTOBIOGRAPHY OF AN ACTRESS; OR, EIGHT YEARS ON THE STAGE. Boston: Ticknor, Reed, and Fields, 1854.

    Her life and travels written in first person. Good account of FASHION and of her touring in America.

1279   MIMIC LIFE; OR, BEFORE AND BEHIND THE CURTAIN. Boston: Ticknor and Fields, 1856.

    "A Series of Narratives," individually entitled "Stella," "The Prompter's Daughter," and "The Unknown Tragedian." Sentimentalized account through eyes of omniscient author of acting conditions, problems, and life in the theatre.

BIBLIOGRAPHY

1280   See entries nos. 4, 29, 33, 34, 45, 48, 1291.

BIOGRAPHY AND CRITICISM

1281   See entries nos. 123, 135, 141, 155.

1282   Barnes, Eric W. THE LADY OF FASHION. New York: Charles Scribner's Sons, 1954.

    The standard biography of her life and career.

1283   Bernard, William Bayle. "Anna Cora Mowatt." In TALLIS'S DRAWING ROOM TABLE BOOK. London: John Tallis, 1851, pp. 9-11.

    A condemnation of her acting in England.

Anna Cora Mowatt Ritchie

1284 Blesi, Marius. "The Life and Letters of Anna Cora Mowatt." Ph.D. dissertation, University of Virginia, 1938.

1285 "Editor's Table." ARTHUR'S LADIES MAGAZINE, 2 (1845), 287-88.

> An early review of FASHION with praise for American work. Emphasis on moral content.

1286 Havens, Daniel F. "Cultural Maturity and the Flowering of Native American Social Comedy: Mowatt's FASHION (1845)." In his THE COLUMBIAN MUSE OF COMEDY: THE DEVELOPMENT OF A NATIVE TRADITION IN EARLY AMERICAN SOCIAL COMEDY, 1787-1845, pp. 129-48. See entry no. 139.

> An extensive analysis of the play and contemporary attempts at social comedy.

1287 Hutton, Laurence. In ACTORS AND ACTRESSES OF GREAT BRITAIN AND THE UNITED STATES. Ed. Brander Matthews and Laurence Hutton, IV, 155-70. See entry no. 681.

> A survey of life and career, "Anna Cora Mowatt."

1288 Mayorga, Margaret G. A SHORT HISTORY OF THE AMERICAN DRAMA. See entry no. 150.

> A brief comment on FASHION (pp. 145-46).

1289 Meserve, Walter J. AN OUTLINE HISTORY OF AMERICAN DRAMA. See entry no. 153.

> A discussion of FASHION (pp. 86-88).

1290 Moses, Montrose J. THE AMERICAN DRAMATIST. See entry no. 157.

> Slight references (pp. 85-86, 104-05).

1291 Quinn, Arthur Hobson. A HISTORY OF THE AMERICAN DRAMA FROM THE BEGINNING TO THE CIVIL WAR. See entry no. 163.

> General review with emphasis upon FASHION (pp. 310-19).

1292 Poe, Edgar Allan. "The New Comedy by Mrs. Mowatt." BROADWAY JOURNAL, 29 March 1845, pp. 203-05.

> A condemnation of FASHION as dramatic art yet superior to "any American play." Based on a reading of the manuscript. In "Mrs. Mowatt's Comedy" (BROADWAY JOURNAL, 5 April 1845) Poe praises the play's production and is pleased with its reception; he sees a revival of interest in American drama. Both reviews are reprinted in THE AMERICAN THEATRE AS SEEN BY ITS CRITICS, 1752-1934. Eds. Montrose J. Moses

and John Mason Brown, pp. 59-63, 63-66. See entry no. 330. They are also reprinted in THE COMPLETE WORKS OF EDGAR ALLAN POE (Ed. James A. Harrison, 1902; rpt. New York: AMS Press, 1965, XII, 112-21, 124-29).

1293 "Things Theatrical." SPIRIT OF THE TIMES, 15 March 1845, p. 32.

> A review of FASHION and discussion of American dramatic literature as "unploughed field for genius."

1294 "Things Theatrical." SPIRIT OF THE TIMES, 2 February 1850, p. 600.

> An extensive comment on FASHION and its reception in America.

1295 Wilson, Garff B. THREE HUNDRED YEARS OF AMERICAN DRAMA AND THEATRE. See entry no. 173.

> Author discusses Mowatt as playwright and actress (pp. 123-26).

RICHARD PENN SMITH (1799-1854)

MAJOR PLAYS

THE EIGHTH OF JANUARY, 1829.
THE SENTINELS; OR, THE TWO SERGEANTS, 1829.
TRIUMPH OF PLATTSBURG, 1830.
THE DEFORMED; OR, WOMAN'S TRIAL, 1830.
CAIUS MARIUS, 1831.
THE ACTRESS OF PADUA, 1836.

PUBLISHED PLAYS

A. Individual Titles

1296 CAIUS MARIUS, A TRAGEDY BY RICHARD PENN SMITH. Ed. Neda McFadden Westlake. Philadelphia: University of Pennsylvania Press, 1968.

> A model of play editing with a full introduction that places Smith in the developing American drama, describes the creation and reception of the play, gives a note on the text, and provides a checklist of Smith's plays.

B. Collected Plays

1297 THE SENTINELS & OTHER PLAYS. Eds. Ralph H. Ware and H.W. Schoenberger. Vol. 13 of AMERICA'S LOST PLAYS. Ed. Barrett H. Clark. See entry no. 100.

> Contains THE SENTINELS, THE BOMBARDMENT OF ALGIERS, WILLIAM PENN, SHAKESPEARE IN LOVE, A WIFE AT A VENTURE, THE LAST MAN.

Richard Penn Smith

NONDRAMATIC WORKS

1298 MISCELLANEOUS WORKS, COLLECTED BY HIS SON, HORACE W. SMITH. Philadelphia: H.W. Smith, 1856.

> Contains a brief biography of the dramatist by Morton McMichael from the PHILADELPHIA SATURDAY NEWS AND LITERARY GAZETTE.

BIBLIOGRAPHY

1299 See entries nos. 4, 29, 48, 1292, 1296, 1304.

BIOGRAPHY AND CRITICISM

1300 See entries nos. 133, 150, 151, 152, 153, 155, 173.

1301 Mabbott, Thomas O. "Richard Penn Smith's Tragedy of CAIUS MARIUS." AL, 2 (1930), 141-56.

> A sketch of dramatist and discussion of the play and its early stage history. Includes Act V, Scene v, from the PHILA-DELPHIA SATURDAY NEWS AND LITERARY GAZETTE, 7 January 1836, pages 150-56.

1302 McCullough, Bruce Welker. THE LIFE AND WRITINGS OF RICHARD PENN SMITH WITH A REPRINT OF HIS PLAY, "THE DEFORMED," 1830. Menasha, Wis.: Banta, 1917.

> The only book-length study of the dramatist; originally a University of Pennsylvania doctoral dissertation, with a bibliography.

1303 [McMichael, Morton?]. "Biography of Richard Penn Smith." BURTON'S GENTLEMAN'S MAGAZINE, 5 (September 1839), 119-21.

> A contemporary biographical sketch, covers all literary work. Verbose.

1304 Quinn, Arthur Hobson. A HISTORY OF AMERICAN DRAMA FROM THE BEGINNING TO THE CIVIL WAR. See entry no. 163.

> See pages 205-19, 411-12, for the best commentary on the plays of R.P. Smith and his contribution to American drama. Bibliography.

1305 "Richard Penn Smith." EVERY BODY'S ALBUM, 1 (1836), 366.

> Facts about his life, anecdotes, activities, particular attention to plays.

JOHN AUGUSTUS STONE (1800-1834)

MAJOR PLAYS

RESTORATION; OR, THE DIAMOND CROSS, 1824.
METAMORA; OR, THE LAST OF THE WAMPANOAGS, 1829.
TANCRED, KING OF SICILY; OR, THE ARCHIVES OF PALERMO, 1831.
THE ANCIENT BRITON, 1833.
THE KNIGHT OF THE GOLDEN FLEECE; OR,THE YANKEE OF SPAIN, 1834.

PUBLISHED PLAYS

A. Collected Plays

1306   METAMORA & OTHER PLAYS. Ed. Eugene R. Page. Vol. 14 of AMERICA'S LOST PLAYS. Ed. Barrett H. Clark. See entry no. 100.

>Includes METAMORA and TANCRED, KING OF SICILY. The reissue of this volume by Indiana University Press includes the previously missing fourth act of METAMORA with Richard Moody's essay.

B. Plays in Anthologies

1307   METAMORA. In DRAMAS FROM THE AMERICAN THEATRE, 1762-1909. Ed. Richard Moody, pp. 205-27. See entry no. 105.

1308   METAMORA. In FAVORITE AMERICAN PLAYS OF THE NINETEENTH CENTURY. Ed. Barrett H. Clark, pp. 1-34. See entry no. 101.

>Includes a prologue and epilogue to METAMORA.

1309   METAMORA. In SIX EARLY AMERICAN PLAYS, 1798-1900. Eds. William Coyle and Harry G. Damaser, pp. 54-95. See entry no. 102.

1310 [METAMORA]. "Lost and Now Found: The Fourth Act of METAMORA." AL, 34 (1962), 353-64.

    The missing act plus a descriptive and analytical commentary by Richard Moody, see entry no. 1306.

BIBLIOGRAPHY

1311 See entries nos. 4, 29, 45, 48, 1318.

BIOGRAPHY AND CRITICISM

1312 See entries nos. 119, 133, 141, 142, 150, 151, 155, 156, 155, 156, 173.

1313 "Dramatic Literature." NORTH AMERICAN MAGAZINE, 1 (1832), 117-24.

    A stimulating analysis of THE ANCIENT BRITON including a long quotation from the play. Praises Stone and American drama.

1314 Eich, L.M. "American Indian Plays." QJS, 30 (1944), 212-15.

    Eich places METAMORA in continuity of Indian plays.

1315 Meserve, Walter J. AN EMERGING ENTERTAINMENT: THE DRAMA OF THE AMERICAN PEOPLE TO 1828. See entry no. 152.

    A brief comment on Stone's early career (pp. 296-97).

1316 _____. AN OUTLINE HISTORY OF AMERICAN DRAMA. See entry no. 153.

    Scattered references with commentary on METAMORA (pp. 78-79).

1317 "The New York Stage. The New Tragedy of METAMORA--A Bird's Eye View of Mr. Forrest's Performance." IRISH SHIELD AND MONTHLY HILENAN, 10 (1829), 467-68.

    This critic thoroughly condemns the play, then applauds Forrest's performance.

1318 Quinn, Arthur Hobson. A HISTORY OF THE AMERICAN DRAMA FROM THE BEGINNING TO THE CIVIL WAR. See entry no. 163.

John Augustus Stone

Scattered comments on various plays by Stone (pp. 243-44, 250-51, 270-72, 293-94).

1319 Reardon, John D. "Verse Drama in America from 1765 to the Civil War." Ph.D. dissertation, University of Kansas, 1957.

Includes commentary on Stone's work, particularly METAMORA.

AUGUSTUS THOMAS (1857-1934)

MAJOR PLAYS

IN MISSOURA, 1893.
NEW BLOOD, 1894.
ARIZONA, 1899.
THE EARL OF PAWTUCKET, 1903.
THE WITCHING HOUR, 1907.
AS A MAN THINKS, 1911.

PUBLISHED PLAYS

A. Individual Titles

1320   Samuel French has published library editions of ten plays, which include interesting accounts of the plays by Thomas: THE WITCHING HOUR, OLIVER GOLDSMITH, THE HARVEST MOON, IN MISSOURA, MRS. LEFFINGWELL'S BOOTS, THE OTHER GIRL, THE EARL OF PAWTUCKET, THE COPPERHEAD, COLONEL GEORGE OF MOUNT VERNON, THE CRICKET OF PALMY DAYS.

B. Plays in Anthologies

1321   AS A MAN THINKS. In MODERN AMERICAN PLAYS. Ed. George P. Baker, pp. 1-100. See entry no. 481.

1322   THE COPPERHEAD. In LONGER PLAYS BY MODERN AUTHORS (AMERICAN). Ed. Helen L. Cohen. New York: Harcourt & Brace, 1922, pp. 55-162.

1323   IN MISSOURA. In REPRESENTATIVE PLAYS BY AMERICAN DRAMATISTS. Ed. Montrose J. Moses. III, 447-519. See entry no. 111.

Augustus Thomas

1324 THE WITCHING HOUR. In REPRESENTATIVE AMERICAN DRAMAS, NATIONAL AND LOCAL. Ed. Montrose J. Moses, pp. 99-142. See entry no. 109.

1325 THE WITCHING HOUR. In REPRESENTATIVE AMERICAN PLAYS. Ed. Arthur Hobson Quinn, pp. 734-69. See entry no. 114.

NONDRAMATIC WORKS

1326 "Augustus Thomas." CURRENT OPINION, 64 (1918), 183-84.
   A slight and folksy comment on the tricks of writing plays.

1327 "How I Wrote My Greatest Play." DELINEATOR, 73 (1909), 221-22.
   Comments on THE WITCHING HOUR.

1328 "Playwright's Views." REVIEW OF REVIEWS, 75 (1927), 402.
   Thomas' opposition to censorship.

1329 THE PRINT OF MY REMEMBERANCE. See entry no. 1129.
   An autobiography that includes a discussion of his theory of playwriting and accounts of his major plays.

BIBLIOGRAPHY

1330 See entries nos. 4, 29, 33, 45, 48, 1353.

BIOGRAPHY AND CRITICISM

1331 See entries nos. 137, 145, 146, 155, 166, 376, 382, 426.

1332 "Arizona." MUNSEY'S, 24 (1900), 413-19.
   General praise for Thomas' playwriting plus background and assessment of ARIZONA.

1333 Bergman, Herbert. "Augustus Thomas, Dramatist of His Age." Ph.D. dissertation, University of Wisconsin, 1953.

1334 Brooks, Van W. "Augustus Thomas." WORLD'S WORK, 18 (1909), 11882-85.

In an interview with Thomas, whom Brooks calls the "most representative playwright," Brooks discusses regional American plays.

1335 Burton, Richard. THE NEW AMERICAN DRAMA. New York: Crowell, 1913.

A comment on Thomas' writing techniques (pp. 27-45).

1336 Bynum, Lucy S. "The Economic and Political Ideas of Augustus Thomas." Ph.D. dissertation, University of North Carolina, 1954.

1337 Clark, Barrett H. BRITISH AND AMERICAN DRAMA TO-DAY. See entry no. 876.

An evaluation of Thomas (pp. 233-42).

1338 Dithmar, E.A. "Augustus Thomas." BOOK-BUYER, 15 (1898), 323.

1339 Eaton, Walter Pritchard. THE AMERICAN STAGE OF TO-DAY. See entry no. 494.

An extensive criticism of THE WITCHING HOUR (pp. 27-44).

1340 Going, William T. "The Prestons of Talladega and the Hubbards of Bowen: A Dramatic Note." In his ESSAYS IN ALABAMA LITERATURE. University: University of Alabama Press, 1975, pp. 142-55.

Author compares Thomas' ALABAMA with Lillian Hellman's LITTLE FOXES and ANOTHER PART OF THE FOREST.

1341 Hamilton, Clayton. "Augustus Thomas." FORUM, 29 (1908), 366-69.

Hamilton condemns THE RANGER while giving effusive praise to THE WITCHING HOUR.

1342 Hapgood, Norman. "August Thomas and the Time Spirit." HARPER'S WEEKLY, 22 November 1913, p. 25.

Author considers Thomas a success in writing light plays, unsuccessful in plays of serious nature; he comments in particular on INDIAN SUMMER.

1343 Hart, R.L. "Enter Augustus Thomas." OUTLOOK, 131 (1922), 672-73.

Hart comments on Thomas' views concerning censorship after his appointment as executive chairman of the Broadway Managers Association.

Augustus Thomas

1344   Herron, Ima Honaker. THE SMALL TOWN IN AMERICAN DRAMA. See entry no. 140.

        See particularly pages 140-49 and 208-10 for comments on Thomas' rural dramas.

1345   Hewitt, Barnard. THEATRE U.S.A. 1668-1957. See entry no. 141.

        Hewitt comments mainly on THE COPPERHEAD and includes Haywood Broun's review in the NEW YORK TRIBUNE, 19 February 1918--see pages 323-26.

1346   Hoole, W. Stanley. "ALABAMA: Drama of Reconciliation." ALABAMA REVIEW, 19 (1966), 83-108.

        Production history, reviews, and an assessment of the play in uniting North and South.

1347   Howells, W.D. "The Recent Dramatic Season." NAR, 172 (1901), 474.

        An enthusiastic review of ARIZONA and summary of Thomas' work, plus comments on Fitch and Herne.

1348   Matthews, Brander. "Augustus Thomas on His Methods." ART WORLD, 2 (1917), 510-11.

        Based on an interview with Thomas in which Matthews praises his plays and critical accounts.

1349   Mayorga, Margaret G. A SHORT HISTORY OF THE AMERICAN DRAMA. See entry no. 150.

        Excerpts from and comments on ARIZONA and THE WITCHING HOUR (pp. 213, 217, 220-27, 293).

1350   Meserve, Walter J. AN OUTLINE HISTORY OF AMERICAN DRAMA. See entry no. 153.

        Discussions of Thomas' efforts in regional, labor, political, and social drama on pages 132-33, 162, 165, 168, 170-71, 189.

1351   Moses, Montrose J. THE AMERICAN DRAMATIST. See entry no. 157.

        Comments on technique and use of realistic detail (pp. 159-63).

1352   Nathan, George J. "In Memoriam." AMERICAN MERCURY, 8 (May 1926), 117-20.

        A bitingly negative view of Thomas' significance as a dramatist.

Augustus Thomas

1353 Quinn, Arthur Hobson. "Augustus Thomas and the Picture of American Life." In his A HISTORY OF THE AMERICAN DRAMA FROM THE CIVIL WAR TO THE PRESENT DAY. I, 239-64. See entry no. 164.

   Extensive biographical information and an analysis of Thomas' plays.

1354 Salem, James M. A GUIDE TO CRITICAL REVIEWS: PART I: AMERICAN DRAMA, 1909-1969. See entry no. 47.

   See pages 479-83 for reviews of Thomas' plays.

1355 Strang, Lewis C. PLAYERS AND PLAYS OF THE LAST QUARTER CENTURY. Vol. 2: THE THEATRE OF TODAY. See entry no. 170.

   Strang sees Thomas as one of four important American dramatists; other general commentary--see pages 183-89.

1356 Wilson, Garff B. THREE HUNDRED YEARS OF AMERICAN DRAMA AND THEATRE. See entry no. 173.

   The contribution of Thomas to American drama with particular reference to THE WITCHING HOUR (pp. 331-34).

1357 Winter, William. "Shadows on the Stage." HARPER'S WEEKLY, 8 October 1910, p. 13.

   Includes brief comment on Thomas' THE JEW.

1358 _____. THE WALLET OF TIME. See entry no. 593.

   An assessment of Thomas' work (II, 529-57).

DENMAN THOMPSON (1833-1910)

MAJOR PLAYS

JOSHUA WHITCOMB, 1876.
THE OLD HOMESTEAD (with George W. Ryer), 1886.

PUBLISHED PLAYS

A. Individual Titles

1359   THE OLD HOMESTEAD. Boston: Walter H. Baker, 1927.
> Complete acting edition. Note: Prior to publication in play form the plot of THE OLD HOMESTEAD was published in a series of "Popular Theatrical Novels" as Denman Thompson's OLD HOMESTEAD. Written from the Celebrated Play of "The Old Homestead." New York: Street and Smith, 1889.

B. Plays in Anthologies

1360   THE OLD HOMESTEAD. In S.R.O. THE MOST SUCCESSFUL PLAYS OF THE AMERICAN STAGE. Comp. Bennett Cerf and Van H. Cartmell, pp. 167-221. See entry no. 98.

BIBLIOGRAPHY

1361   See entries nos. 4, 29, 48.

BIOGRAPHY AND CRITICISM

1362   See entries nos. 140, 146, 150, 151, 157, 173, 371, 943.

1363   Brock, H.I. "'The Old Homestead' Comes Homes Again." NEW YORK TIMES MAGAZINE SECTION, 13 August 1933, pp. 12, 16.

> A glib comment on the production history of this play at a revival for two-hundredth anniversary of Keene, New Hampshire.

1364   Gaillard, Eva Ryman. "How Denman Thompson Wrote 'The Old Homestead.'" THEATRE MAGAZINE, 7 (1907), 296.

> Not a detailed or dependable essay.

1365   Heydrick, Benjamin A. "The Drama." CHATAUQUAN, 65 (1911), 30-31.

> Praises the realism in THE OLD HOMESTEAD.

1366   Hodge, Francis. YANKEE THEATRE: THE IMAGE OF AMERICA ON THE STAGE, 1825-1850. See entry no. 139.

> Brief mention of THE OLD HOMESTEAD (p. 262). (Many books and essays on the Yankee character refer to Josh Whitcomb in this play.)

1367   Howells, W.D. "Editor's Study." HARPER'S MONTHLY, 79 (1889), 317.

> Howells praises THE OLD HOMESTEAD as a "representation of American life."

1368   Meserve, Walter J. AN OUTLINE HISTORY OF AMERICAN DRAMA. See entry no. 153.

> Discussion and plot of THE OLD HOMESTEAD, pp. 128-9.

1369   THE OLD HOMESTEAD. Significant reviews in NEW YORK HERALD, 3 September 1787, p. 6; NEW YORK TIMES, 3 September 1878, p. 5; NEW YORK DRAMATIC MIRROR, 15 January 1887, p. 4; NEW YORK TIMES, 11 January 1887, p. 5.

1370   "'The Old Homestead'--The Greatest Popular Success of the American Stage." CURRENT LITERATURE, 45 (1908), 663-69.

> Early published excerpts from THE OLD HOMESTEAD.

1371   Patterson, Ada. "A Chat with Old Josh Whitcomb." THEATRE MAGAZINE, 8 (1908), 194.

> A brief personal comment on the Yankee hero of THE OLD HOMESTEAD, with a good quote from Eugene Field.

Denman Thompson

1372 "A Play That Ran for Thirty Years." WORLD'S WORK, 22 (1911), 14439-40.

> An account of the development of THE OLD HOMESTEAD in which dates are invariably inaccurate.

1373 Quinn, Arthur Hobson. A HISTORY OF THE AMERICAN DRAMA FROM THE CIVIL WAR TO THE PRESENT DAY. See entry no. 164.

> Background of THE OLD HOMESTEAD (I, 128-29).

1374 "Religion and the Stage: Christians Advised to See OLD HOMESTEAD." NEW YORK TIMES, 4 December 1888, p. 2.

1375 Sedgwick, Ruth W. "Those Were the Heart Throbs of a Nation." STAGE, 11 (July 1934), 29-33.

> THE OLD HOMESTEAD is included in this sentimental reverie.

1376 "The Significance of Joshua Whitcomb." CURRENT LITERATURE, 50 (1911), 648-50.

> Poorly argued thesis.

1377 Stevenson, E. Irenaeus. "Denman Thompson and Our Rural Life Drama." In FAMOUS AMERICAN ACTORS OF TO-DAY. Eds. Frederic Edward McKay and Charles E.L. Wingate, pp. 389-94. See entry no. 922.

> Slight information in this biographical essay comparing Thompson's work to contemporary rural plays.

1378 "Thompson, Denman." Useful obituary notices in NEW YORK TIMES, 15 April 1911, p. 13; NEW YORK DRAMATIC MIRROR, 19 April 1911, p. 13.

1379 "Uncle Josh Goes Back to 'The Old Homestead.'" NATIONAL MAGAZINE, 50 (April 1921), 42.

> A notice of a revival with William Laurence.

1380 Walsh, William H. "Reminiscences of Denman Thompson." NEW ENGLAND MAGAZINE, 48 (1910), 43-50.

> This essay is valuable mainly for the quotes attributed to Thompson.

1381 "Where American Drama Began." See entry no. 945.

> Author considers influence of Harrigan, Hoyt, and Thompson on American drama.

1382 White, Matthew, Jr. "The Stage." MUNSEY'S, 57 (1916), 510.
Reference to a film version of THE OLD HOMESTEAD.

ROYALL TYLER (1757-1826)

MAJOR PLAYS

THE CONTRAST, 1787.
MAY DAY IN TOWN, 1787.
THE GEORGIA SPEC; OR, LAND IN THE MOON, 1797.
THE ISLAND OF BARRATARIA, pub. 1940.
THE ORIGIN OF THE FEAST OF PURIM, pub. 1940.
JOSEPH AND HIS BRETHREN, pub. 1940.
THE JUDGEMENT OF SOLOMON, pub. 1940.

PUBLISHED PLAYS

A. Individual Titles

1383 THE CONTRAST, A COMEDY. Philadelphia: Prichard & Hall, 1790; rpt., introd. Thomas J. McKee, New York: Dunlap Society, 1887; new ed., ed. James B. Wilbur, with introd. and bibliog. by Helen Tyler Brown. Boston: Houghton Mifflin, 1920.

1384 THE CONTRAST, WITH A HISTORY OF GEORGE WASHINGTON'S COPY. Ed. James Benjamin Wilbur. Boston: Houghton Mifflin, 1920; rpt. New York: AMS Publications, 1970.

B. Collected Plays

1385 FOUR PLAYS BY ROYALL TYLER. Eds. Arthur Wallace Peach and George Floyd Newbrough. Vol. 15 of AMERICA'S LOST PLAYS. Ed. Barrett H. Clark. See entry no. 100.

> Contains THE ISLAND OF BARRATARIA, THE ORIGIN OF THE FEAST OF PURIM, JOSEPH AND HIS BRETHREN, THE JUDGEMENT OF SOLOMON in this 1940 publication.

C. Plays in Anthologies

1386   THE CONTRAST. In AMERICAN DRAMA. Ed. Alan S. Downer, pp. 13-47. See entry no. 103.

1387   THE CONTRAST. In AMERICAN PLAYS. Ed. Allan G. Halline, pp. 1-34. See entry no. 105.

1388   THE CONTRAST. In BEST PLAYS OF EARLY AMERICAN THEATRE. Eds. John Gassner and Mollie Gassner, pp. 1-37. See entry no. 104.

1389   THE CONTRAST. In DRAMAS FROM THE AMERICAN THEATRE, 1762-1909. Ed. Richard Moody, pp. 33-59. See entry no. 108.

1390   THE CONTRAST. In REPRESENTATIVE AMERICAN PLAYS. Ed. Arthur Hobson Quinn, pp. 47-77. See entry no. 114.

1391   THE CONTRAST. In REPRESENTATIVE PLAYS BY AMERICAN DRAMATISTS. Ed. Montrose J. Moses. I, 431-98. See entry no. 111.

BIBLIOGRAPHY

1392   See entries nos. 4, 29, 30, 33, 34, 45, 48, 1398, 1410, 1413.

1393   Coates, Walter J. "Royall Tyler." DRIFTWIND, 6 (1932), 27-31.

1394   Peladeau, Marius B. THE PROSE OF ROYALL TYLER. Montpelier: Vermont Historical Society; Rutland, Vt.: Charles E. Tuttle, 1972.
    Contains a scholarly checklist and bibliography of prose works.

1395   Tanselle, G. Thomas. "Some Uncollected Authors XLII: Royall Tyler, 1757-1826." BOOK COLLECTOR, 15 (1966), 303-20.

BIOGRAPHY AND CRITICISM

1396   See entries nos. 123, 137, 141, 144, 145, 151, 154, 155, 159, 161.

1397   Bishop, W. "First American Comedy; THE CONTRAST." MENTOR, 15 (1928), 39.
    Slight comment on comic aspects.

Royall Tyler

1398 Blandford, Lucy. "The Production History of Royall Tyler's THE CONTRAST." M.A. thesis, University of Virginia, 1970.

> A good study, carefully researched. Lists thirty-eight productions from 1787 to 1804.

1399 [Candour]. "The Contrast." DAILY ADVERTISER, 18 April 1787; rpt. in THE AMERICAN THEATRE AS SEEN BY ITS CRITICS, 1752-1934. Eds. Montrose J. Moses and John Bason Brown, pp. 24-25. See entry no. 330.

> The first review of the play by a critic calling himself "Candour."

1400 Halline, Allan Gates. "Main Currents of Thought in American Drama." Ph.D. dissertation, University of Wisconsin, 1935.

> A discussion of historical background of THE CONTRAST in Chapter 1, "Nationalism: Royall Tyler" (pp. 15-30).

1401 Havens, Daniel F. "Enter Jonathan." In his THE COLUMBIAN MUSE OF COMEDY: THE DEVELOPMENT OF A NATIVE TRADITION IN EARLY AMERICAN SOCIAL COMEDY, 1787-1845, pp. 8-51. See entry no. 136.

> A thorough study of THE CONTRAST, emphasizing possible sources, noting comparisons with THE SCHOOL FOR SCANDAL, and examining the Yankee character.

1402 Jarvis, Katherine S. "Royall Tyler's Lyrics for MAY DAY IN TOWN." HARVARD LIBRARY BULLETIN, 23 (1975), 188-98.

> Jarvis reproduces and discusses Tyler's verse for this light opera. Mainly for "historical interest."

1403 Lauber, John. "THE CONTRAST: A Study in the Concept of Innocence." ENGLISH LANGUAGE NOTES, 1 (1963), 33-37.

> Lauber sees play as important stage in development of a distinctly American literature with the outline of national character based on concept of innocence. Play foreshadows international thesis of Henry James's novels.

1404 Meserve, Walter J. AN EMERGING ENTERTAINMENT: THE DRAMA OF THE AMERICAN PEOPLE TO 1828. See entry no. 152.

> A discussion of Tyler's contribution to American drama with an emphasis upon THE CONTRAST (pp. 95-102).

1405 _____. AN OUTLINE HISTORY OF AMERICAN DRAMA. See entry no. 153.

    A brief comment mainly on THE CONTRAST (pp. 20-23).

1406 Nethercot, Arthur H. "Dramatic Background of Royall Tyler's THE CONTRAST." AL, 12 (1941), 435-46.

    Nethercot questions theory that Tyler never studied drama prior to writing THE CONTRAST and provides an excellent analysis of play to show Tyler's knowledge of the work of many dramatists and of the rules of dramatic composition.

1407 Newbrough, G.F. "Mary Tyler's Journal." VERMONT QUARTERLY, 20 (1952), 19-31.

    A detailed journal of Royall Tyler's last days.

1408 "Our First Truly National Play: THE CONTRAST." DELINEATOR, 85 (July 1944), 7.

    A slight patriotic statement.

1409 Péladeau, Marius B. "Royall Tyler's Other Plays." NEQ, 40 (1967), 48-60.

    Author considers four manuscript plays and three fragments. Most of the information is on the manuscript plays, but Péladeau erroneously gives Tyler credit for THE MEDIUM by Judith Sargent Murray.

1410 Quinn, Arthur Hobson. A HISTORY OF THE AMERICAN DRAMA FROM THE BEGINNING TO THE CIVIL WAR. See entry no. 163.

    A commentary on Tyler's work with emphasis on THE CONTRAST (pp. 64-73).

1411 _____. THE LITERATURE OF THE AMERICAN PEOPLE. See entry no. 165.

    General comments on Tyler (pp. 198-200).

1412 Rourke, Constance. THE ROOTS OF AMERICAN CULTURE AND OTHER ESSAYS. Ed. Van Wyck Brooks. New York: Harcourt, Brace, 1942.

    An important evaluation of Tyler's contribution to the development of the Yankee character (pp. 114-24).

1413 Seilhamer, George O. HISTORY OF THE AMERICAN THEATRE. See entry no. 913.

A detailed discussion of the reception of THE CONTRAST (II, 225-39).

1414 Stein, Roger B. "Royall Tyler and the Question of Our Speech." NEQ, 38 (1965), 454-74.

Stein finds THE CONTRAST a "suggestive register" of American speech during a critical period. A study of the play as a "linguistic drama" in search of a native idiom.

1415 Tanselle, G. Thomas. "Author and Publisher in 1800: Letters of Royall Tyler and Joseph Nancrede." HARVARD LIBRARY BULLETIN, 15 (1967), 129-39.

The correspondence between Tyler and a Boston bookseller reveals awkward situation of the gentleman of letters trying to avoid the taint of commercialism. There is evidence that Tyler did not regard writing as his profession.

1416 _____. ROYALL TYLER. Cambridge, Mass.: Harvard University Press, 1967.

A scholarly treatment of man and writer. In a historical study of the plays, Tanselle provides a chapter-length discussion of THE CONTRAST and concludes that the play was the product of "brief idle moments."

1417 Tupper, Frederick. "Royall Tyler, Man of Law and Man of Letters." PROCEEDINGS OF THE VERMONT HISTORICAL SOCIETY, 4 (1928), 65-101.

Concerned with Tyler's entire career, Tupper emphasizes his literary work.

1418 Tyler, Thomas Pickman. "Royall Tyler." PROCEEDINGS OF THE VERMONT BAR ASSOCIATION, 1 (1878-1881), 44-62.

A general survey of Tyler's life, based on a memoir by his son.

1419 Wilson, Garff B. THREE HUNDRED YEARS OF AMERICAN DRAMA AND THEATRE. See entry no. 170.

A discussion of THE CONTRAST (pp. 42-45).

MERCY OTIS WARREN (1728-1814)

MAJOR PLAYS

THE ADULATEUR, 1772.
THE DEFEAT, 1773.
THE GROUP, 1775.
THE LADIES OF CASTILE, 1790.
THE SACK OF ROME, 1790.

PUBLISHED PLAYS

A. Individual Titles

1420   THE ADULATEUR. In MASSACHUSETTS SPY, 2 (26 March, 23 April 1772), 15, 32; rpt. in MAGAZINE OF HISTORY, 16 (1917-18), 227-59.

       Includes additional scenes by someone other than Mercy Warren.

1421   THE ADULATEUR. Boston: Printed and sold at the New Printing Office, near Concert Hall, 1773.

1422   THE BLOCKHEADS; OR, THE AFFRIGHTED OFFICERS. Boston: Printed in Queen Street, 1776.

       Frequently attributed to Mercy Warren.

1423   THE DEFEAT. In BOSTON GAZETTE, 24 May, 19 July 1773.

1424   THE GROUP. Boston: Sold by Edes and Gall, In Queen Street, 1775.

       Other editions were published in Philadelphia and New York; a Jamaican edition referred to by John Adams, however, has never been found.

Mercy Otis Warren

1425 THE GROUP. Foreword by Colton Storm. Ann Arbor: William L. Clements Library, University of Michigan, 1953.

> This edition contains a descriptive foreword.

1426 THE MOTLEY ASSEMBLY. Boston: Printed and sold by Nathaniel Coverly, in Newberry-Street, 1779.

> Frequently attributed to Mercy Warren.

B. Collected Plays

1427 POEMS, DRAMATIC AND MISCELLANEOUS. Boston: T. Thomas and E.T. Andrews, 1790.

> Includes THE LADIES OF CASTILE and THE SACK OF ROME.

C. Plays in Anthologies

1428 THE BLOCKHEADS; OR, THE AFFRIGHTED OFFICERS. In TRUMPETS SOUNDING: PROPAGANDA PLAYS OF THE AMERICAN REVOLUTION. Ed. Norman Philbrick, pp. 151-68. See entry no. 113.

1429 THE GROUP. In REPRESENTATIVE PLAYS BY AMERICAN DRAMATISTS. Ed. Montrose J. Moses. I, 209-32. See entry no. 111.

1430 THE MOTLEY ASSEMBLY. In TRUMPETS SOUNDING: PROPAGANDA PLAYS OF THE AMERICAN REVOLUTION. Ed. Norman Philbrick, pp. 348-58. See entry no. 113.

BIBLIOGRAPHY

1431 See entries nos. 4, 29, 30, 45, 48.

BIOGRAPHY AND CRITICISM

1432 See entries nos. 133, 141, 155, 173.

1433 Anthony, Katherine. FIRST LADY OF THE REVOLUTION: THE LIFE OF MERCY OTIS WARREN. 1958; rpt. Port Washington, N.Y.: Kennikat Press, 1972.

> Substantial general work.

Mercy Otis Warren

1434 Brown, Alice. MERCY OTIS WARREN. New York: Charles Scribner's Sons, 1896.

    A standard work of uneven value.

1435 Ford, Worthy C. "Mrs. Warren's 'The Group.'" PROCEEDINGS OF THE MASSACHUSETTS HISTORICAL SOCIETY, 62 (October 1928), 15-22.

    A description of existing copies of THE GROUP and identification of characters in GROUP, BLOCKHEADS, and MOTLEY ASSEMBLY.

1436 Hutchinson, Maud M. "Mercy Warren, A Study of Her Life and Works." Ph.D. dissertation, American University, 1951.

1437 Marble, A.R. "Mistress Mercy Warren: Real Daughter of the American Revolution." NEW ENGLAND MAGAZINE, n.s. 27 (1903), 163-80.

    Laudatory appraisal of Warren's work.

1438 Mayorga, Margaret G. A SHORT HISTORY OF THE AMERICAN DRAMA. See entry no. 150.

    A brief discussion of THE GROUP (pp. 33-35).

1439 Meserve, Walter J. AN EMERGING ENTERTAINMENT: THE DRAMA OF THE AMERICAN PEOPLE TO 1828. See entry no. 152.

    Warren is considered a major protagonist in "War of Belles Lettres" (pp. 65-75).

1440 _____. AN OUTLINE HISTORY OF AMERICAN DRAMA. See entry no. 153.

    Warren is treated as a "partisan satirist" (pp. 14-17).

1441 Moses, Montrose J. AN AMERICAN DRAMATIST. See entry no. 157.

    A brief appraisal of Warren (pp. 47-49).

1442 Quinn, Arthur Hobson. A HISTORY OF THE AMERICAN DRAMA FROM THE BEGINNING TO THE CIVIL WAR. See entry no. 163.

    An analysis with ample quotations of THE ADULATEUR and THE GROUP (pp. 33-47).

JOHN BLAKE WHITE (1781-1859)

MAJOR PLAYS

FOSCARI, THE VENETIAN EXILE, 1806.
THE MYSTERIES OF THE CASTLE, 1806.
MODERN HONOR, 1812.

PUBLISHED PLAYS

A. Individual Titles

1443 THE FORGERS. SOUTHERN LITERARY JOURNAL, 1 (1837), 118-25, 218-26, 354-62, 435-43, 509-18.

1444 FOSCARI. Charleston, S.C.: J. Hoff, 1806.

1445 MODERN HONOR. Charleston, S.C.: J. Hoff, 1812.

1446 THE MYSTERIES OF THE CASTLE. Charleston, S.C.: J. Hoff, 1807.

BIBLIOGRAPHY

1447 See entries nos. 4, 29, 48, 1450, 1451.

BIOGRAPHY AND CRITICISM

1448 See entries nos. 133, 135, 150, 155, 298.

1449 Meserve, Walter J. AN EMERGING ENTERTAINMENT: THE DRAMA OF THE AMERICAN PEOPLE TO 1828. See entry no. 152.

John Blake White

A discussion of his major works; also other references--see pages 195-96, 201-03.

1450 Partridge, Paul W., Jr. "John Blake White: Southern Romantic Painter and Playwright." Ph.D. dissertation, University of Pennsylvania, 1951.

A valuable source.

1451 Quinn, Arthur Hobson. A HISTORY OF THE AMERICAN DRAMA FROM THE BEGINNING TO THE CIVIL WAR. See entry no. 163.

A brief comment on White's plays (pp. 188-90).

1452 Watson, Charles S. "John Blake White." In his ANTEBELLUM CHARLESTON DRAMATISTS, pp. 80-109. See entry no. 312.

The most complete assessment to date of the man and his plays.

1453 Weidner, Paul R., ed. "The Journal of John Blake White." SOUTH CAROLINA HISTORY AND GENERAL MAGAZINE, 42 (1941), 55-71, 169-86; 43 (1942), 35-46, 103-17, 161-74.

NATHANIEL PARKER WILLIS (1806-67)

MAJOR PLAYS

BIANCA VISCONTI, 1837.
THE KENTUCKY HEIRESS, 1837.
TORTESA THE USURER, 1839.

PUBLISHED PLAYS

A. Individual Titles

1454   BIANCA VISCONTI. New York: S. Colman, 1839.

1455   TORTESA THE USURER. New York: S. Colman, 1839.

B. Collected Plays

1456   THE COMPLETE WORKS OF N.P. WILLIS. New York: J.S. Redfield, 1846.

1457   TWO WAYS OF DYING FOR A HUSBAND. London: Hugh Cunningham, 1839.
      Contains DYING TO KEEP HIM; OR, TORTESA THE USURER and DYING TO LOSE HIM; OR, BIANCA VISCONTI.

C. Plays in Anthologies

1458   BIANCA VISCONTI. In AMERICAN PLAYS. Ed. Allan Gates Halline, pp. 199-230. See entry no. 105.

Nathaniel Parker Willis

1459 TORTESA THE USURER. In REPRESENTATIVE AMERICAN PLAYS. Ed. Arthur Hobson Quinn, pp. 241-76. See entry no. 114.

1460 TORTESA THE USURER. In REPRESENTATIVE PLAYS BY AMERICAN DRAMATISTS. Ed. Montrose J. Moses. II, 253-377. See entry no. 111.

BIBLIOGRAPHY

1461 See entries nos. 4, 29, 48, 1464, 1472.

BIOGRAPHY AND CRITICISM

1462 See entries nos. 135, 142, 150, 151, 152, 153, 155, 157, 165, 173.

1463 "The American Drama." In THE COMPLETE STORIES AND POEMS OF EDGAR ALLAN POE: WITH SELECTIONS FROM HIS CRITICAL WRITING. 2 vols. Eds. Arthur Hobson Quinn and E.H. O'Neill. New York: Knopf, 1958. II, 953-78.

   Poe assesses Willis as a dramatist.

1464 Auser, Courtland P. NATHANIEL PARKER WILLIS. New York: Twayne Publishers, 1969.

   A very brief comment on Willis as "Romantic Playwright" in a book which contains play plots but no critical evaluation. Bibliography.

1465 Beers, Henry E. NATHANIEL PARKER WILLIS. Boston: Houghton Mifflin, 1885.

   The first full-length biography. Inadequate on verse drama.

1466 Benton, Richard P. "The Works of N.P. Willis as a Catalyst of Poe's Criticism." AL, 39 (1967), 315-24.

   Author argues that Willis not only influenced Poe throughout TORTESA but prompted Poe to elaborate his critical principles on the creative process.

1467 "Editor's Table." FEDERAL AMERICAN MONTHLY, 10 (1837), 353-55.

   Detailed comments on BIANCA VISCONTI. Praises play as literature and tragedy.

Nathaniel Parker Willis

1468 [Felton, C.C.]. "Dramas of N.P. Willis." NAR, 51 (1840), 141-58.

> An extended review of TORTESA and BIANCA VISCONTI, which are described as "two dramatic poems." Many quotations from plays.

1469 Grigsby, Hugh Blair. "N.P. Willis." SOUTHERN LITERARY MESSENGER, 1 (1834), 88-90.

> Author, who looks back to their college days, praises Willis for his use of language.

1470 Peck, H.T. "N.P. Willis and His Contemporaries." BOOKMAN 24 (September 1906), 33-43.

> A sympathetic view of Willis' life and works. Peck considers Willis a writer of courage and manliness who was not prudent with his reference to Forrest and his divorce.

1471 Poe, Edgar Allen. "N.P. Willis." In THE COMPLETE WORKS OF EDGAR ALLEN POE. Virginia Edition. 14 Vols. Ed. James A. Harrison. New York: Thomas Y. Crowell, 1902; rpt. New York: AMS Press, 1965. X, 27; XIII, 33.

> A contemporary reaction to TORTESA with an evaluation of Willis' work, first published in BURTON'S GENTLEMAN'S MAGAZINE, August 1839, and later included in Poe's discussion entitled "The American Drama" in the AMERICAN WHIG REVIEW, August 1845.

1472 Quinn, Arthur Hobson. A HISTORY OF THE AMERICAN DRAMA FROM THE BEGINNING TO THE CIVIL WAR. See entry no. 163.

> A generous assessment of Willis' work with particular attention to TORTESA THE USURER (pp. 255-59).

1473 "Theatricals." EXPOSITOR, 13 April 1839, pp. 199-200.

> A commentary on Willis with particular attention to the language of TORTESA.

1474 "Tortesa, the Usurer." BOSTON QUARTERLY REVIEW (July 1839), 390.

> Author condemns the play and the author as not worthy of notice.

SAMUEL WOODWORTH (1785-1842)

MAJOR PLAYS

LA FAYETTE; OR, THE CASTLE OF OLMUTZ, 1824.
THE WIDOW'S SON; OR, WHICH IS THE TRAITOR? 1825.
THE FOREST ROSE; OR, AMERICAN FARMERS, 1825.

PUBLISHED PLAYS

A. Individual Titles

1475 THE DEED OF GIFT. New York: C.N. Baldwin, 1822.

1476 LA FAYETTE; OR, THE CASTLE OF OLMUTZ. New York: Circulating Library and Dramatic Repository, 1824.

1477 THE FOREST ROSE; OR, AMERICAN FARMERS. New York: Hopkins and Morris, 1825.

1478 THE FOREST ROSE; OR AMERICAN FARMERS. Boston: William V. Spencer, 1855.

1479 THE WIDOW'S SON; OR, WHICH IS THE TRAITOR? New York: Circulating Library and Dramatic Repository, 1825.

B. Plays in Anthologies

1480 THE FOREST ROSE. In DRAMAS FROM THE AMERICAN THEATRE, 1762-1909. Ed. Richard Moody, pp. 155-74. See entry no. 108.

Samuel Woodworth

BIBLIOGRAPHY

1481 See entries nos. 4, 29, 48, 1491.

1482 Wegelin, Oscar. A BIBLIOGRAPHICAL LIST OF THE LITERARY AND DRAMATIC PRODUCTIONS AND PERIODICALS WRITTEN AND COMPILED BY SAMUEL WOODWORTH. Heartman's Historical Series, No. 18. New Orleans: Heartman, 1953.

BIOGRAPHY AND CRITICISM

1483 See entries nos. 133, 135, 151, 153, 155, 157, 173.

1484 Coad, Oral Sumner. "The Plays of Samuel Woodworth." SEWANEE REVIEW, 27 (1919), 163-75.

  Coad surveys the plays in terms of Woodworth's contemporaries; he sees the plays as stage pieces only, of no literary value.

1485 Duffy, Charles. "'Scenes of My Childhood.'" AL, 13 (1941), 167.

  Duffy suggests Wordsworth as a possible source for Woodworth's poem "The Old Oaken Bucket."

1486 Havens, Daniel F. THE COLUMBIAN MUSE OF COMEDY: THE DEVELOPMENT OF A NATIVE TRADITION IN EARLY AMERICAN SOCIAL COMEDY, 1787-1845. See entry no. 139.

  Analysis of THE FOREST ROSE (pp. 113-16).

1487 Herron, Ima Honaker. THE SMALL TOWN IN AMERICAN DRAMA. See entry no. 140.

  Discussions of THE FOREST ROSE (pp. 48-50, 89-90).

1488 Hodge, Francis. YANKEE THEATRE: THE IMAGE OF AMERICA ON THE STAGE, 1825-1850. See entry no. 142.

  On Woodworth and THE FOREST ROSE (pp. 54-59). Other scattered references to Woodworth's plays. (Most essays and books on the Yankee character in American drama refer to THE FOREST ROSE.)

1489 Mayorga, Margaret G. A SHORT HISTORY OF THE AMERICAN DRAMA. See entry no. 150.

  A brief comment with emphasis on THE FOREST ROSE (pp. 85-88).

1490 Meserve, Walter J. AN EMERGING ENTERTAINMENT: THE DRAMA OF THE AMERICAN PEOPLE TO 1828. See entry no. 152.

    An evaluation of Woodworth's plays as contribution to developing American drama (pp. 236-41).

1491 Quinn, Arthur Hobson. A HISTORY OF THE AMERICAN DRAMA FROM THE BEGINNING TO THE CIVIL WAR. See entry no. 163.

    A survey of Woodworth's plays (pp. 156-59); and a comment on THE FOREST ROSE (pp. 294-95).

1492 _____, ed. THE LITERATURE OF THE AMERICAN PEOPLE. See entry no. 165.

    References to Woodworth's plays (pp. 207-08, 503, 511).

1493 Taft, Kendal B. SAMUEL WOODWORTH. Chicago: Privately printed, 1938.

    A revised Ph.D. dissertation, University of Chicago.

1494 _____. "'Scenes of My Childhood': A Comment." AL, 13 (1942), 410-11.

    Wordsworth is discussed as a possible source for Woodworth's poem "The Old Oaken Bucket."

AUTHOR INDEX

In addition to authors this index includes editors, compilers, and contributors. References are to entry number and alphabetization is letter by letter.

A

Abrahamson, Doris M. 212
Adair, Douglas 1183
Adams, William D. 1
Adkins, Nelson F. 57-58, 213
Aiken, George L. 104, 110
Alfriend, Edward M. 100, 101
Allen, Ralph G. 116, 963
Alman, Miriam 16
Amacher, Richard E. 214
Anderson, John 117
Angotti, Vincent L. 6, 215
Anthony, Catherine 1433
Arata, Esther S. 7
Archer, William 423, 623, 1017
Argetsinger, Gerold 799
Arndt, K.J. 216
Ash, Lee 76
Aston, Anthony 175
Atkinson, Brooks 118, 836
Auser, Courtland P. 1464
Austin, Mary 176
Avery, Laurence G. 177

B

Baine, Rodney M. 1190
Baker, Blanche M. 9-10
Baker, George P. 481, 1321
Balch, Marston 343

Ball, Robert Hamilton 100, 474
Barck, Dorothy C. 793
Barker, James N. 104, 105, 110, 114
Barnard, Charles 100
Barnes, Eric W. 1282
Barnes, James 565
Barnett, Morris 112
Barras, Charles 107
Barrett, Lawrence 402
Barry, S. 112
Bartholet, Carolyn 32
Bass, Althea 1237
Bateman, Mrs. Sidney 110
Bates, Alfred 96, 119, 668, 791, 1233
Beatly, Richmond C. 566
Beaumont, Fletcher 360-61, 872
Becker, Samuel L. 13
Beers, Henry E. 1465
Behrman, Alfred 800
Belasco, David 99, 100, 101, 109, 110, 114, 437
Bell, Archie 837
Bender, Jack E. 424
Bennett, Clarence 100
Bennison, Martin J. 362
Benton, Richard P. 1466
Bergman, Herbert 492, 1333
Bergquist, William G. 11
Bernard, William Bayle 279, 1283
Bernbaum, Martin 838

Author Index

Best, Mrs. A. Starr 130
Bidwell, Barnabas 222
Bird, Mary Mayer 528
Bird, Robert M. 100, 105, 108, 114
Birdoff, Harry 351
Bishop, W. 1397
Black, John 341, 342
Blake, W.S. 922
Blakeley, Sidney H. 1238
Blanc, Robert E. 217
Blanck, Jacob 12
Blandford, Lucy 1398
Blesi, Marius 1284
Blitgen, Sister Carol 62
Bloomfield, Maxwell 1018
Blower, B.O. 968-69
Boker, Henry p. xiii, 100, 105, 108, 110, 114
Booth, Michael R. 97, 218, 732
Boucicault, Dion 101, 102, 104, 114
Boulter, E. Merton 1239
Bowman, Mary R. 801
Boyle, Charles John 1019
Brackenridge, H.H. 110, 113
Bradley, Edward Sculley 120, 553-54, 562, 567-69
Brainard, Charles H. 1240
Brewer, E. 570
Bridenbaugh, Carl 178
Bridenbaugh, Jessica 178
Briggs, E.B. 219
Briggs, H.E. 219
Briscoe, Johnson 1020
Bristol, Roger Pattrell 81
Brock, H.I. 873, 1363
Brockett, L. 363
Brockett, Oscar G. 13, 121, 363, 815
Bronson, Daniel R. 529
Brooks, Noah 689
Brooks, Van Wyck 802, 1334
Brougham, John 96, 108
Brown, Alice 1434
Brown, Charles Brockden 258
Brown, D.P. 110
Brown, Helen Tyler 1383

Brown, Herbert 179
Brown, John Mason 330, 342, 817, 818, 841, 930, 963, 1024, 1099, 1134, 1182, 1399
Brown, William W. 238
Brownell, Atherton 1117
Brownson, Orestes Augustus 418
Brougham, John 100
Bruce, Philip A. 180
Bruntjen, Carol 81
Bruntjen, Scott 81
Bryant, Donald C. 13
Bucks, Dorothy S. 959-60
Bunce, O.B. 110
Burk, John Daly 108
Burke, Charles 96, 110, 112
Burton, Richard 122, 874, 1335
Busacca, Basil 14
Bynum, Lucy S. 1336

C

Cairns, W.B. 181
Campbell, Bartley 100, 101
Campbell, Charles 699
Campbell, Louis W. 878
Canary, Robert H. 803-4
Candour 1399
Carleton, Henry Guy 437
Carlson, C.L. 903-4
Cartmell, Van H. 98, 1360
Cerf, Bennett 98, 1360
C.G.S. 1167
Chaplin, Leila Bowie 220
Chapman, John 99, 477, 864
Chicorel, Marietta 63
Chiles, Rosa P. 1241
Clapp, H.A. 364
Clapp, J.B. 1021
Clapp, William W., Jr. 123, 700
Clark, Barrett H. 100, 101, 124-25, 126, 473, 474, 554, 598, 601, 669, 708, 719, 730, 790, 839, 876, 946, 961, 1004, 1002-23, 1111, 1114, 1161, 1226, 1227, 1297, 1308, 1337, 1385
Clifford, James L. 221
Clinch, Charles P. 100
Cloak, F. Theodore 598
Clough, Peter H. 64

Author Index

Coad, Oral Sumner 100, 127, 222, 783, 805-7, 1484
Coates, Walter J. 1393
Cohen, Helen L. 1322
Cohen, Hennig 8
Colby, Elbridge 182
Coleman, A.I. 739
Coleman, William S.E. 365
Comstock, Sarah 223
Conrad, Joseph 374
Conrad, R.T. 110, 571
Conway, H.J. 100
Cook, Doris E. 877
Cooper, Gayle 81
Cooper, J.F. 96
Cooper, M. Frances 81
Corbett, Elizabeth 352
Corbin, John 962
Cornyn, Stan 65
Cowie, Alexander 128
Coyle, William 102, 605, 785, 950, 1277, 1309
Crain, W.H., Jr. 28
Crane, Stephen 374
Crawford, Mary Caroline 129
Crick, B.R. 16
Crinkle, Nym 443
Cronin, James F. 808
Crowley, John W. 457
Culp, Ralph Borden 183-84
Curry, Wade 1168
Curvin, Jonathan 185
Custis, George Washington Parke 114

D

Dahl, Curtis 530
Dale, Alan 493
Dallett, Frances J. 186
Dalton, Frank 625
Daly, Augustin 97, 105, 422
Daly, Joseph Francis 626, 740-41
Damaser, Harry G. 102, 605, 785, 950, 1277, 1309
Davis, Blanche E. 224
Davis, Owen 366
Davis, Richard Harding 925
DeBaillou, Clemens 1242
Deering, Nathaniel 220
Defoe, Louis V. 489

Degen, John A. 627
DeMille, Henry C. 100
DeMille, William C. 100
Dewsnap, James W. 226
Dickinson, T.H. 1169
Dithmar, Edward A. 742, 963, 1024, 1338
Doddrige, Joseph 227
Dolmetsch, Carl R. 187
Dorson, Richard M. 228, 344
Downer, Alan S. 103, 952, 954, 1386
Downs, Robert Bingham 79
Drake, Frank C. 1091
Drama League of America 130
Drummond, A.M. 188, 353
Dube, Anthony 1092
Duffy, Charles 1485
Dunlap, William 96, 100, 102, 105, 108, 110, 114, 131, 265, 454, 1204
Dupee, F.W. 1139
Durang, Charles 532
Durang, John 532
Durham, F.H. 1140
Durivage, O.E. 112
Duyckinck, Evert A. 132
Duyckinck, George L. 132
Dyson, Jane 42-43

E

Eames, Wilberforce 46
Earnhart, Phyllis H. 458
Eaton, Walter Pritchard 231, 367, 494-97, 674, 841, 862, 926, 1170, 1339
Eddleman, Floyd E. 18
Edel, Leon 1121, 1141
Edgett, E.F. 1021
Edmonds, Randolph 116
Edwards, Herbert J. 965-67, 1093-94
Egan, Michael 1142
Eich, Louis M. 345, 1314
Elfenbien, Josef Aaron 232
Ellis, Milton 233
Engle, Gary 80
Enkvist, Nils Erik 234, 630
Enneking, J.J. 972

Author Index

Evans, Charles 81
Ewing, Robert 235

F

Fabre, Geneviève 20
Fagin, N. Bryllion 236, 328
Falk, Armand E. 237
Farrison, W.E. 238-39
Faulkner, Seldon 631
Fay, Theodore Sedgwick 1243
Fechter, Charles 101, 104
Felhein, Marvin 743-44, 1025
Felton, C.C. 1468
Fergusson, Francis 1143
Ferrer, Lloyd A. 1027
Field, J.M. 100
Findlay, Robert R. 121
Fine, L.H. 368-69
Finley, Katherine P. 21
Firkins, Ina Ten Eyck 67
Fitch, Clyde 109, 110
Flory, Claude R. 572
Flower, B.O. 972
Floyd, W.R. 112
Folland, Harold 632
Forbes, Elizabeth L. 1144
Ford, James L. 1026
Ford, Paul Leicester 189, 789
Ford, Worthy C. 1435
Foust, Clement E. 520, 533-34
Fox, D.R. 240
Foxen, John 409
Fracchia, Charles Anthony 82
Freedley, George 83-84, 85, 126
Frenz, Horst 712, 878
Frohman, Daniel 370-71, 498, 633 713
Fyles, Franklin 100

G

Gaffney, Fannie H. 372
Gafford, Lucile 241-42
Gaillard, Eva Ryman 1364
Gallagher, Kent G. 133, 573, 701
Gambone, Kenneth 634
Garland, Hamlin 373, 425, 970-72, 990
Garrison, L. McK 973

Gassner, John 104, 602, 963, 1084, 1230, 1388
Gassner, Mollie 104, 602, 1084, 1230, 1388
Gay, F.L. 190
Gegenheimer, Albert F. 905
Geisinger, Marion 134
George, Dorothy 906
Gerson, Virginia 825, 840
Gilbert, Vedder Morris 1244
Gilder, Rodman 723
Gilder, Rosamond 85
Gillespie, Patti P. 974
Gillette, William 99, 104, 114, 422
Glenn, Stanley 243-44
Godfrey, Thomas 110, 114
Gohdes, Clarence 22-23, 165
Going, William T. 1340
Goldberg, Isaac 100, 1205
Goldstein, Malcolm 3
Gordon, John D. 374
Grigsby, Hugh Blair 1469
Grimsted, David 135, 354, 535, 809, 1245
Grinchuk, Robert A. 810
Grover, Leonard 100
Grover, Osgood Edwin 1171

H

Hackett, James 248, 349
Hagemann, E.R. 415
Hall, Margaret 745
Hall, Roger A. 375
Halline, Allan G. 100, 105, 450, 522, 731, 786, 1003, 1005, 1028, 1272, 1387, 1400, 1458
Hamar, Clifford E. 68
Hamilton, Clayton 879-80, 1029, 1341
Hanshew, T.W. 96
Hanson, Willis T., Jr. 1246
Hapgood, Norman 136, 746, 844, 881, 975, 1118, 1342
Harbert, Earl N. 380
Harrigan, Edward 108
Harris, H.A. 499
Harris, Richard A. 524, 536-37
Harris, William E. 635

Author Index

Harrison, A. Cleveland 636-39
Harrison, Gabriel 1247
Harrison, James A. 1471
Hart, R.L. 1343
Hartman, John Geoffrey 137, 845
Hartnoll, Phyllis 138
Haskell, David C. 86
Haskins, William 376
Hatch, James V. 24-25
Hatcher, Joe B. 1145
Hatlen, Theodore 976-77
Hatton, Anne K. 214
Havens, Daniel F. 139, 460, 538, 1401, 1486
Hawes, David S. 675-77
Hazelrigg, Charles Tabb 245
Hazelton, George C. 100
Heartman, C.F. 1235
Heffner, Hubert 100
Hench, John B. 81
Henderson, Archibald 191-92, 574, 898, 907
Hennequin, Alfred 377
Hennessee, Don A. 27
Herne, Chrystal 978
Herne, James A. p. xiv, 102, 103, 107, 108, 114, 387, 393, 437
Herne, Julia A. 967
Herne, Mrs. James A. 947
Herold, Amos L. 246
Herron, Ima Honaker 140, 461, 500, 747, 846, 979, 1119, 1344, 1487
Hewitt, Barnard 141, 1345
Heydrick, Benjamin A. 378, 1365
Heywood, Blanche E. 379
Hill, Frank Pierce 26
Hill, George H. 247
Hislop, Codman 100, 1226, 1227
Hixon, Don L. 27
Hodge, Francis 142, 248, 346, 1366, 1488
Hogan, Robert 640
Holman, C. Hugh 249, 380
Hoole, William Stanley 250-51, 1346
Hope, John F. 1146
Hopkinson, Francis 108
Hornblow, Arthur 143, 381-82
Howard, Bronson 100, 101, 102, 105, 108, 110, 114

Howe, Julia Ward 100
Howells, Mildred 1098
Howells, William Dean 104, 108, 383-84, 882, 930-31, 980-82, 1030-32, 1120-21, 1347, 1367
Hoyt, Charles H. 101, 108, 109
Hoyt, Harlowe R. 144
Hubbell, Jay B. 193, 573-76, 1183
Hudson, Long E. 34
Hughes, Glenn 100, 145, 473
Huneker, James G. 501
Hunt, Douglas L. 100, 1111, 1122-23
Hunter, Frederick J. 87
Hunter, Jack W. 641
Hunter, Robert 100
Hurley, Doran 194
Hutchinson, Ellen Mackay 1011
Hutchinson, Maud M. 1436
Hutton, Joseph 110
Hutton, Laurence 6, 146-47, 385, 678-79, 681, 932, 1095-96, 1248, 1287

I

Ingersoll, Charles Jared 254
Irving 104, 112, 114
Isaacs, Edith J.R. 148

J

James, Henry 374, 1134
Jarvis, Katherine S. 1402
Jessop, George H. 100
Johnson, Albert E. 28, 386, 642-43
Johnson, Allen 674
Johnston, W. 195
Jones, J.S. 96, 100, 110
Jones, Joseph 29
Jorgenson, C.E. 253

K

Kahan, Gerald 265
Kahn, E.J., Jr. 934-35
Kalb, Deborah S. 387
Kames, Lord 335
Kaplan, Sidney 644

Author Index

Keese, W.L. 680
Keller, Dean H. 69, 1160
Kenney, Charles Lamb 645
Kenton, Edna 1147
Kernodle, Portia 347
Kibles, James E., Jr. 255
Killheffer, Marie 348
Kirby, David K. 722, 1089, 1136, 1148
Kirk, Clara Marburg 1097
Kirk, Rudolph 1097
Kobbe, Gustav 748
Kohut, G.A. 1201
Koster, Donald Nelson 388, 749
Krause, David 597, 646
Krutch, Joseph W. 577
Kuhn, John G. 462
Kussrow, Van Carl, Jr. 196

L

Lancaster, A.E. 256
Lathrop, George Parsons 578-79, 750
Lauber, John 1403
Laurie, Joe, Jr. 355
LaVerne, Sister Mary 502
Law, Robert A. 197
Lawson, James 329
Leacock, John 110, 113
Leary, Lewis G. 30-32, 257, 1249
Leder, Lawrence H. 198
Leggett, William 329, 349
Leland, Charles G. 580-82
Lescarbot, Marc 199
Leverton, Garrett H. 100, 599
Lewis, Philip C. 149
Linn, John Blair 258
Lippman, Monroe 356
Litto, Frederic M. 33
Lockwood, Samuel 1206
Logan, Olive 389
Long, Luther 114
Long, Robert Emmet 1137
Longfellow, H.W. 96
Lovell, John, Jr. 106
Low, Samuel 110
Lowe, John A. 833
Lown, Charles R., Jr. 259-60
Luquer, Thatcher 1250-52
Lynch, Gertrude 883

Lynn, Kenneth 1191

M

Mabbott, Thomas O. 1301
Mabie, Hamilton W. 390, 1034
McCloskey, James 100, 108
McCoskey, John C. 35
McCullough, Bruce Welker 1302
MacDougall, A.R. 1253
McDowell, John H. 36
McElderry, Bruce R., Jr. 1149
Macfarlane, Peter Clark 884
McGaw, Charles J. 36
McGinnis, William C. 811
McGraw, Rex T. 885
Mackay, Ellen 385
McKay, Frederic Edward 660, 922, 1377
Mackaye, Arthur Loring 1172
MacKaye, Percy 100, 1173-74
MacKaye, Steele 100, 110, 114, 422
McKee, Thomas J. 769, 1383
MacKenzie, R. Shelton 666
McMichael, Morton 1298, 1303
McNicall, Robert E. 200
Makover, Abraham B. 1207
Mantle, Burns 426, 503
Marble, A.R. 1437
Marchiafava, Bruce T. 262
Marder, Carl J. III 70
Marder, Daniel 263
Marker, Lise-Lone 504
Marsh, John L. 427
Marshall, Thomas F. 391, 1035
Masters, Robert W. 847
Mates, Julian 37, 264, 784
Matlaw, Myron 107, 557, 603, 812, 948, 1006, 1273
Matthews, Brander 428-31, 681, 694, 724, 765, 868, 1033, 1036-38, 1099-1100, 1150, 1287, 1348
Matthews, F. Annie 392
Mawson, Harry P. 1033
Maxwell, William Bulloch 265
Mayorga, Margaret G. 150, 201, 463, 848, 908, 1208, 1288, 1349, 1438, 1489

Author Index

Mendelsohn, Michael J. 1151
Menelly, John Henry 202
Meserve, Ruth I. 357
Meserve, Walter J. 3, 38, 100, 151-53, 266, 357, 393, 464-65, 505, 539-40, 583, 647, 669, 702, 720, 725, 752, 790, 813, 849, 909-10, 954, 984, 1039, 1077, 1101-4, 1124, 1175, 1177, 1192, 1209, 1255-56, 1289, 1315-16, 1350, 1368, 1404-5, 1439-40, 1449, 1490
Metcalf, John C. 584
Middleton, George 506
Millard, Bailey 394
Miller, Joaquin 105, 379
Miller, Jordan Y. 3, 154
Miller, Tice L. 432-33
Miller, William 76
Minns, Edwin, Jr. 127
Mitchell, Langdon 100
Moise, Abraham 267
Moise, Lusius Clifton 268
Molnar, John Edgar 71
Montgomery, Evelyn 269
Montgomery, George E. 395, 714, 936, 1040
Moody, Richard 108, 109, 188, 353, 358, 523, 558, 670, 696, 792, 826, 917, 937, 953, 1007, 1083, 1112, 1176, 1186, 1199, 1274, 1307, 1389, 1480
Mooney, James E. 81
Moramarco, Fred 814
Morris, Clara 648, 753-54
Morris, Lloyd 156
Morris, Muriel 1257
Mortimer, Lillian 100
Morton, Frederick 985
Moses, Montrose J. 110, 111, 157-58, 270, 330, 342, 396, 449, 475, 476, 482, 507-8, 560, 649, 755, 787, 817, 818, 825, 827, 830, 840, 841, 850, 886-87, 899, 930, 963, 986-87, 1009, 1010, 1024, 1041, 1099, 1113, 1125, 1134, 1163, 1182, 1200, 1229, 1258, 1276, 1290, 1323, 1324, 1351, 1391, 1399, 1429, 1441, 1460

Moss, James E. 331
Mowatt, Anna Cora 102
Munford, Robert 108, 113
Murdoch, Frank 100, 101
Murdock, Kenneth B. 165
Murray, James J. 851
Murray, Judith Sargent 233
Musser, Paul H. 452, 466

N

Naeseth, Henriette 397
Nannes, Caspar Harold 159
Nardin, James T. 398
Nathan, George Jean 509, 1352
Neidig, William J. 203
Nelligan, Murray H. 272
Nethercot, Arthur H. 959-60, 1406
Nevins, Allen 206
Newbrough, George Floyd 100, 1385, 1407
New York Public Library 88-89
Nichols, Harold J. 274, 888
Nicoll, Allardyce 84, 100, 598, 651-52
Noah, M.M. 108, 110
Nolan, Paul T. 21, 41, 160, 399-403
Northall, W.K. 350
Norton, Elliot 116

O

Oakes, James 332-33, 682
O'Neill, Edward H. 100, 519, 1463
O'Neill, James 100
Orr, Lynn Earl 653
Ota, Thomas 275
Ottemiller, John H. 72
Overmeyer, Grace 1259-60

P

Page, Eugene R. 100, 276, 667, 1306
Pagel, Carol Ann Ryan 277
Pallard, Anna 683
Palmer, A.M. 405
Palmer, Helen H. 42-43
Parks, Edd Winfield 278

Author Index

Partridge, Paul W., Jr. 1450
Patterson, Ada 852, 1371
Paulding, James K. 105, 279-81
Paulding, William Irving 280-81
Pawley, Thomas D. 406
Payne, John Howard 96, 104, 110, 112, 114
Payne, T. 1250-52
Peach, Arthur Wallace 100, 1385
Pearson, Harlan C. 1126
Peavy, C.D. 282
Peck, H.T. 1470
Péladeau, Marius B. 1394, 1409
Pence, James H. 73
Perkins, Alice J. 283
Perry, John 957, 989
Perry, Thomas Sargent 1105
Phelps, William Lyon 853
Philbrick, Norman 113, 815, 1187, 1428-30
Pierce, John H. 480
Pizer, Donald 990-91
Poe, Edgar Allan 1292, 1471
Poggi, Jack 992
Pollock, Thomas Clark 161, 911
Popkin, Henry 1152-53
Potter, Helen 407
Pratt, William W. 97
Pray, Isaac C., Jr. 284

Q

Quinn, Arthur Hobson 84, 100, 114, 162-65, 204, 451, 467, 479, 510, 518, 521, 541-43, 559, 585-87, 604, 655, 703, 715, 756, 788, 816, 828, 829, 854, 889, 900, 912, 941-42, 946, 949, 993-95, 1008, 1043, 1106, 1127-28, 1162, 1178, 1193, 1210, 1232, 1261, 1275, 1291, 1304, 1318, 1325, 1353, 1373, 1390, 1410-11, 1442, 1451, 1459, 1463, 1472, 1491-92

R

Rahill, Frank 166, 408, 511, 656-57, 716, 890
Rappolo, Joseph 285-86, 359

Reardon, John D. 1319
Reardon, William R. 100, 287, 336, 409, 669, 790
Reed, Perley I. 167
Rees, James 168, 288, 544-45
Rees, Robert A. 380
Richardson, W.R. 100, 1226, 1227
Ritchie, Anna C.M. 102, 105, 107, 108, 110, 114
Robbins, J. Albert 29
Robinson, Alice Jean McDonnell 205, 996
Roden, Robert F. 44
Rogers, Cleveland 341, 342
Rogers, Robert 110, 206
Rossman, K.R. 290
Roth, Catherine 32
Rothman, John 434
Rotoli, Nicholas J. 7
Rourke, Constance 1412
Rowell, George 600
Rubin, Louis D., Jr. 53
Rugg, Harold G. 207
Russak, J.B. 100
Ryan, Pat M., Jr. 45, 684, 726

S

Sabin, Joseph 46
Salem, James M. 47, 512, 855, 1354
Saraceni, Gene A. 997
Sargent, Epes 332
Sargent, M.E. 291
Sarlos, Robert K. 90-91
Sata, Mansanori 468
Savage, George 100, 473
Sawyer, Lemuel 292-93
Saxon, Arthur H. 1262
Scanlan, Tom 410
Scherting, John A. 294
Schneider, Robert W. 411
Schoenberger, Harold William 100, 295, 1297
Schuttler, Georg W. 891
Schwab, Arnold T. 435
Scott, Clement 436, 658, 892
Sederholm, Frederick L. 337

Author Index

Sedgwick, Ruth W. 1375
Seilhamer, George O. 913, 1413
Sewall, Jonathan 96
Shafer, Yvonne 893
Shaw, Bernard 1107
Shaw, Ralph R. 81
Sherk, H. Denis 894
Sherr, Paul C. 588
Sherwood, Garrison P. 99, 477, 864
Shillingsburg, Miriam J. 296
Shipton, Clifford K. 81
Shockley, Martin S. 297
Shoemaker, Richard H. 81
Shulim, Joseph I. 704
Shuman, R.B. 589
Sievers, W. David 169, 513
Simms, William Gilmore 298
Sitton, Fred 299
Skloot, Robert 1263
Slout, William L. 412
Smeal, J.F.S. 338
Smith, John 108
Smith, R.P. 100
Smith, Sol 1211
Smith, Talbot 742
Smith, William 108, 914
Snowden, Yates 300-301
Sperber, Ann 92
Spillane, Daniel 943, 1179
Spiller, Robert E. 48, 120, 128
Spitz, Leon 1212
Srnka, Alfred H. 74
Stafford, William T. 1154
Stallings, Roy 413
Stallman, Robert W. 414-15
Staub, August W. 1155
Steadman, Edmund Clarence 385, 1011
Stearns, B.M. 1264
Steele, S.S. 100
Steele, William Paul 606, 659
Steele, Willis 857
Steer, Helen Vane 1156
Stein, Roger B. 1414
Stevenson, E. Irenaeus 1377
Stoddard, Richard H. 590
Stoddard, Roger E. 49-50
Stone, Henry Dickinson 303

Stone, John A. 100, 101, 102, 108, 279
Stone, P.M. 895
Storm, Colton 1425
Strang, Lewis C. 170, 717, 757, 858, 944, 998, 1355
Stratman, Carl J. 51-52
Streubel, Ernest J. 302
Stronks, James B. 727
Sturtevant, Catherine 100, 730
Syle, Dupont 437

T

Taft, Kendal B. 1493-94
Tanselle, G. Thomas 1395, 1415-16
Tarkington, Booth 1108
Taubman, Howard 171
Tayleure, C.W. 110
Taylor, Charles A. 100
Taylor, G.H. 563
Teunissen, John J. 208
Thomas, A.E. 98
Thomas, Augustus 109, 110, 863, 1011, 1044, 1129-30
Thomas, Louis F. 305
Thompson, C. Seymour 546
Thompson, Denman 98
Thompson, James 314
Thompson, Laurance 304
Thompson, Lawrence S. 75
Thompson, Vance 660
Ticki, Cecelia 209
Tidwell, James 279
Tiempo, Marco 999
Timberlake, Craig 514
Tolson, Julius H. 661
Towse, John Ranken 438, 758, 1045-46
Trent, William P. 158, 162, 439
Trinka, Zdena 1265
Tupper, Frederick 1417
Turner, Arlin 1249
Twain, Mark 383, 417
Tyler, Moses Coit 915
Tyler, Royall P. xii, 100, 103, 104, 105, 110, 114
Tyler, Thomas Pickman 1418

Author Index

U

Urban, Gertrude 591

V

Vail, R.W.G. 307
Van Lennep, William 308
Voelker, Paul D. 592
Von Chorba, Albert, Jr. 93

W

Wade, Allan 1157
Wagenknecht, Edward 1109
Waggoner, Hyatt A. 1000
Walbridge, Earl F. 172
Walbrook, H.H. 1158
Walker, Phillip 728
Wallack, Lester 100
Walser, Richard 310
Walsh, Robert 339
Walsh, Townsend 662
Walsh, William H. 1380
Waltermire, Alfred, Jr. 76
Ware, Ralph H. 100, 1297
Warren, John Ernest 1033
Warren, Mercy 110, 113
Waterman, W.R. 311
Watson, Charles S. 53, 312-14, 340, 1452
Watson, Margaret G. 417
Wayne, John Lakmond 547
Wayne, Palma 759
Wegelin, Oscar 54, 315, 418, 796, 819, 1266, 1482
Weidner, Paul R. 1453
Weiss, H.B. 1235
Wells, H.G. 374
Wells, Henry W. 11, 94
Welsh, Willard 419
Wemyss, Francis C. 548
Westlake, Neda McFadden 1296
Wheeler, A.C. [Nym Crinkle] 100, 101, 663, 718, 1182
Whicher, George F. 165
White, Matthew, Jr. 760, 896, 1382
Whitman, Walt 341-42

Whitford, Kathryn 420
Whitton, Joseph 688
Wiggins, Robert A. 729
Wilbur, James Benjamin 1383, 1384
Wilkins, J.H. 100
Wilkins, Thurman 1267
Willey, Malcolm 1001
Williams, Alfred 227
Williams, Espy 403
Williams, Stanley T. 549
Willis, Nathaniel P. 105, 110, 114
Wills, J. Richard 421
Wilson, Garff B. 173, 469, 761, 859, 1213, 1295, 1356, 1419
Wilson, J.H. 1002
Wilson, John Grosvenor 422
Wilt, Napier 100, 719
Wingate, Charles E.L. 660, 922, 1377
Wingfield, Lewis 664
Winter, Jefferson 515
Winter, William 422, 440-42, 515, 593, 665, 689, 762, 1357-58
Wise, Jennings C. 210
Witham, Barry B. 362
Wolf, H.B. 916
Wolf, S. 1214
Wood, Mrs. Henry 98
Wood, William Burk 317
Woodress, James 55
Woods, Alan 594
Woods, Walter 100
Woodworth, Samuel 108
Woolf, Benjamin E. 101
Woolsey, T.S. 820
Wright, Richardson 174
Wright, Thomas K. 443
Wright D'Arusmont, Frances 316
Wroth, Laurence C. 211
Wyatt, Edward A. 705
Wyld, Lionel D. 318, 821, 1159

Y

Young, Stark 516-17
Young, William C. 95

Z

Zanger, Jules 595

TITLE INDEX

This index includes all titles and plays cited in the text; in some cases the titles have been shortened. References are to entry number and alphabetization is letter by letter.

A

Abaellino, the Great Bandit 763, 782
Accusation 1215
Across the Continent 100, 108
Actors and Actresses of Great Britain and the United States 681, 1287
Actor's Heritage, The 926
Adeline 1216
Adulateur, The 1420-21, 1442
Alabama 1340
Albany Depot, The 1047, 1079
Ali Pacha 1217
American, The 1131
American Bibliography 81
American Bibliography: A Chronological Dictionary of All Books, Pamphlets and Periodical Publications Printed in the United States of America, from the Genesis of Printing in 1639 Down to and Including the Year 1820
American Bibliography: A Preliminary Checklist for 1801-1819 81
American Bibliography of Charles Evans, The. Vol. 13 81
American Bibliography of Charles Evans, The. Vol. 14 81
American Comedies 280

American Dissertations on the Drama and the Theatre, a Bibliography 33
American Drama (Downer) 103, 952, 1386
American Drama. Vol. 19 96, 119, 791
American Drama. Vol. 20 96, 119
American Drama and Its Critics 954
American Drama as Seen by Its Critics, 1752-1934, The 1099
American Drama Bibliography, a Checklist of Publications in English 45
American Drama Criticism 42
American Drama Criticism. Supplement I 43
American Drama Criticism. Supplement II 18
American Drama from Its Beginnings to the Present 34
American Dramatic Literature 154
American Dramatist, The 157, 507, 755, 886, 938, 1125, 1177, 1258, 1290, 1351, 1441
American Library Resources 79
American Literary Manuscripts 29
American Literary Pioneer 245
American Literary Realism 2
American Literary Scholarships 3
American Literature 4
American Literature Abstracts 5
American Musical Stage before 1800, The 264

227

Title Index

American Periodical Series, 1800-1850. A Guide to Years 21-31 of the Microfilm Collection, Reels 817-1151 with the Title Index to Years 1-31 60
American Periodical Series, 1800-1850. A Guide to Years 21-31 of the Microfilm Collection, Reels 1152-1408 with Title Index to Years 1-37 61
American Periodical Series, 19th Century--1800-1850 59
American Plays 105, 786, 1005, 1272, 1387, 1458
American Plays Printed, 1714-1830 26
American Playwrights of Today 426, 503
American Stage, The 127
American Stage of To-Day, The 494, 1339
American Theatre, The 117
American Theatre: A Sum of Its Parts, The 116
American Theatre as Seen by Its Critics, 1752-1934 330, 342, 841, 930, 963, 1024, 1134, 1182, 1292
American Theatre to 1900 p. xv
American Theatrical Arts 95
American Theatrical Periodicals, 1798-1967 51
America's First Hamlet 1259
America's Lost Plays 100, 367, 790, 946, 1003, 1111, 1161, 1226, 1227, 1297, 1306, 1385
America's Lost Plays. Vol. 1 598
America's Lost Plays. Vol. 18 473
America Takes the Stage 155, 176
Among Thieves 862
Ancient Briton, The 1313
André 102, 105, 110, 114, 764, 765, 785-88
Androboros 100
Annals of an Era 1171
Anne Boleyn 550, 555, 580
Annie 418
Annotated Bibliography and Subject Index to the Microfilm Collection 6
Another Part of the Forest 1340

Antebellum Charleston Dramatists 312
Anti-Bellum Charleston Theatre, The 250
Antipathies 280
Archers, The 766
Aristocracy 1021
Armand 1268, 1271
Arrant Knave, An 100, 1161
Arrant Knave & Other Plays, An 1161
Articles in American Studies, 1954-1968 8
Articles on American Literature, 1900-1950 31
Articles on American Literature, 1950-1967 32
Articles on American Literature Appearing in Current Periodicals, 1920-1945 30
Arizona 1332, 1347, 1349
As a Man Thinks 1321
At the New Theatre and Others 841
Autobiography of an Actress 1278
Autobiography of a Play 1011
Autobiography of Lemuel Sawyer, The 292
Awkward Age, The 1144

B

Banker's Daughter, The 100, 101, 1003, 1004, 1038, 1043
Banker's Daughter & Other Plays 1003
Bankrupt, The 100, 554
Baron Rudolph 100, 1003
Barbara Frietchie 822, 825
Battle of Brooklyn, The p. xii, 100, 113
Battle of Bunker's Hill, The 110
Battle of Stillwater, The 100
Beau Brummell 825
Becky Sharp 100
Belle Lamar 599
Best Plays of 1894-99, The 99
Best Plays of the Early American Theatre 104, 1084, 1230, 1388
Bethlehem Gabor 690
Betrothal, The 555, 580
Bianca Visconti 105, 1454, 1458
Bibliographical Checklist of the Plays and Miscellaneous Writings of William Dunlap 796

Title Index

Bibliographical Guide to Research in Speech and Dramatic Art, A 13
Bibliographical Guide to the Study of the Literature of the U.S.A. 22
Bibliographical List of the Literary and Dramatic Productions and Periodicals Written and Compiled by Samuel Woodworth 1482
Bibliographic Guide to the Theatre Arts 77
Bibliography of American Literature 12
Bibliography of the American Theatre, excluding New York City 52
Bibliotheca Americana 46
Big Bonanza, The 100, 730
Billy the Kid 100
Biography and Notes 316
Biography of Isaac Harby 268
Bishop of Broadway, The 514
Black American Playwrights, 1800 to the Present 7
Blackbeard 293
Black Crook and Other Nineteenth-Century American Plays, The 107, 948, 1006, 1273
Black Images and the American Stage, a Bibliography of Plays and Musicals, 1770-1970 24
Black Man, The 100, 1226
Blockheads, The 113
Blockheads; Or the Affrighted Officers, The 1428
Boarding School, The 1218
Boarding Shools, The 100, 1227
Broker of Bogota, The 114, 520, 521, 536
Bombardment of Algiers, The 100, 1297
Brass Monkey 1125
Bride Roses 1048, 1079
Brief Survey Course on American Drama 130
British and American Drama of To-Day, The 124, 876, 961, 1022, 1337
Broadway 118, 836
Brougham's Dramatic Works 666
Brutus 110, 1219, 1228-29, 1256

Bucktails, The 105, 280
Bunch of Keys, A 100, 1111
Bunker-Hill 691, 692, 693, 694

C

Caius Marius, a Tragedy by Richard Penn Smith 1296
Calaynos 551, 555, 580
Candidates, The 108, 310, 1183, 1186
Captain Jinks of the Horse Marines 823, 825
Carabasset 220
Career of Boucicault, The 645
Career of Dion Boucicault, The 662
Careless Husband, The 187
Caricatures of Americans on the English Stage Prior to 1870 234
Caridorf 100, 519
Carl Ehrlichkeit 418
Caroline 418
Catalog of the Theatre and Drama Collections 77
Catalog of the Theatre and Drama Collections. Part 1, Drama Collection: Author Listing 88
Catalog of the Theatre and Drama Collections. Part 1, Drama Collection: First Supplement, Listing of Cultural Origins 89
Catalogue of Additions to the Manuscripts in the British Museum 15
Century of Innovation 121
Change at Heart, A 1131
Chaperon, The 1131
Character of Melodrama, The 659
Charity Ball, The 100
Charles the Second 104, 112, 114, 1220, 1230, 1231-32
Chicorel Theater Index to Plays in Anthologies, Periodicals, Discs and Tapes 63
City, The 109, 825, 826, 827
City Looking Glass 139, 518, 538
Clairvoyants 220
Clari 1221
Climbers, The 825
Cloud of Witnesses p. xii
Clyde Fitch and His Letters 840

Title Index

Clyde Fitch I Knew 837
Collection of Plays and Poems, by the Late Colonel Robert Munford, of Mecklenburg, in the State of Virginia 1185
Collections of the New York Historical Society 793
Colleen Bawn, The 597, 600
Colonel George of Mount Vernon 1320
Colonel Sellers as a Scientist 720
Columbian Muse of Comedy, The 139, 460, 538, 1486
Columbus 682
Columbus el Filibustero 686
Complete Plays, The 1141
Complete Plays of Henry James, The 1131
Complete Plays of W.D. Howells, The 720, 725, 1077
Complete Works of Edgar Allan Poe, The 1292
Complete Works of N.P. Willis, The 1456
Contrast p. xii, 103, 104, 105, 108, 110, 114, 185, 344, 348, 1386-91, 1401, 1404, 1405
Contrast, a Comedy, The 1383
Contrast, with a History of George Washington's Copy, The 1384
Copperhead, The 1320, 1332, 1345
Counterfeit Presentment, A 1049
Counterfeit Presentment and the Parlor Car, A 1078
Count of Monte Cristo 104
Cowled Lover, The 100
Cowled Lover & Other Plays by Robert Montgomery Bird 519
Cricket of Palmy Days 1320
Crock of Gold, The 100
Crumbling Idols 425
Cure for the Spleen, A 96
Curiosities of the American Stage 146, 932
Curtain Time 156
Cyclopaedia of American Literature 132

D

Daniel Frohman Presents 370, 498, 713

Daisy Miller 1131
Dangerous Ruffian, A 1107
Danites in the Sierras, The 105
Darby's Return 100, 767, 782, 789-90
Darling of the Gods, The 475
David Belasco 504
David Copperfield 666
Davy Crockett 100, 101
Death of General Montgomery, The 113
Deed of Gift, The 1475
Defeat, The 1423
Development of American Social Comedy, 1787-1936, The 137, 845
Dialogue and Ode, A 108
Diary of a Dramatist, 1766-1839 793
Diary of Elihu Hubbard Smith, The 808
Diary of William Dunlap 793
Dialogue between an Englishman and an Indian, A 108, 207
Dialogue between a Southern Delegate, and His Spouse, on His Return from the Grand Continental Congress 113
Dictionary Catalogue of the Harris Collection of American Poetry and Plays 78
Dictionary of the Drama, A 1
Digests of Great American Plays 106
Dion Boucicault 596, 640
Disappointment, The 310
Disengaged 1131, 1132
Discussions of Modern American Drama 954
Dissertations in American Literature, 1891-1966 55
Divorce 100, 730
Doll's House 959
Dolman Press Boucicault, The 597
Dombey and Son 666
Dot 100, 598
Drama, The 96, 119
Drama of Yesterday and Today, The 658

Title Index

Dramas from the American Theatre, 1762-1909 108, 696, 826, 917, 953, 1007, 1083, 1112, 1186, 1199, 1274, 1307, 1389
Dramatic Authors of America, The 168, 544
Dramatic Bibliography 9
Dramatic Compositions Copyrighted in the United States, 1870-1916 17
Dramatic Index for 1909-49 66
Dramatic Opinions and Essays 1107
Dramatic Works of William Dunlap, The 782
Drifting Apart 946, 971, 980
Drunkard, The 108
DuBarry 475
Duke's Motto, The 100
Duke's Motto: Or I Am Here!, The 667
Dying to Keep Him 1457
Dying to Lose Him 1457

E

Earl of Pawtucket, The 1320
Early American Imprints (First Series, Evans) 1639-1800 81
Early American Imprints (Second Series, Shaw-Shoemaker) 1801-1819 81
Early American Periodicals Index to 1850 57
Early American Plays, 1714-1830 54
Early Life of John Howard Payne with Contemporary Letters Heretofore Unpublished, The 1246
Early Plays of James A. Herne 946
Electricity 860
Elements of Criticism 335
Elevator, The 1050, 1079, 1082
Emerging Entertainment, An 152, 464, 539, 702, 813, 909, 1192, 1209, 1255, 1315, 1404, 1439, 1449, 1490
Enciclopedia Dello Spettacolo 1180
English and American Drama of the Nineteenth Century 27
English and American Plays of the 19th Century 84
English Dramatists of Today 1017

Epoch 1168, 1169, 1170, 1172, 1173
Escape, The 212
Esmeralda 861
Essays in Dramatic Criticism with Impressions of Some Modern Plays 437
Evening Dress 1051, 1079
Experience 238

F

Fairfax 100, 708
Fall of British Tyranny, The 110
False Shame 100, 783
Fashion 102, 105, 108, 110, 114, 139, 234, 266, 1269-70, 1272-73, 1274-77, 1288, 1293
Fashionable Follies 110
Father, The 139, 768, 769
Father of an Only Child, The 96, 339, 782, 784, 791
Favorite American Plays of the Nineteenth Century 101, 1004, 1114, 1308
Female Patriotism 695
Fire-Tribe and the Pale Face, The 368, 369
First Lady of the Revolution 1433
Five O'Clock Tea 1052, 1079, 1080
Five Plays by Charles Hoyt 1111
Flying Scud 100, 101, 598, 601
Fontainville Abbey 782
Fool's Errand, A 1160
Fool's Opera, The 175
Forbidden Fruit 100, 598
Forbidden Fruit & Other Plays 598
Foreigner in Early American Drama, The 133, 701
Foreigners in America, The 418
Forest Rose 108, 1477-78, 1480
Forgers, The 1443
Fortress of Sorrento, The 1194
'Forty-Niners, The 96
Foscari 1444
Four in a Green Room 1035
Four Plays by Royall Tyler 1385
Four Plays by William Dunlap, 1789-1812 784

Title Index

Francesca Da Rimini 105, 108, 110, 114, 266, 362, 555, 556, 557, 558, 559, 560, 573, 586, 589
Frances Wright 311
Frances Wright, Free Enquirer 283
Fraternal Discord 770, 782
Freud on Broadway 169, 513
From Rags to Riches 100

G

Galley Slave, The 100, 708
Game of Life 666
Game of Love 666
Garroters, The 1053, 1079, 1080, 1107
Gathering of Forces, The 341, 342
George Henry Boker, Poet and Patriot 562, 567
Ghosts 959
Girl I Left behind Me, The 100, 473
Girl of the Golden West, The 109, 470, 475, 476
Girl with the Green Eyes, The 825, 828
Gladiator, The 105, 108, 520, 522, 523, 536
Glaucus and Other Plays 100, 554
Gleanings from a Gathered Harvest 1201
Gleeson Library Associates, University of San Francisco 82
Glory of Columbia, The 108
Good Neighbor, The 782
Grand Historical Allegory of America 706
Great Diamond Robbery, The 100, 101
Grecian Captive, The 1195
Griffith Davenport 982, 998
Group, The 110, 1424-25, 1429, 1442
Group of Comedians, A 680
Guide to Critical Reviews, A 512, 1354
Guide to Critical Reviews: Part I, A 47, 855

Guide to Manuscripts Relating to America in Great Britain and Ireland, A 16
Guide to the Theatre and Drama Collection at the University of Texas 87
Guy Domville 1131

H

Handy Andy 112
Harvest Moon, The 1320
Hazard of New Fortunes, A 1091
Hazel Kirke 114, 1162, 1175, 1177
Heart of Maryland, The 100, 101, 473, 477
Heart of Maryland and Other Plays, The 473
Held by the Enemy 128
Henrietta, The 105, 1005, 1021, 1046
Henry James 1131
Henry James: The Ibsen Years 1142
Her Great Match 829
Her Opinion of His Story 1054, 1079
Her Own Way 825
High Bid, The 1131
Hippolytus 100
Hiss the Villain 97
History of American Literature during Colonial Times, A 915
History of English Drama, 1660-1900. Vol. IV, A 651
History of English Drama, 1660-1900. Vol. V, A 652
History of Modern Drama, A 126
History of the American Drama from the Beginning to the Civil War, A 163, 467, 703, 912, 1193, 1210, 1291, 1304, 1318, 1410, 1442, 1451, 1472, 1491
History of the American Drama from the Civil War to the Present Day, A 164, 510, 715, 941, 1106, 1127, 1178, 1373
History of the American Theatre (Dunlap) 131, 794, 1204

Title Index

History of the American Theatre (Seilhamer) 913, 1413
History of the American Theatre, 1700-1950, A 145
History of the Theatre in America from Its Beginnings to the Present Time, A 143
Home, Sweet Home 1265
Horizon 105, 731
Horseshoe Robinson 110
How to Try a Lover 444
Hugh Henry Brackenridge 263
Hurricane 100, 1003

I

Image of America on the Stage, 1825-1850 1366
Impossible, a Mystery Play, The 1055
Indian Giver, An 1056, 1079
Indian Princess, The 110, 445, 449
Indian Summer 1342
In Memoriam, Bronson Howard 1033
In Missoura 110, 1320, 1323
In Spite of All 100, 1161
Index of Early American Periodicals 58
Index to Early American Periodical Literature, 1728-1870 57
Index to Plays 1800-1826 67
Index to Plays in Collections 72
Index to Plays in Periodicals 69
Island of Barrataria, The 100, 1385
Italian Bride, The 100, 1226
Italian Father, The 771, 782, 784

J

Jack Cade 110
James A. Herne, the American Ibsen 989
James A. Herne: The Rise of Realism in the American Drama 967
James Gibbons Huneker, Critic of the Seven Arts 435
James Kirk Paulding 246
James Nelson Barker, 1784-1858 466
Jam Jehan Nima 1237
Jessie Brown 596

Job and His Children 100
John Howard Payne, a Biographical Sketch of the Author of "Home Sweet Home" with a Narrative of the Removal of His Remains from Tunis to Washington 1240
John Howard Payne, Dramatist, Poet, Actor, and Author of "Home, Sweet Home!" His Life and Writings 1247
John Howard Payne to His Countrymen 1242
Johnny Johnson 344
Joseph and His Brethren 100, 1385
Judgement of Solomon, The 100, 1385
Julia 1222
Juvenile Poems 1247

K

Kentuckian, The 248, 279
Knave and Queen 100, 1003
Konigsmark, the Legend of the Hounds and Other Poems 552

L

La Belle Ruse 100, 473
Ladies of Castile 1427
Lady of Fashion, The 1282
La Fayette 1476
Last Duel in Spain, The 100, 1226
Last Duel in Spain & Other Plays, The 1226
Last Man, The 100, 1297
Later American Plays, 1831-1900 44
Leicester 782, 784
Leonor de Guzman 555
Letter of Introduction, A 108, 1057, 1079, 1083, 1095
Library of American Literature from the Earliest Settlement to the Present Time, A 1011
Life and Dramatic Works of Robert Montgomery Bird, The 520, 533
Life and Recollections of Yankee Hill 350
Life and Work of Charles H. Hoyt, The 1123

Title Index

Life and Writings of Richard Penn Smith with a Reprint of His Play, "The Deformed", The 1302
Life in Letters of William Dean Howells 1098
Life of Augustin Daly, The 626, 740, 741
Life of David Belasco, The 515
Life of Edwin Forrest with Reminiscences and Personal Recollections, The 545
Life of Robert Montgomery Bird 528
Life on the Border 403
Likely Story, A 1058, 1079, 1080
Lion of the West, The 279, 281
Literary Biography of Mordecai Manuel Noah 1201
Literary History of the United States 48
Literary Life of James Kirk Paulding 281
Literature and Theatre of the States and Regions of the U.S.A. 23
Literature of the American People, The 165, 543, 995, 1411, 1492
Little Foxes 1340
Little Sunshine 707
Little Tea Table Chitchat 108, 207
London Assurance 610, 612
Longer Plays by Modern Authors (American) 1322
Lord Chumley 100
Louis XI 100, 598
Love and Murder 666
Love in '76 110
Lover's Lane 825
Lover's Vows 772, 782, 1223

M

Madame Butterfly 114, 475, 479
Madmen All 280
Magazine and the Drama, The 73
Main Line, The 100
Major Noah 1205
Making of the American Theatre, The 171
Man and Wife 100, 730
Man and Wife & Other Plays 730
Margaret Fleming 102, 107, 114, 362, 948-50, 959, 968, 970, 981-83, 991, 996, 1002, 1196
Mark Twain and Southwestern Humor 1191
Marmion 339, 446, 459, 462
Masque of Alfred, The 204
Masterpiece of Diplomacy, A 1059, 1079
Mazeppa 100, 1227
Medium, The 1409
Melodrama Unveiled 135, 535, 1245
Member of the Third House 991
Memoirs of John Howard Payne, The American Roscius 1254
Memorial Edition of the Plays of Clyde Fitch 825
Memories of Daly's Theatres 742
Men and Women 100
Mercenary Match, The 222
Mercy Dodd 100, 598
Mercy Otis Warren 1434
Merry Partners, The 934
Metamora 100, 101, 102, 108, 1306, 1307-10, 1314, 1319
Metamora & Other Plays 1306
Mimic Life 1279
Midnight Bell, A 100, 1111
Mighty Dollar, The 101, 428
Mignon 216
Milk White Flag, A 100, 1111
Minor Dramas 1079
Minute Men of 1774-1775, The 100, 946
Miscellaneous Works, Collected by His Son, Horace W. Smith 1298
Mistress Nell 100
MLS International Bibliography of Books and Articles on the Modern Languages and Literatures 39
Modern American Plays 1321
Modern Drama 40
Modern Honor 1445
Monologue 1131
Monte Cristo 100, 101
Moors and the Christians, The 176
Mordecai Manuel Noah 1214
Mordecai M. Noah--His Life and Work 1207
Moth and the Flame 110, 830
Mother and the Father, The 1060

Title Index

Motley Assembly, The 113, 1426, 1430
Mount Savage 100, 1227
Mouse Trap, The 104, 1061, 1079, 1080, 1084
Mouse Trap and Other Farces, The 1080
Mr. George Jean Nathan Presents 509
Mrs. Leffingwell's Boots 1320
Much Ado about the Merchant of Venice 677
Mulligan Guard Ball, The 108, 917
My First Fifty Years in the Theatre 366
My Partner 100, 101, 708
Mysteries of the Castle 1446
Mysterious Father, The 265

N

Nathan Hale 824, 825
National Index of American Imprints through 1800 81
Naughty Anthony 100, 473
Needles and Pins 100, 730
Negro in the American Theatre, The 148
Nathaniel Parker Willis (Auser) 1464
Nathaniel Parker Willis (Beers) 1465
New American Drama, The 12, 1335
New Sabin, The 75
News of the Night 100, 519
New York Drama, a Choice Collection of Tragedies, Comedies, Farces, Comediettas, etc. 112, 1228, 1231
Night before Christmas, The 1062
Nineteenth-Century American Drama 27
Noble Exile, The 280
No Mother to Guide Her 100
Notes on the Settlement and Indian Wars, of the Western Parts of Virginia and Pennsylvania from the Year 1763 until the Year 1783 Inclusive 227

Nydia 553

O

Octoroon, The 102, 104, 107, 114, 602, 603, 604, 605, 615
Old Homestead, The 344, 345, 348, 1359-60, 1365, 1366, 1367, 1370, 1371, 1372, 1375, 1382
Old Lavender 928
Old Love Letters 100, 1003
Oliver Goldsmith 1320
One of Our Girls 100, 1003, 1030
Oralloossa 520, 536
Origin and Development of Dramatic Criticism in the "New York Times," 1851-1880, The 434
Origin of the Feast of Purim 100, 1385
Other Days 441, 665
Other Girl, The 1320
Other House, The 1131
Our Boarding House 100
Out of the Question 1063
Out of the Question and at the Sign of the Savage 1063
Outcry, The 1131, 1141
Outline History of American Drama, An 153, 465, 505, 540, 583, 647, 752, 849, 910, 984, 1039, 1102, 1124, 1175, 1256, 1289, 1316, 1350, 1368, 1405, 1440
Oxford Companion to the Theatre, The 138

P

Papers on Playmaking 1038
Parlor Car, The 1064, 1079, 1082
Parlor Car and the Sleeping Car, The 1081
Parting Friends 1065
Patriots, The 113, 1184, 1185, 1187
Paul Kauvar 110, 1163
Pelopidas 520, 536
People's Lawyer, The 10, 348
Persecuted Dutchman, The 112
Personal Recollections of the Drama or Theatrical Reminiscences

Title Index

Embracing Sketches of Prominent Actors and Actresses, Their Chief Characteristics, Original Anecdotes of Them, and Incidents Connected Therewith 303
Personal Recollections of the Stage, Embracing Notices of Actors, Authors, and Auditors, during a Period of Forty Years 317
Peter the Great 782
Philadelphia Theatre in the Eighteenth Century, The 161
Pique 100, 730
Pizarro in Peru 773
Players and Plays of the Last Quarter Century 170, 717, 757, 858, 944, 1355
Playing with Fire 687
Plays, Players and Playwrights, an Illustrated History of the Theatre 134
Plays and Players 147, 679
Plays and Players: Leaves from a Critic's Scrapbook 497
Plays and Poems 555
Plays of Henry C. DeMille Written in Collaboration with David Belasco, The 474
Plays of the Present 1021
Playwrights on Playmaking 724, 1150
Po-Ca-Hon-Tas 96, 100, 108, 114, 666, 668, 669, 670, 685
Poems, Dramatic and Miscellaneous 1427
Politian 216
Politician Outwitted, The 110
Politics in the American Drama 159
Ponteach 111, 185, 206
Poor of New York, The 606
Previous Engagement, A 1066, 1079, 1096
Prince of Parthia, The p. xii, 110, 114, 191, 440, 897-900, 908, 912, 913
Print of My Rememberance, The 1129, 1329
Prose of Royall Tyler, The 1394
Provincial Drama in America, 1870-1916 160
Pseudonymous Publications of William Gilmore Simms 255

Pyramus and Thisbe 1131

R

Ranger, The 1341
Realistic Presentation of American Characters in Native American Plays Prior to 1870, The 167
Rebels and Gentlemen, Philadelphia in the Age of Franklin 178
Record of the Boston Stage, A 123, 700
Red Owl, The 863
Register, The 1067, 1079, 1082
Reilly and the 400 925
Representative American Dramas, National and Local 109, 110
Representative American Plays 111, 114, 787, 788, 828, 829, 830, 899, 900, 1008, 1009-10, 1162, 1163, 1200, 1229, 1232, 1275, 1276, 1323, 1391, 1459, 1460
Reprobate 1131
Return of Peter Grimm, The 100, 471, 475, 481, 482
Revels in Jamaica, 1682-1838 174
Reverend Griffith Davenport, The 100, 946, 951, 962
Ribbemont 774
Richelieu 1224
Rip Van Winkle 96, 107, 110, 112, 114, 437
Robert Emmet 100, 598
Robert Montgomery Bird 530
Robert Munford, America's First Comic Dramatist 1190
Romance and Reality 666
Romance of the American Theatre, The 129
Romulus 1226
Romulus the Shepherd King 100
Room Forty-Five 1068, 1079
Roots of American Culture and Other Essays, The 1412
Rosedale 100
Rose Michel 100, 1161
Rose of Rancho, The 472
Royall Tyler 1416
Royal Slave, A 100

Title Index

Runaway Colt, A 1121

S

Sack of Rome, The 1427
Saloon, The 1131
Sam'l of Posen 100
Samson 1069
Samuel Woordworth 1493
Saratoga 1021
Saved 1070
Scenes from the Life of an Actor 247
Scenic Art, The 1134
School for Scandal, The 1401
Sea Change, A 1071
Secret Service 104, 114, 128, 864, 882, 894, 896
Selective Index to Theatre Magazine 65
Self 110
Self-Sacrifice 1072
Sentinels, The 100, 1297
Sentinels & Other Plays 1297
Sertorius 110
Shadows of the Stage 442
Shakespeare in Love 100, 1297
Shaughraun, The 597
Shenandoah 102, 107, 108, 110, 114, 1006-9, 1021, 1031
Shepherd King, The 1226
Sherlock Holmes and Much More 877, 894
She Would Be a Soldier 1208, 1213, 1197, 1199-1200
Shore Acres 103, 108, 345, 437, 952-53, 969, 985, 991
Shore Acres and Other Plays by James A. Herne 947
Short History of the American Drama, A 150, 463, 848, 908, 1208, 1288, 1349, 1438, 1489
Signor Marc 100
Silas Lapham 966, 1094
Silver Theatre, Amusements of the Mining Frontier in Early Nevada, 1850-1864 417
Simpson 418
Six Early American Plays, 1798-1900 102, 785, 950, 1277, 1309
Six Plays 475

Sixty Years of the Theatre 438
Sketch of the Life of John Howard Payne, A 1243
Sleeping Car, The 1073, 1079, 1082, 1097
Sleeping Car and Other Farces, The 1082
Small Town in American Drama, The 140, 461, 500, 747, 846, 979, 1119, 1344, 1487
Smoking Car, The 1074, 1079
Solon Shingle 96
Some Correspondence and Six Conversations 856
Some Materials to Serve for a Brief Memoir of John Daly Burk, Author of a History of Virginia 699
South Carolina Players and Playwrights 300
Spanish Background of American Literature, The 549
Spanish Husband, The 100, 1227
Spanish Student, The 96
Spirit of the Times 325
Spy, The 100
Squatter Sovereignty 939
S.R.O. The Most Successful Plays of the American Stage 98
Stage Confidences 754
Stage in America, 1897-1900, The 136, 746, 844, 881, 1118
Stage-Struck Yankee, The 112
Still Waters 1131
Stranglers of Paris, The 100, 473
Stubborness of Geraldine, The 825
Study of the Modern Drama, A 125, 839, 1023
Subject Collections 76
Summersoft 1131
Superstition 104, 114, 339, 451, 461, 462
Supplement to Charles Evans' American Bibliography 81
Susanna Haswell Rowson 307

T

Tancred, King of Sicily 100, 1306
Tears and Smiles 139, 447, 452, 461

Title Index

Tell Truth and Shame the Devil 775
Temperance Town, A 100, 108, 1111, 1112
Temptation 666
Tenants 1131, 1132
Ten Nights in a Bar-Room 97
Ten Squaws, The 418
Texas Steer, A 109, 1113, 1124
Theatre and Allied Arts, The 10
Theatre and Drama in the Making 963
Theatre Collections in Libraries and Museums 85
Theatre in America, the Impact of Economic Forces, 1870-1967 992
Theatre of Augustin Daly, The 743, 744
Theatre of Neptune in New France, The 199
Theatre through Its Stage Door, The 489
Theatre U.S.A. 1668-1957 141, 1345
Theatrical Comicalities, Whimsicalities, Oddities and Drolleries 115
Theatrical Contributions of "Jacques" to the United States Gazette, The 235
Theatrical Management in the West and South for Thirty Years 1211
Theatricals: Second Series 1133
Theatricals, Two Comedies 1132
Theme of Divorce in American Drama, 1871-1939, The 388
Thérèse 1225
Thérèse, the Orphan of Geneva 96, 1233
Thirty Years 100, 783
Three Centuries of English and American Plays 11
Three Centuries of English and American Plays, 1500-1830 94
Three Hundred Years of American Drama and Theatre 173, 469, 761, 859, 1213, 1295, 1356, 1419
Tortesa the Usurer 110, 114, 1455, 1459-60
Town Hall Tonight 144

Tragedy of Superstition, The 448
Trial of Atticus before Justice Beau for a Rape 100
Trial without Jury 100
Trial without Jury & Other Plays 1227
Trip to Chinatown, A 100, 101, 1111, 1114, 1122
Trip to Niagara, A 108, 776, 792, 821
Triumphs of Love 310
Trouping 149
True Hero, A 1075
Trumpets Sounding 113
Truth, The 825
'Twas All for the Best 100, 519
Twenty-Six Years of the Life of an Actor and Manager 548
Two Sons-In-Law, The 100, 1227
Two Ways of Dying for a Husband 1457

U

Uncle Tom's Cabin p. xv, 98, 104, 108, 110, 266, 358-59
Under the Gaslight 97, 732
Unexpected Guests, The 1076, 1079
Usurper, The 100

V

Valerian, a Narrative Poem Intended, in Part, to Describe the Early Persecution of Christians and to Illustrate the Influence of Christianity on the Manners of Nations 258
Virginian, The 100, 708
Virgin of the Sun, The 777
Voice of Nature, The 778, 782

W

Wags of the Stage 688
Wallet of Time, The 593, 1358
Warrens of Virginia, The 100
Washington and the Theatre 789
Wept of Wish-ton-wish, The 96
White Slave, The 100, 708

Title Index

White Slave and Other Plays by Bartley Campbell, The 708, 719
Widow's Marriage, The 555
Widow's Sons, The 1479
Wife, The 100
Wife at a Venture, A 100, 1297
Wife of Two Husbands, The 779, 782
Wild Goose Chase, The 780
William Dean Howells, the Friendly Eye 1109
William Dunlap (Canary) 803
William Dunlap (McGinnis) 811
William Dunlap: A Study of His Life and Works and of His Place in Contemporary Culture 806
William Dunlap and His Writings 819
William Gilmore Simms as Literary Critic 278
William Penn 100, 1297
William Wells Brown 239
Witching Hour, The 109, 1320, 1324-25, 1327, 1341, 1349, 1356
Within an Inch of His Life 100, 946

Wolfville, 1905 857
Woman in the Case, The 825
Woman's Revenge 100, 1226
Won at Last 100, 1161
World a Mask, The 100, 554, 580
World of Melodrama, The 166, 511, 656, 716
World's Greatest Hit, The 351
Writings of John Howard Payne, The 1226

Y

Yankee Chronology 781, 784
Yankee Peddler, The 112
Yankee Theatre 142, 346, 1488
Yankey in England, The 348
Ye Beare and Ye Cub 180
Ye Kingdome of Accawmacke on the Eastern Shore of Virginia in the Seventeenth Century 210
Yorker's Strategem 310
Young Mrs. Winthrop 1023

SUBJECT INDEX

This index includes all topics discussed in the text. References are to entry numbers and underlined numbers refer to main areas within the subject. Alphabetization is letter by letter.

A

Acting
 biographies concerning 1
 of Brougham 675, 678, 681, 683, 688
 in burlesque 678
 criticism of 325, 330, 342, 364, 432, 436
 Gillette on 867
 of Gillette 873, 889
 of Harrigan 922, 926
 of Herne 997
 historical approaches to 145-47, 149
 Howard on 1013
 in 19th century Boston theater 230
 of Mackaye 1182
 of Payne 1244, 1246, 1248, 1254, 1258-60
 Puritan condemnation of 209
 of Ritchie 1278-79, 1283, 1287, 1295
 trade unions 997
Acting companies. See Theater companies
Adams, John, on Judah's ODOFRIEDE, THE OUTCAST 308
Agrarianism in drama 314

Aiken, George L.
 biography and criticism of 354
 plays of in anthologies 104, 108, 110
Alabama, checklist of the drama of 41
Alfriend, Edward M., plays of in anthologies 100-101
American College Theatre Festival, First (1969), papers of 116
American Company 192
American Revolution. See Revolutionary War
Andre, John (Major), dramatic characterizations of 296, 815
Aristotle, comparison of Boucicault to 607, 636-37
Aston, Tony 192

B

Baker, Benjamin, biography and criticism of 306
Ball, Michael, Valentine 427
Bannister, Nathaniel Harrington, biography and criticism of 288, 391
Barker, James Nelson
 bibliographies on 455
 biography and criticism of 163, 223, 297, 322, 456-69

Subject Index

nondramatic works of 453-54
plays of 444-48
 in anthologies 104-5, 110, 115, 449-52
Barnard, Charles, plays of in anthologies 100
Barnett, Morris, plays of in anthologies 112
Barnum, P.T. 650
Barras, Charles, plays of in anthologies 107
Barrett, Lawrence 402, 572
Barry, S., plays of in anthologies 112
Bateman, Sidney (Mrs.)
 obituary 271, 436
 plays of in anthologies 110
Beaver Dam, Wis., theater in 144
Belasco, David
 bibliographies on 490
 biography and criticism of 164, 382, 437, 491-517, 890
 nondramatic works of 483-89
 plays of 470-75
  in anthologies 99, 100-101, 109-10, 114, 476-82
Bennett, Clarence, plays of in anthologies 100
Bernard, William Bayle, biography and criticism of 248, 279
Bidwell, Barnabas, biography and criticism of 222
Bird, Robert Montgomery
 bibliographies of 523, 525
 biography and criticism of 163, 523, 526-49
 plays of 518-20
  in anthologies 100, 105, 108, 114, 521-24
Blacks in drama 24-25, 116, 146, 148, 155
 dialect of 310
 on the English stage 234
 in pre-Civil War comedy 243
 See also Drama, black; Playwrights, black
Boccaccio, Giovanni, as a source for Boker 589

Boker, George H.
 bibliographies on 561-63
 biography and criticism of 564-95
 plays of 550-55
  in anthologies 100, 105, 107-8, 110, 114, 556-60
Booth, Edwin 436
Boston, theater in 62, 123, 230, 700, 977, 996, 1002
 censorship of 287
 racial drama of 991
 UNCLE TOM'S CABIN productions 358
 War of 1812 and 241
Boucicault, Dion
 bibliographies on 621
 biography and criticism of 163, 290, 371, 408, 622-26
 nondramatic works of 607-20
 plays of 596-98
  in anthologies 100-102, 104, 107, 114, 599-606
Brackenridge, Hugh Henry
 biography and criticism of 263
 plays of in anthologies 110, 113
British Museum, catalog of additions to the manuscripts in 15
Broadway 118
Broadway Managers Association 1343
Brook Farm, use of drama at 242
Brougham, John
 bibliographies on 671
 biography and criticism of 147, 214, 290, 436, 666, 672-89
 plays of 666
  in anthologies 100, 108, 667-70
Brougham's Theatre (New York City) 677
Brown, Charles Brockden, biography and criticism of 258
Brown, D.P., plays of in anthologies 110
Brown, William Wells, biography and criticism of 212, 238-39
Brownson, Orestes Augustus, bibliography of the plays of 418

Subject Index

Brown University. Library. Harris Collection, catalog of 78
Brune, Clarence, correspondence with E. Williams 399
Buckstone, John, Brougham compared to 673
Buffalo Bill. See Cody, William F.
Bunce, O.B., plays of in anthologies 110
Burk, John Daly
    bibliographies of 697
    biography and criticism of 698-705
    plays of 690-95
        in anthologies 108, <u>696</u>
Burke, Charles, plays of in anthologies 96, 110, 112
Burlesque 116, 146
    actors who specialize in 678
    Brougham as a writer of 685
    UNCLE TOM'S CABIN in 356
Businessmen in drama 259-60
    in Howard's works 1018, 1034
Byrd, William II 187

C

California, University of (Davis), facilities and theater collections at 90-91
Campbell, Bartley
    bibliographies on 709
    biography and criticism of 370, 395, <u>710-19</u>
    plays of <u>706-8</u>
        in anthologies 100-101
Carleton, Henry Guy, biography and criticism of 382, 437
Carpenter, Stephen Cullen 340
Censorship
    in Boston 287
    Thomas's views on 1328, 1343
Characters and characterization 146, 155, 228, 428
    of Americans on the English stage 234
    based on real people 172
    Bird's 529
    of blacks 24, 243
    Boker's development of 577
    Boucicault's 620, 636, 654
    of Buffalo Bill 365, 403
    Burk's 701
    in comedy 243-44
    of foreigners 133, 701
    Harrigan's 925
    of the Irish 252, 654
    of Major Andre 296, 815
    nationalism in 27
    of Pocahontas 193, 302, 458
    race in 27
    realism and 167, 372
    Thomas's 1366, 1371, 1376
    Tyler's 1401, 1412
    Woodworth's 1488
    of the Yankee 343-50, 1366, 1371, 13<u>76</u>, <u>1</u>401, 1412, 1488
Charleston
    antebellum theater of 250, 312
    colonial theater of 203
Chaucer, Geoffrey, influences on Godfrey 916
Chicago, University of. Library. Atkinson and Morton Collection, catalog of 80
Chickering, Hall (Boston) 996
Chinese Spring Willow Society 357
Civil War in drama 363, 419
Clarke, J.I., biography and criticism of 394
Clemens, Samuel
    bibliographies of 721-22
    biography and criticism of 370, 383, 417, <u>723-29</u>, 755, 1101, 1191
    plays of in anthologies 100-101, 720
Clinch, Charles P., plays of in anthologies 100
Cody, William F., dramatic characterization of 365, 403
College drama and theater
    bibliography on 36
    Bidwell's MERCENARY MATCH in 222
Colonial period. See Drama, American, during the colonial period (to 1783)
Comedies 163, 465
    anthologies of 19th century 115, 280

Subject Index

blacks in pre-Civil War 243
   of Brougham 683
   of Daly 751-52
   of Fitch 845, 854
   of Harrigan 938, 942, 1128
   of Howard 1029
   of Hoyt 942, 1118, 1128
   ludicrous characterization in 244
   of Munford 1190-91
   proverbs in 269
   of the Revolutionary War era 182
   of Ritchie 1286, 1292
   social 137, 139, 752, 845, 854, 1286, 1401, 1486
   theories of 335, 337
   of Tyler 1397, 1401
   of Woodworth 1486
   See also Musical comedies
Conrad, Joseph 374
Conrad, R.T., plays of in anthologies 110
Cooper, James Fenimore, plays of in anthologies 96
Copyright 324, 332-33, 360, 392
   Boucicault and 614, 631, 657
Costumes
   criticism of Belasco's ideas on 495
   in Harrigan's Old Lavender 928
Crane, Stephen, biography and criticism of 368-69, 374, 411, 414-15
Crinkle, Nym. See Wheeler, Andrew Carpenter
Critics, dramatic
   biography of 434
   of the Boston theater 123
   checklists of 18, 42-43
   dictionaries concerned with 28
   Dunlap as 801, 804, 814
   in early St. Louis 331
   from 1861-1900 364, 422-23
   historical approaches to 116, 141, 152-53, 173
   James as 1150, 1157
   from 1784-1860 213, 235-37, 319-42
   Twain as 726
Crockett, Davy, dramatic characterization of 347, 428

Custis, George Washington Parke
   biography and criticism of 214, 272
   plays of in anthologies 114

D

Daly, Augustin
   bibliographies on 735
   biography and criticism of 164, 626, 736-62
   nondramatic works of 442, 733-34
   plays of 730
      in anthologies 97, 100, 105, 731-32
Dartmouth College. Library. Mackaye Collection 1168, 1171
Deadwood, S. Dak., drama and theater in 397
Deering, Nathaniel, biography and criticism of 220
DeMille, Henry C., plays of in anthologies 100
DeMille, William C.
   biography and criticism of 394
   plays of in anthologies 100
Dialects in drama 348
   black 310
Dialogue
   Boker's 585
   Fitch's 856
   Howard's 1042
   Tyler's 1414
   Willis's 1469, 1473
Divorce in drama 388
   Daly and 749
Drama, American
   anthologies and collected plays of 96-115
   bibliographies and checklists of 1-55, 124
   during the colonial period (to 1783) 175-211
   during the rise of realism (1861-1900) 360-443
   effect on Europe 376
   histories of 116-74
   indexes to 56-75

Subject Index

library and microreproduced collections of 76-95
in the period of national development (1784-1860) 212-359
purposes of 177
research opportunities in 37-38
See also Acting; Censorship; College drama and theater; Comedies; Copyright; Critics, dramatic; Dialects in drama; Dialogue; Farces; Folk drama; Historical drama; Melodrama; Miracle plays; Musical comedies; Musicals; Playwrights; Social drama; Theater, American; Tragedies; names of individual playwrights (e.g., Boker, James Nelson)
Drama, black, checklists of 20, 25. See also Blacks in drama; Playwrights, black
Drama, French, American adaptations of 295
Drama, Spanish
in the early Southwest 176, 195
at the Spanish Mission in Florida 200
Dramatic theory 319-42
of Belasco 492, 504
of Boucicault 607-8, 636-39
of Howard 1011, 1041
of Howells 1092
of James 1143
of Thomas 1329
Dramatist's Club 1041
Dunlap, William
bibliographies on 795-96, 803, 806
biography and criticism 135, 163, 214, 223, 265, 297, 319, 454, 797-821
nondramatic works of 793-94
plays of 763-84
in anthologies 96, 100, 105, 108, 110, 114, 785-92
Durivage, O.E., plays of in anthologies 112

E

Economics in drama 336

in Thomas's works 1336
Emerson, Ralph Waldo, comments on drama by 242
EVENING POST (New York), theater criticism of (1807-30) 237

F

Farces 377, 398
audience craving for 336
of Howells 1108
Farfán, Marcos, de los Godos 176, 195
Fechter, Charles, plays of in anthologies 101, 104
Fiction, dramatization of 277, 361, 393
James's works 1140, 1151
Field, Eugene 1371
Field, J.M., plays of in anthologies 100
Fisk, Jim, partnership with Brougham 677
Fitch, Clyde
bibliographies on 832-33, 850
biography and criticism of 137, 164, 170, 423, 834-59, 1347
nondramatic works of 831
plays of 822-25
in anthologies 109-10, 826-30
Florida, first theater production in Spanish 200-201
Floyd, W.R., plays of in anthologies 112
Folk drama 318
Foreigners in drama 133
Burk's characterizations of 701
Forrest, Edwin 330, 545, 726, 1317, 1470
Forrest's Prize Play Contests 274
Freudianism. See Psychology in dramatic interpretation
Frontier in drama 146, 155, 164
on the English stage 234
Fuller, Margaret, comments on drama by 242
Fyles, Franklin, plays of in anthologies 100

Subject Index

G

Garland, Hamlin 373
  biography and criticism of 420, 965, 991, 996
  comments on Mark Twain by 727
George, Henry, influence on Herne 965
Gillette, William
  bibliographies on 870
  biography and criticism of 164, 170, 361, 370-71, 382, 511, 871-96, 975
  nondramatic works of 422, 867-69
  plays of 860-61
    in anthologies 99, 104, 114, 861-66
Godfrey, Thomas
  bibliographies on 901
  biography and criticism of 191, 902-16
  plays of 897-98
    in anthologies 110, 114, 899-900
Godwin, William 436
Goethe, Johann Wolfgang von, Poe compared to 216
Grover, Leonard, plays of in anthologies 100

H

Hackett, James, biography and criticism of 248, 349
Hanshew, T.W., plays of in anthologies 96
Harby, Isaac, biography and criticism of 236, 267-68, 298, 312
Harrigan, Edward
  bibliographies on 919
  biography and criticism of 382, 920-45, 1128, 1130, 1381
  nondramatic works of 442, 918
  plays of in anthologies 108, 917
Hart, Tony 926, 935
Harte, Bret
  attempted collaboration with Boucicault 626
  biography and criticism of 360, 1099
  relations with Daly 755
Hatton, Anne K. 214

Hawkins, Micah, biography and criticism of 315
Hayne, Paul Hamilton, views on Boker's plays 576
Hazelton, George C., plays of in anthologies 100
Herne, James A.
  bibliographies on 956-57
  biography and criticism of 164, 170, 382, 387, 393, 408, 423, 437, 958-1002, 1094, 1347
  nondramatic works of 954-55
  plays of 946-47
    in anthologies 100-103, 107-8, 114, 948-53
Heroes in drama 225
See also Villains in drama
Hicks, Angie 566
Hill, George H. 247
Hill, Yankee 350
Hillhouse, James A., biography and criticism of 245, 289
Historical drama 140, 256, 575
Holland, George, biography and criticism of 298
Honky tonks 116
Honor in drama, Boker and 592
Hope, John F., review of James's THE OUTCRY 1146
Hopkinson, Francis 204
Howard, Bronson
  bibliographies on 1015
  biography and criticism of 164, 170, 371, 376, 382, 396, 423, 1016-46
  nondramatic works of 422, 1010-14
  plays of 1003
    in anthologies 100-102, 105, 107-8, 110, 1004-9
Howe, Julia Ward, plays of in anthologies 100
Howells, William Dean
  bibliographies of 1077, 1088-89
  biography and criticism of 164, 404, 440, 755, 1090-1110
  estimate of Howard 1032
  nondramatic works of 1085-87

Subject Index

plays by 1047-82
  in anthologies 104, 108, 1083-84
  reactions to Herne 966
Hoyt, Charles
  bibliographies on 1115
  biography and criticism of 164, 382, 426, 942-43, 945, 1116-30, 1381
  plays of 1111
    in anthologies 100-101, 108-9, 1112-14
Humor. See Comedies
Huneker, James Gibbons 435
Hunter, Robert
  biography and criticism of 187, 198
  plays of in anthologies 100
Hypnotism 497

I

Ibsen, Henrik
  as an influence on American drama 425, 1010, 1085
  on Herne 959-60, 993
  on James 1143
  reaction to his GHOSTS 1087
Illinois, drama and theater in 413
Independent Theatre (Boston) 977, 996, 1002
Indians
  in drama 146, 155, 214, 282, 299, 465, 1314
  treaties of as first American drama 188, 211
Ingersoll, Charles Jared, biography and criticism of 254
Ioor, William, biography and criticism of 312, 314
Irish-American theater 935
Irish in drama 252, 290
  Boucicault's characterizations of 654
Irving, Washington
  correspondence with Payne 1250
  plays of in anthologies 104, 112, 114

J

James, Henry
  bibliographies of 1135-37
  biography and criticism of 374, 755, 1138-59, 1403
  nondramatic works of 1134
  plays of 1131-33
Jefferson, Joseph 436
  Rip Van Winkle as played by 98, 107, 114, 410, 416
Jeffersonian Republicanism in drama 314
Jessop, George N., plays of in anthologies 100
Jones, J.S., plays of in anthologies 96, 100, 110
Judah, Samuel, biography and criticism of 308
Judd, Sylvester, comments on drama by 242

K

Kidder, Edward, biography and criticism of 382
Klein, Charles, biography and criticism of 394
Kotzebue, August von, success of in America 800, 812

L

Labor and laboring classes in drama 378, 420
  in Thomas's works 1350
Language in drama. See Dialects in drama; Dialogue
Leacock, John
  biography and criticism of 186
  plays of in anthologies 110, 113
Library of Congress, catalogs of 77
Lincoln Center. Library and Museum for Performing Arts 92
Linn, John Blair, biography and criticism of 257
Localism in drama 378, 393. See also Rural areas in drama
Logan, Olive 421
Long, Luther, plays of in anthologies 114

Subject Index

Longfellow, Henry Wadsworth
  biography and criticism of 273, 304
  plays of in anthologies 96
Longworth, David and Thomas, catalog of the dramatic imprints of 49
Lotus Club (New York City) 689
Louisiana in drama 313
Love in drama, Boker and 592
Low, Samuel, plays of in anthologies 110

M

McCloskey, James, plays of in anthologies 100, 108
McHenry, James, biography and criticism of 217
MacKaye, Steele
  bibliographies on 1165
  biography and criticism of 1166-1182
  nondramatic works of 422, <u>1164</u>
  plays of 1160-61
    in anthologies 100, 114, <u>1162-63</u>
McMichael, Morton 1298
Mathews, Cornelius, biography and criticism of 335
Matthews, Brander 404, 424, 439
Matthews, Charles 610
Medley, Mat 175
Melodrama 135, 144, 163, 166, 265, 367, 377
  Belasco's 511, 890
  Bird's 535
  Boucicault's 408, 656, 659
  Campbell's 716
  Daly's 752
  Dunlap's 809
  Gillette's 511, 885, 888, 890
  Herne's 408
  Howard's 1018
  James's 1149
  Payne's 1245
  production of 514
  realism as a rebellion against 969
Menken, Adah I. 726
Merry, Robert, biography and criticism of 221

Miles, George Henry, biography and criticism of 194
Miller, Arthur 410
Miller, Joaquin
  biography and criticism of 376, 379
  plays of in anthologies 105
Mining towns, theater of 417
Minstrel shows and minstrelsy 116
  background of American 389
  in England 234
Miracle plays 318
Miscegenation in drama, Boucicault's reaction to 644
Mississippi, checklist of the drama of 21
Mississippi Valley area, early theater in 219
Mitchell, Langdon, plays of in anthologies 100
Morality in drama 377
  Garland and 991
  Herne and 991
Morris, George, biography and criticism of 248
Mortimer, Lillian, plays of in anthologies 100
Morton, Martha, biography and criticism of 394
Mowatt, Anna Cora. See Ritchie, Anna Cora Mowatt
Munford, Robert
  bibliographies on 1188
  biography and criticism of 1189-93
  plays of 1183-85
    in anthologies 108, 113, 1186-87
Murdock, Frank, plays of in anthologies 100-101
Murdock, John, biography and criticism of 310
Murray, Judith Sargent 233
  biography and criticism of 253, 1409
Musical comedies 375
Musicals 412
  production of before 1800 264

Subject Index

N

Nancrede, Joseph, correspondence with Tyler 1415
Nationalism in drama 27, 135, 165
  in the colonial period 205
  from 1861-1900 381, 404
  from 1784-1860 270, 272, 274, 319-42
    Boker on 457
  in Tyler's works 1403, 1408
  See also Patriotism
National Theatre (Boston), UNCLE TOM'S CABIN at 358
Nevada, theater in 417
New Mexico, drama in Spanish 176
New Orleans
  Nineteenth-century theater in 286
  UNCLE TOM'S CABIN productions in 359
New Theatre (Philadelphia), criticisms of performances at 235
New York City, colonial theaters of 203
NEW YORK MAGAZINE, Dunlap's connection with 801, 814
New York Public Library. Theatre and Drama Collections, catalogs and descriptions of 77, 83, 86, 88-89
NEW YORK TIMES, origin and development of dramatic criticism in 434
Noah, Mordecai M.
  bibliographies on 1202
  biography and criticism of 297, 1203-14
  nondramatic works of 1201
  plays of 1194-98
    in anthologies 108, 110, 1199-1200
North Carolina, early drama and entertainment in 191-92
Nude in drama 412, 421

O

Old American Company 794
O'Neill, Eugene 410
O'Neill, James, MONTE CRISTO as played by 100

Opera, light, Tyler's lyrics for 1402

P

Patriotism, influence on drama and the theater 262. See also Nationalism in drama
Paulding, James Kirk
  biography and criticism of 246, 248, 281
  plays of in anthologies 105
Payne, John Howard
  bibliographies on 1234-35
  biography and criticism of 163, 223, 297, 1236-67
  plays of 1215-27
    in anthologies 96, 100, 104, 110, 112, 114, 1228-33
Pennsylvania, University of. Library, checklist of plays to 1865 held by 93
Periodicals
  bibliography of theater 51
  indexes to plays in 69, 73
Philadelphia, theater in 161, 178, 235, 532
Playwrights
  actors as 174
  biography of and comments on 1, 48, 118, 123-27, 136, 138, 140, 143, 145, 149, 151, 156-57, 168-69, 171, 366, 431, 442
  checklist of Southern 160
  lack of talent among 336
  rejection of the work of 405
  of South Carolina 300-301
  variety of creativity among 152
  women as 484
  See also Critics, dramatic; Drama, American; names of playwrights (e.g., Boker, George H.)
Playwrights, black 406
  bibliographies and checklists of 7, 14, 24
  See also Drama, black; names of black playwrights (e.g., Brown, William Wells)

Subject Index

Playwriting 170
  Belasco and 485-86
  Boucicault and 612, 640
  Gillette and 868, 873, 880, 888
  Harrigan and 918, 937
  Howard and 1043
  Noah and 1204
  Thomas and 1326, 1329, 1335
Plots, Gillette's use of 872
Pocahontas, dramatic characterization of 193, 302, 458
Poe, Edgar Allan
  assessment of Willis 1463, 1466, 1471
  compared to Goethe 216
  corrections to his POLITIAN 261
  as a critic 328, 1292
  indebtedness of Boker to 569
Poetic drama 163, 465
  Boker's 583
  Stone's 1319
Poetry, Boker's attitude toward 576
Politics
  in drama 159, 163
  in Boker's works 592
  in Thomas's works 1336, 1350
  of Herne 997
  of Noah 1206
Power, Tyrone, biography and criticism of 252
Pratt, T.S., plays of in anthologies 97
Propaganda, drama as 409
Proverbs in drama 269
Psychology in dramatic interpretation 169, 507, 513
Puritans, attitudes toward drama 209, 233

Q

Quebec, colonial theater of 203

R

Race in drama 27
Radio 173
Raymond, John T., biography and criticism of 383, 436
Realism in drama 185, 377, 393
  Belasco and 483, 493, 502, 505
  bibliography of studies on 2
  Boker and 57
  Boucicault and 611, 664
  in characterization 167, 372
  Daly and 752
  Gillette and 889
  Harrigan and 930, 945, 1130
  Herne and 954, 967-69, 972, 976, 984, 986, 994, 999-1001
  Howells and 1092, 1102
  Hoyt and 945, 1130
  Thomas and 1351
  Thompson and 1365
Repertory theater 433
Revolutionary War
  comedy in the time of 182
  drama and theater as an influence on 183-84, 208
  treatment of in drama 296
Richmond Theatre 297
Ritchie, Anna Cora Mowatt
  bibliographies on 1280
  biography and criticism of 234, 1281-95
  nondramatic works of 1278-79
  plays of 1268-71
    in anthologies 102, 105, 107-8, 110, 114, <u>1272-77</u>
Rogers, Robert
  biography and criticism of 181, 206
  plays of in anthologies 110
Romanticism in drama 155, 164
  Bird and 542
  Boker and 573, 587
  Boucicault and 663
  MacKaye and 1176
  White and 1450
  Willis and 1464
Rowe, Nicholas, influence on Godfrey 911
Rowson, Susanna, biography and criticism of 291, 307
Rural areas in drama 140, 461, 500
  Daly and 747
  Fitch and 846

Subject Index

Herne and 979
Hoyt and 1119
Thomas and 1344
Thompson and 1377
Woodworth and 1487
See also Localism in drama

S

St. Louis, dramatic criticism of the theater in 331
San Francisco, drama and the theater in 437
San Francisco, University of. Library. George W. Poultney Collection of Theatre Manuscripts, catalog of 82
Sargent, Epes, biography and criticism of 309, 332
Satire, dramatic
 bibliography on 35
 Brougham's 684
Sawyer, Lemuel 292
Science, influence on Herne 1000
Sellers (Colonel), dramatic characterization of 347, 428
Sentiment in drama 362
Sewall, Jonathan
 biography and criticism of 208
 plays of in anthologies 96
Shakespeare, William 616
 Gillette's adaptation of HAMLET 891
 influence on drama 619
Shaw, George Bernard, admiration for James 1145
Shelley, Mary, romance with Payne 1257
Simms, William Gilmore
 biography and criticism of 226, 249, 251, 278, 312
 comment on drama by 255
 letters of Boker to 575
Slote (Judge), dramatic characterization of 428
Smith, Elihu Hubbard 808
Smith, John
 biography and criticism of 207
 plays of in anthologies 108

Smith, Richard Penn
 bibliographies on 1296, 1299
 biography and criticism of 1300-1305
 nondramatic works of 1298
 plays of 1296-98
 in anthologies 100
Smith, William
 authorship of THE MASQUE OF ALFRED 204
 influence on Godfrey 905, 916
 plays of in anthologies 108
Social drama 140, 232, 378
 comedic 137, 139, 752, 845, 854, 1286, 1401, 1486
 Daly's 751-52
 Fitch's 845, 849, 854
 Garland's 991
 Herne's 991
 Howard's 1018
 realism in 377
 Ritchie's 1286
 Thomas's 1350
 Tyler's 1401
 Woodworth's 1486
Song in drama 377. See also Musicals
South Carolina, plays and playwrights of 300-301. See also Charleston
Southern states
 bibliographies on drama and the theater of 380, 400
 checklist of playwrights in (1870-1916) 160
Stage. See Theater, American
Steele, S.S., plays of in anthologies 100
Stoddard, Charles Warren 576
Stone, John Augustus
 bibliographies on 1311
 biography and criticism of 214, 248, 279, 297, 1312-19
 plays of 1306
 in anthologies 100-102, 108, 1307-10
Stowe, Harriet Beecher. See UNCLE TOM'S CABIN

Subject Index

T

Tayleure, C.W., plays of in anthologies 110
Taylor, Bayard 566
Taylor, Charles A., plays of in anthologies 100
Television 173
Temperance in drama 218
Texas, University of. Library. G.C. Howard Collection, catalog of 87
Thalian Association 191
Theater, American
  adaptation of French plays in 295
  advertising of the colonial 192
  attitudes of the transcendentalists toward 242
  bibliographies on 9-10, 13, 22-23, 33, 52
    in the South 380
  black 25, 148
  in Boston 62, 123, 230, 241, 287, 358, 700, 977, 991, 996, 1002
  in Charleston 203, 250, 312
  condemnation of the nineteenth century 229
  criticism of 432-33
  dictionaries concerning 203
  history of 121, 127, 129, 131, 134-35, 141, 143, 145, 156, 163-65, 171, 173, 203, 240, 294, 364
  in Illinois 413
  image of the American in 142
  indexes to 63, 66, 68
  influence of patriotism on 262
  lack of good playhouses for 342
  library collections devoted to 77
  lights and lighting in 495
  management of 405, 625, 675, 742, 761, 1122, 1211
  in the mining towns 417
  in the Mississippi Valley area 219
  periodicals 51
  in Philadelphia 161, 178, 235, 532
  production and direction in 214, 223, 489, 503-4, 594,
  719, 740, 750, 755, 759, 800, 804, 808, 812, 815-16, 1122, 1129, 1143, 1168, 1210, 1346, 1363, 1398
  public arguments in favor of colonial 196
  research opportunities in 38
  in the Revolutionary War 182-84, 208
  in St. Louis 331
  in San Francisco 437
  setting and scenery in 970, 1164
  See also Broadway; Censorship; College drama and theater; Musicals; Repertory theater; names of theaters (e.g., New Theatre [Philadelphia])
Theater, English
  characterizations of Americans in 234, 347
  first American play in 458
Theater audiences 392, 932
  Harrigan's theories on 929
  James's failure to satisfy 1143, 1155
  manners of 1145
  taste of 321, 327, 336
Theater companies 320, 433
  black 406
  criticism of 325
  See also names of companies (e.g., Old American Company)
Thomas, A.E., plays of in anthologies 98
Thomas, Augustus
  bibliographies on 1330
  biographies and criticism of 164, 170, 376, 382, 423, 426, 1331-58
  nondramatic works of 1326-29
  plays of 1320
    in anthologies 109-10, 1321-25
Thomas, Louis F., scene from an unpublished play by 305

Subject Index

Thompson, Denman
   bibliographies on 1361
   biography and criticism of 371, 943, 1120, 1362-82
   plays of 1359
      in anthologies 98, 1360
Thompson, James, biography and criticism of 314
Towse, John Ranken 432, 443
Tragedies 163, 284, 309
   of Boker 573, 587, 595
   criticism of 320
   of Dunlap 799
   of Longfellow 273
   of Smith 1301
   of Willis 1467
Transcendentalists, attitudes toward drama and the theater 242
Twain, Mark. See Clemens, Samuel
Tyler, Royall
   bibliographies on 1392-95
   biography and criticism of 223, 1396-1419
   plays of 1383-85
      in anthologies 100, 103-5, 108, 114, 1386-91

U

UNCLE TOM'S CABIN, dramatic adaptations of 98, 104, 108, 110, 351-59, 409

V

Van Winkle, Rip
   English characterizations of 234
   musical versions of 437
   as played by J. Jefferson 98, 107, 114, 410, 416
Very, Jones, comments on drama by 242
Villains in drama, Gillette's 885. See also Heroes in drama; Melodrama
Villareal (Brother) 200-201
Virginia, drama in colonial 180

W

Wallack, Lester, plays of in anthologies 100
Wallack's Theatre 685
War in drama 155. See also names of wars (e.g., Revolutionary War)
War of 1812
   the Boston theater and 241
   in drama 274
   the New Orleans theater and 285
Warren, Mercy Otis
   bibliographies on 1431
   biography and criticism of 208, 1432-42
   plays of 1420-27
      in anthologies 110, 113, 1428-30
Wells, H.G. 374
West Point in drama 296
Wetmore, Prosper, biography and criticism of 248
Wheeler, Andrew Carpenter
   as a critic 443
   plays of in anthologies 100-101
White, John Blake
   bibliographies on 1447
   biography and criticism of 298, 312, 1448-53
   plays of 1443-46
Wilkins, G.P., obituary of 225
Wilkins, J.H., plays of in anthologies 100
Williams, Barney, biography and criticism of 290
Williams, Espy, biography and criticism of 399, 401-2
Williams, Tennessee 410
Willis, Nathaniel Parker
   bibliographies on 1461
   biography and criticism of 1462-74
   plays of 1454-57
      in anthologies 105, 110, 114, 1458-60
Wilson, John Grosvenor 422
Winter, William 422, 443

Subject Index

Winter Garden Theatre 631
Wit and humor. See Comedies
Women
   in drama 387
   as playwrights 484
Wood, Henry (Mrs.), plays of in anthologies 98
Wood, William Burk 74, 317
Woods, Walter, plays of in anthologies 100
Woodworth, Samuel
   bibliographies on 1481-82
   biography and criticism of 1483-94
   plays of 1475-79
      in anthologies 108, 1480
Woolf, Benjamin E.
   biography and criticism of 428
   plays of in anthologies 101
Wordsworth, William, as a source for S. Woodworth 1485, 1494
Workman, James, biography and criticism of 313

Wright, Frances, biography and criticism of 283, 311, 316

Y

Yale College, 18th century student dramatics at 275
Yankee (The), characterizations of 142, 155, 343-50, 428
   on the English stage 234, 347
   in Thomas's works 1366, 1371, 1376
   in Tyler's works 1401, 1412
   in Woodworth's works 1488

Z

Zola, Emile, Harrigan compared to 936